MW01008054

NTC's
Dictionary
of
FRENCH
FAUX PAS

Ann Crowe   Maureen Wesolowski

Printed on recyclable paper

NTC Publishing Group
Lincolnwood, Illinois USA

1995 Printing

Published by National Textbook Company, a division of NTC Publishing Group.
© 1994 by NTC Publishing Group, 4255 West Touhy Avenue,
Lincolnwood (Chicago), Illinois 60646-1975 U.S.A.
Manufactured in the United States of America.

5 6 7 8 9 BC 9 8 7 6 5 4 3 2

Introduction

The purpose of the book

NTC's Dictionary of French Faux Pas is a reference guide to potential pitfalls for the English-speaking learner of French. It provides a practical tool—quick and easy to use—that leads the learner across the barrier from "English" French to "French" French.

Organized in alphabetical order (by the English word) for convenient reference, the entries focus on what learners most need to master for everyday communication. Examples are carefully selected to alert learners to common blunders, to steer them clear of *faux amis* or other anglicisms, as well as to provide idiomatic French equivalents for hard-to-translate English concepts. Short grammar notes serve to remind learners of essential rules they may have forgotten.

NTC's Dictionary of French Faux Pas can be used for individual study or in a formal classroom setting. It can be a valuable reference for learners at all proficiency levels and an ideal guide for travelers who want to "bone up" in preparation for a trip to France.

Suggestions for Using This Dictionary

Browse through it

Pick out words and phrases you would like to be able to use. Mark the items you want to learn so you can find them easily.

As you go through the book, you may discover you have been using expressions that are not authentic, idiomatic French. Pay special attention to these entries, so that you can avoid making the same *faux pas* in the future. Watch for the warning signal Ø that flags special pitfalls called *faux amis*. These are words that may look similar in French and English but have totally different meanings. For example, *la monnaie* means "change" and not "money."

Practice regularly

As English speakers, it is much easier for us to read French or understand it than it is to express ourselves in that language. We can frequently recognize words we "half know" and guess what we don't know from the contest. But when we actually try to speak French, "half-knowing" and guessing don't help much. There is no substitute for knowing.

You may learn best if you make a regular study plan. Start with the entries you have marked for review or pick a section you want to learn. Repeat the French aloud until you master it. Come back in a few days, cover up the French side of the text and see if you remember the key phrases without looking. You will find your fluency improves with practice. And the results are better if the practice is regular and systematic.

Use for quick reference

When you are looking for a common word or expression, check this book first—before going to a standard French-English dictionary. There's a good chance you will find what you need. All vocabulary is presented in context—both in English and French—to guide you to the right selection and warn you of possible pitfalls. When you do need to look up an English word in a standard French-English dictionary, be sure to consider the options available. If you cannot identify the right one, double-check any likely choices by looking them up in the French-English section to be certain you have the right meaning. In this way, you will avoid blunders like this one: *"J'ai trouvé de beaux obus* ("bombshells") *sur la plage."* ("Seashells" are *coquillages.*)

How to choose the right word

Sometimes the same English word may be translated into French in several ways, depending on context. This book highlights the possible choices and provides clear examples to illustrate the various uses. For instance, under the entry for the word "time," there are six subheadings that guide the user to the correct choice. Examples of usage include: "How time flies!" *(Comme le temps passe vite!)*; "What time is it?" *(Quelle heure est-il?)*; "several times" *(plusieurs fois)*; "at the present time" *(en ce moment);* "at the time of Napoleon" *(à l'époque de Napoléon).*

What part of speech is it?

When you are looking up a word, it is helpful to know what part of speech it is. Beware of English words that may be two different parts of speech.

Here are some examples of distinctions to make:

rent (*verb*) "to rent a house" *louer une maison*
rent (*noun*) "to pay the rent" *payer le loyer*
light (*noun*) "to turn off the light" *éteindre la lumière*
light (*adjective*) "a light color" *une couleur claire*

fast (*adverb*) "Run fast!" *Cours vite!*
fast (*adjective*) "a fast train" *un train rapide*

When looking up a verb, you may need to know if it is transitive (can take an object) or intransitive (cannot take an object), for example:

grow (*verb trans*) "In the Southwest they grow a lot of wheat." *Dans le sud-ouest on cultive beaucoup de blé.*
grow (*verb intrans*) "Asparagus grows well in this climate." *Les asperges poussent bien dans ce climat.*

Pay special attention to prepositions

Prepositions are often used differently in English and in French. For instance, depending on context, "with" could be translated as *avec, de, or à*. If you are not sure, take a moment to verify your choice. Every preposition entry in this dictionary gives a broad selection of phrases illustrating French usage. Here are some examples: "to France" *(en France)*; "at the butcher shop" *(chez le boulanger)*; "on the bus" *(dans l'autobus)*; "in the picture" *(sur la photo)*; "That's very nice of you!" *(C'est très gentil à vous!)*

Don't leave home without it

Carry *NTC's Dictionary of French Faux Pas* with you wherever you go—to class, the Post Office, the beach. Consult it often to review phrases that you want to remember when speaking or writing. And, of course, don't leave it behind when you go to France or any other French-speaking country.

Abbreviations

adj	adjective	*invar*	invariable
adv.	adverb	*m*	masculine
art	article	*m pl*	masculine plural
conj	conjunction	*n*	noun
dem	demonstrative	*obj*	object
dir	direct	*pl*	plural
disj	disjunctive	*prep*	preposition
emph	emphatic	*pron*	pronoun
excl	exclamation	*sing*	singular
fam	familiar	*subj*	subject
f	feminine	*v*	verb
f pl	feminine plural	*v intrans*	verb intransitive
indir	indirect	*v trans*	verb transitive
inter	interrogative		

Parts of speech

Please note that the part of speech indicated for each entry is for the English word. The French equivalent will not necessarily be the same part of speech as the English.

Abbreviations used in the examples

sb	somebody
sth	something
qqn	quelqu'un
qqch	quelque chose
∅	Warning signal

≡ A ≡

a/an *art*
with measurements
That costs 15 francs a meter/a kilogram/a liter.

It's 20 francs a bottle/a bag/a packet.

He makes 40 francs an hour.

with a profession, nationality, religion
He is a mechanic.
He is an excellent mechanic.

I am a protestant/a Catholic/a Jew.

He's an American; she's a German.

Ça coûte 15 francs **le** mètre/**le** kilo/**le** litre. [*Note: definite article*]
C'est 20 francs **la** bouteille/**le** sac/**le** paquet.
Il gagne 40 francs de l'heure.

Il est mécanicien. [*Note: no article*]
C'est **un** excellent mécanicien. [*Note: Article is used when noun is modified.*]
Je suis protestant(e)/catholique/juif/ juive. [*Note: no article*]
Il est américain; elle est allemande. [*Note: no article*]

ability *n*
to have a lot of ability

to the best of one's ability
I answered to the best of my ability.
to have the ability to do sth

Ø **abilité** is not French.

avoir beaucoup de talent
être très habile/capable
de son mieux
J'ai répondu de mon mieux.
être capable de faire qqch

able *adj*
capable, adept
She is very able.

to be able to (do sth)

I was able to convince them.
She will not be able to pay her debts.

Elle est très habile/capable.
Elle a beaucoup de talent.

être capable de/pouvoir/réussir à faire qqch
J'ai pu les convaincre.
Elle ne réussira pas à payer ses dettes.

about *prep*
concerning
They told me a lot about their trip.

Ils m'ont beaucoup parlé de leur voyage.

Oh, about that magazine . . .

Tiens, à propos de cette revue/au sujet
   de cette revue . . .

Here's an article about French canals.
Voici un article sur les canaux français.

What's this play about?
De quoi s'agit-il dans cette pièce?

This play is about three boys who . . .
Dans cette pièce, il s'agit de trois
   garçons qui . . . [Note: *s'agir* always
   takes the impersonal subject, **il.**]

verb + about

to talk about

parler de

to ask about

poser des questions/se renseigner sur/
   au sujet de

I asked about the price.
Je me suis renseigné sur le prix.

to hear about
entendre parler de

I've heard a lot about you.
J'ai beaucoup entendu parler de vous.

on the point of

I was about to ask you.
J'allais vous demander.

I was just about to leave.
J'étais sur le point de partir.

approximately [*see* **around**]

above   *adv*
above
au dessus/en haut

on the floor above
à l'étage au-dessus

above all [*especially*]
surtout/avant tout

see above [*in a text*]
voir ci-dessus

above   *prep*
above
au-dessus de

The picture is above the fireplace.
Le tableau est au-dessus de la
   cheminée.

academic   *adj*
the academic year
l'année scolaire

an academic record
un dossier scolaire

That's an academic question.
La question est toute théorique.

accent   *n*
He speaks French well, and with a
   good accent.
Il parle bien le français, et sans accent.

You have a good accent.
Vous n'avez pas d'accent.

He has a southern [*French*] accent.
Il a l'accent du Midi.

2

accidentally *adv*
by chance
I met him by chance.

par hasard
Je l'ai rencontré par hasard.

unintentionally
He did it accidentally.

par mégarde
Il ne l'a pas fait exprès.

account *n*
a bank account
on account of the heat

un compte en banque
à cause de la chaleur

Ø **acompte** [m] means "a deposit on a purchase."

ache *n & v*
I have a headache.
I have toothache.
I have muscle aches.
I ache all over.
[*see also* **hurt**]

J'ai mal à la tête.
J'ai mal aux dents.
J'ai des courbatures.
J'ai mal partout.

across *prep*
The movie theater is across the street.
right across (the street) from the hotel
to go across the street/the square/the hills
to walk/drive across the bridge

Le cinéma est en face.
juste en face de l'hôtel
traverser la rue/la place/les collines

traverser le pont en marchant/en conduisant

actually *adv*
Actually, I'm not sure.
She claims she speaks five languages, but she actually speaks only two.
What did she actually say?
Did she actually do that?

A vrai dire, je ne suis pas sûr.
Elle prétend parler cinq langues, mais en fait elle n'en parle que deux.
Qu'est-ce qu'elle a dit exactement?
Est-ce qu'elle a vraiment fait ça?

Ø **actuellement** means "at present."

add *v*
in general
to add mustard
to add a comment
Value Added Tax (VAT)

ajouter
ajouter de la moutarde
ajouter une observation
la taxe à la valeur ajoutée (TVA)

in math
to add up the bill

additionner/faire une addition
faire l'addition de la note

addict n/addicted adj

a drug addict	un(e) drogué(e)/un(e) toxicomane
to be addicted to drugs	être adonné(e) à la drogue/aux stupéfiants
to be addicted to golf	être un(e) fanatique/un(e) fana [fam] du golf
	se passionner pour le golf

addition n

in addition [what's more/besides]	de plus/en plus/en outre
In addition, you're always late.	En plus, vous arrivez toujours en retard.
In addition to her poodles she has a spaniel.	En plus de ses caniches elle a un épagneul.

Ø ~~en addition~~ is not French.

additional adj

an additional [extra] week	une semaine supplémentaire
an additional charge	un supplément

admission n

Free admission.	Entrée gratuite.
There's a charge for admission.	L'entrée est payante.
admission to a school/a club	l'admission [f]

admit v

to own up to

to admit a mistake	reconnaître/avouer
I'm lazy, I must admit.	reconnaître une faute
	Je suis paresseux, je l'avoue.

to let in

to be admitted to a university	être admis(e) à une université
to be admitted to a club	se faire admettre à un club

advantage n

to take advantage of sb	abuser de qqn
to take advantage of the good weather to...	profiter du beau temps pour...

advertise v

to advertise a product	faire de la publicité/de la réclame pour un produit

advertisement *n*
an advertisement

classified advertisements
to put an ad in the paper
a TV ad [*a commercial*]

une publicité/une réclame/un message
   publicitaire
les petites annonces
mettre une annonce dans le journal
une publicité/une pub

Ø **avertissement** [*m*] means "warning" or "notice."

advice *n*
advice
to ask sb for advice
He always has advice to give.
That's a good piece of advice.

le conseil
demander conseil à qqn
Il a toujours des conseils à donner.
C'est un bon conseil.

Ø **avis** [*m*] usually means "opinion."

advise *v*
to advise sb to do sth

conseiller à qqn de faire qqch

Ø **aviser** means "to notify."

affair *n*
a love affair

une affaire de coeur/une liaison

Ø **affaires** [*f pl*] means "business," "events," or "things."

affluent *adj*
an affluent family

une famille riche

Ø **affluent** [*m*] means a "tributary."

afford *v*
I can't afford a car like that.

I can't afford it/that.

Je n'ai pas les moyens d'acheter une
   telle voiture.
Je n'en ai pas les moyens.
Je ne peux pas me payer ça/me
   permettre ça.

afraid *adj*
to be afraid of sb/sth

Don't be afraid of the dog.

to be afraid that. . .
I'm afraid (that) he'll fall.
I'm afraid of falling

to regret
I'm afraid I'm not free tonight.

avoir peur de qqn/qqch
craindre qqn/qqch
N'aie pas peur du chien.

avoir peur que [+*subjunctive*]
J'ai peur qu'il (ne) tombe.
J'ai peur de tomber. [*Note: The infinitive form is used if the subject of both verbs is the same.*]

Je regrette, je ne suis pas libre ce soir.

after *adv*
after(wards)
That happened afterwards.
soon after

après/ensuite
Cela s'est passé après.
peu après

after *prep & conj*
after
That was after the war.
She arrived after we had left.

I'll phone you after you've seen him.

He burned the letter after reading it.

après [*prep*]/après que [*conj*]
C'était après la guerre.
Elle est arrivée après que nous étions partis.
Elle est arrivée après notre départ.
[*Note: The noun form is preferred.*]
Je vous téléphonerai après que vous l'aurez vu. [*Note:* **Après que** *takes future tense when meaning is future.*]
Il a brûlé la lettre après l'avoir lue.
[*Note: The infinitive form is used when the subject of both verbs is the same.*]

again *adv*
once more
Try again.
Here we are, lost again.
You forgot your umbrella again.
She is sick again.

encore une fois/de nouveau/encore
Esssaye encore une fois.
Nous voici perdus de nouveau.
Tu as encore oublié ton parapluie.
Elle est encore malade. [*Note: This sentence can also mean "She is still sick."*]

in a negative
I won't say it again.

ne. . .plus
Je ne le dirai plus.

verb + again
to do sth again — refaire qqch
to go out again — ressortir
to go up/down again — remonter/redescendre
to leave again — repartir
to read again — relire
to see again — revoir
to start again — recommencer

agenda *n*
[*in general*] — le programme
agenda for an official meeting — l'ordre du jour

Ø **agenda** [*m*] means "appointment book."

aggravated *adj*
to be aggravated at sb/sth — être agacé(e)/exaspéré(e) par qqn/qqch

Ø **aggraver** means "to make worse."

ago *adv*
a long time ago — il y a longtemps
many years ago — il y a bien des années
a few minutes ago — il y a un moment/tout à l'heure
I spent a month in France two years ago. — J'ai passé un mois en France il y a deux ans.

agree *v*
to have the same opinion — être d'accord
I agree with him. — Je suis d'accord avec lui.
He doesn't agree. — Il n'est pas d'accord.
Do you agree? — D'accord?/Tu es d'accord?
We must agree on the price. — Il faut se mettre d'accord sur le prix.

to consent — consentir à/accepter de
They agreed to help us. — Ils ont consenti à nous aider.
Ils ont accepté de nous aider.

in grammar
In French, the adjective agrees with the noun. — En français, l'adjectif s'accorde avec le nom.

of food
Cucumbers don't agree with me. — Je n'arrive pas à digérer les concombres.

Ø **agréer**, used in business correspondence, means "to accept."

7

all

all *adj*

	tout tous
	toute toutes
all the time	tout le temps
all the ice cream	toute la glace
all (of) the children	tous les enfants [*Note: "Of" is not translated.*]
all (of) the churches	toutes les églises

all *pron*

	tout tous
	toute toutes
That's all.	C'est tout.
They have all arrived.	Ils sont tous arrivés. [*Note: When **tous** is used as a pronoun, the "s" is pronounced.*]
Come, all of you.	Venez tous. [*Note: "Of" is not translated.*]
Don't all leave together.	Ne partez pas tous ensemble.

all (that)

	tout ce qui [*subj*]
	tout ce que [*obj*]
That's all that's left.	C'est tout ce qui reste.
Eat all (that) you want.	Mangez tout ce que vous voulez.

all right [*see **okay***]

allow *v*

to permit

to allow sb to do sth	permettre à qqn de faire qqch
Smoking is not allowed.	Il est interdit/défendu de fumer.
	Défense de fumer.
No dogs allowed.	Les chiens ne sont pas admis.
	Les chiens sont interdits.
Is parking allowed here?	Est-ce que le stationnement est permis/autorisé ici?

to estimate

	prévoir/compter
You should allow half a liter per person.	Il faut prévoir un demi-litre par personne.
Allow at least ten minutes to get across town.	Comptez au moins dix minutes pour traverser la ville.

Ø **allouer** means "to allocate."

almost *adv*
The washing is almost dry.
We've almost finished.
I almost fell/fainted/laughed.

Le linge est presque sec.
Nous avons presque fini.
J'ai failli tomber/m'évanouir/rire.

along *prep*
to go along the river
The road runs along the river.
all along the beach/the street

longer le fleuve
La route longe le fleuve.
tout le long de la plage/la rue

also *adv*
They also heard the noise.
We went to the park and also to the zoo.

Eux aussi ont entendu le bruit.
Nous sommes allés au parc et aussi au zoo.

in addition
Also, I have things to do.

de plus/en plus/en outre
En plus, j'ai des choses à faire. [*Note: Do not use* **aussi** *at the start of a sentence to express "also"; in this position* **aussi** *means "therefore."*]

although *conj*
although

Ginette can read, although she's only four.

bien que [+*subjunctive*]
quoique [+ *subjunctive*]
Ginette sait lire, bien qu'elle n'ait que quatre ans.

alumni/alumnae *n*
[*graduates of a school*]

les anciens étudiants/les anciennes étudiantes

A.M.
two A.M.

deux heures du matin

angry *adj*
to be angry
to get angry with sb

Don't get angry.

être en colère/fâché(e)/furieux(-euse)
se mettre en colère/se fâcher **contre** qqn
Ne te fâche pas./Ne vous fâchez pas.

anniversary *n*
the anniversary

l'anniversaire [*m*]

announcer

the fiftieth anniversary of the liberation   le cinquantième anniversaire de la libération

a wedding anniversary   un anniversaire de mariage

Ø **anniversaire** [m] also means "birthday."

announcer *n*
radio/TV announcer   un speaker/une speakerine/un présentateur/une présentatrice/un annonceur

Ø **annonceur** [m] also means "advertiser."

another *adj*
additional   encore un(e)
Will you have another cookie?   Tu veux encore un petit gâteau?

different   autre
She's wearing another skirt today.   Elle porte une autre jupe aujourd'hui.

another (one) *pron*
additional   encore un(e)/un(e) de plus
I already have two seats. I need another.   J'ai déjà deux places. Il m'en faut encore une.

different   un(e) autre
My shirt is torn. I'll put on another one.   Ma chemise est déchirée. Je vais en mettre une autre.

antique *n*
[*an object*]   un objet ancien
[*a piece of furniture*]   un meuble ancien
an antique shop   un magasin d'antiquités
[*second-hand bric-a-brac*]   la brocante
an antique dealer   un antiquaire/un brocanteur

anxious *adj*
eager   impatient(e)/désireux(-euse)
He's anxious to leave right away.   Il est impatient de partir tout de suite.

apprehensive   inquiet(-ète)/soucieux(-euse)/anxieux(-euse)
She's anxious about her children.   Elle est inquiète au sujet de ses enfants. Elle s'inquiète pour ses enfants.

[*see also* **worried**]

any *adj*
no matter which
Read any magazine.
Any teacher could tell you that.

n'importe quel (quelle)
Lisez n'importe quelle revue.
N'importe quel professeur pourrait vous
   le dire.

in a question
Is there any milk?

du/de la/de l'/des
Est-ce qu'il y a du lait?

after a negative
I don't have any brothers.

de
Je n'ai pas de frère. [*Note: singular*]

any *pron*
any (one) at all
Which tie will you wear? — Any one
   will do.

n'importe lequel/laquelle
Quelle cravate veux-tu porter? —
   N'importe laquelle fera l'affaire.

any (of it, of them)
A little sugar? — No, I don't want any.

en
Un peu de sucre? — Non, je n'en veux
   pas.

I have no more matches. Do you have
   any?

Je n'ai plus d'allumettes. Tu en as?

anybody/anyone *pron*
no matter who
Ask anybody.
Anybody would know.

n'importe qui
Demandez à n'importe qui.
N'importe qui le saurait.

in the negative
She doesn't know anybody.
We haven't seen anybody.

ne . . . personne
Elle ne connaît personne.
Nous n'avons vu personne.

in a question
Is anybody home?
Have you found anybody for the job?

quelqu'un
Il y a quelqu'un?
Avez-vous trouvé quelqu'un pour le
   poste?

anyhow/anyway *adv*
in any case
I was tired but I went anyway.

de toute façon/quand même
J'étais fatigué mais j'y suis allé quand
   même.

any old how/way
It was put together any old how.

n'importe comment/à la va-vite
C'était assemblé n'importe comment.

11

anyone [see *anybody*]

anything *pron*
no matter what
They will eat anything if they're hungry. | n'importe quoi
Ils mangeront n'importe quoi s'ils ont faim.

something
If I find anything I'll bring it. | quelque chose
Si je trouve quelque chose je l'apporterai.

in a question
Did you hear anything? | quelque chose
As-tu entendu quelque chose?
Anything else? [in a store] | Il vous faut autre chose?
Et avec ça?

in a negative
He didn't see anything. | ne...rien
Il n'a rien vu.
I never buy anything expensive. | Je n'achète jamais rien de cher.

any time *adv*
[no matter when] | n'importe quand
You can phone her any time. | Tu peux lui téléphoner n'importe quand.

anyway [see *anyhow*]

anywhere *adv*
no matter where
You can buy them anywhere. | n'importe où
Vous pouvez les acheter n'importe où.

in a question
Have you seen her anywhere (around)? | Tu l'as vue quelque part?

in a negative
I didn't see her anywhere. | Je ne l'ai vue nulle part.

apology *n*/**apologize** *v*
to make an apology/to apologize | s'excuser/faire ses excuses
I apologize for the delay. | Je m'excuse du retard.
You should apologize to them. | Tu devrais t'excuser auprès d'eux.
I apologize for not writing sooner. | Excusez-moi de pas avoir écrit plus tôt.

Ø **apologie** [f] means "apologia."

12

appear *v*
to seem, look
He appears tired.

sembler/paraître/avoir l'air
Il semble fatigué./Il a l'air fatigué.

to become visible
They appeared on the balcony.

Ils ont paru au balcon.

Ø **apparaître** has limited use in spoken French.

application *n*
to make an application
a job application
to fill out an application form

faire une demande
une demande d'emploi
remplir un formulaire de demande

Ø **application** [*f*] means "implementation" or "use."

apply *v*
to apply for a job

faire une demande d'emploi/poser sa
  candidature pour un poste/solliciter
  un emploi

to apply for a passport
to apply to a university

faire une demande de passeport
faire une demande d'inscription

appointment *n*
an appointment
to make an appointment with sb

un rendez-vous
prendre rendez-vous avec qqn/donner
  rendez-vous à qqn

Do you have an appointment?
He has a doctor's appointment.
by appointment (only)

Avez-vous pris rendez-vous?
Il a rendez-vous chez le médecin.
(uniquement) sur rendez-vous

Ø **appointements** [*m pl*] means "salary."

appreciate *v*
to be grateful
I really appreciate all she did for me.

Je lui suis très reconnaissant de tout ce
  qu'elle a fait pour moi.

to like sth
I don't appreciate your attitude.

Je n'aime pas votre attitude.
Je n'apprécie pas votre attitude.

area

in a business letter

We would appreciate a prompt reply.	Nous vous serions obligés de bien vouloir répondre dans les plus brefs délais.

Ø **apprécier** also means "to evaluate" or "to assess."

area *n*

area (in square meters)	la superficie (en mètres carrés)
[*region of a country*]	la région
[*section of town*]	le quartier
area (of expertise)	le domaine (de compétence)
[*see also* **field**]	

argument *n*

to have an argument with sb	avoir une dispute avec qqn/se disputer avec qqn
She had an argument with her husband.	Elle s'est disputée avec son mari.
We had an argument.	Nous nous sommes disputés.

Ø **argument** [*m*] is used mainly in law and philosphy.

around *adv & prep*

approximately

They worked for around two days.	à peu près/environ
	Ils ont travaillé environ deux jours.
around 50 employees	à peu près 50 employés/une cinquantaine d'employés
around 20/around 30	une vingtaine/une trentaine

time

Come back around two o'clock.	vers
	Revenez vers deux heures.

round, all around

to walk around the park	faire un tour/se promener dans le parc
They've made a circular route around the city.	On a construit une route périphérique autour de la ville.
We gathered around the fire.	Nous nous sommes réunis autour du feu.
There was smoke all around.	Il y avait de la fumée tout autour.

other expressions

the first house around the corner	la première maison après le coin
Is she around?	Elle est là?

Have you seen her around?	Tu l'as vue quelque part?
When he's around his friends, he...	Quand il est avec ses amis, il...

arrangements *n*

I'll make all the arrangements.	Je vais m'occuper de tout.
	Je ferai tout le nécessaire.
	Je prendrai toutes les dispositions nécessaires.

arrest *n & v*

He was arrested by the police.	Il a été arrêté par la police.
to be under arrest	être en état d'arrestation

as *conj & prep*
in comparisons

as...as	aussi...que
as big as	aussi grand que
as fast as	aussi rapidement que
as long as [see **long**]	
as much as [see **much**]	
as many as [see **many**]	

other expressions

as for me...	quant à moi...
As an engineer, I...	En tant qu'ingénieur, je...
as [since] he was late	puisqu'il était en retard/comme il était en retard
as [when] he was leaving	au moment où il partait/comme il partait
She is working as a saleswoman.	Elle travaille comme vendeuse. [Note: no article]
disguised as/dressed as	déguisé **en**/habillé **en**
She was dressed as a witch.	Elle était déguisée en sorcière. [Note: no article]

ask *v*

to ask for sth	demander qqch [Note: "For" is not ··translated.]
to ask sb (for) sth	demander qqch à qqn
to ask sb to do sth	demander à qqn de faire qqch
to ask a question	poser une question [Note: not **demander**]

15

asleep

asleep [see *sleep*]

assist *v*

to asist sb	aider/assister qqn
Can I assist you?	Est-ce que je peux vous aider?

Ø **assister à** means "to be present at" or "to attend."

assume *v*

to assume [*suppose*]	supposer/présumer
I assume he's coming.	Je suppose qu'il viendra.

Ø **assumer** means "to take over" (e.g., responsibilities).

at *prep*
a place

at the office	**au** bureau
at school	**à** l'école
at the baker's (shop)	**à la** boulangerie
at the Galeries Lafayette	**aux** Galeries Lafayette

somebody's home or place of work — **chez** quelqu'un

at the baker's	**chez** le boulanger [*Note the difference between* **chez** *and* **à**: **chez** *le boulanger (a person) but* **à** *la boulangerie (a place).*]
at Paul's (house)	**chez** Paul
at my aunt's (house)	**chez** ma tante
at the wine merchant's	**chez** le marchand de vins
at my house/my place	**chez** moi

time

at that time	à ce moment-là/à cette époque-là
at the moment	pour l'instant/en ce moment
at times	parfois
three at a time	trois à la fois
at night	la nuit

with verbs

to look at sb/sth	regarder qqn/qqch
to stare at sb/sth	fixer qqn/qqch
to aim at sb/sth	viser qqn/qqch
to be angry at sb	être fâché/se fâcher **contre** qqn

to be irritated/furious at sb	être irrité/furieux **contre** qqn
to rush at sb/sth	se précipiter sur qqn/qqch
to fire at sb/sth	tirer **sur** qqn/qqch
to laugh at sb/sth	rire **de** qqn/qqch
	se moquer **de** qqn/qqch
to be surprised at sb/sth	être surpris **de** qqn/qqch
to be astonished at sb/sth	être étonné **de** qqn/qqch
to point at sb/sth	montrer qqn/qqch du doigt

other expressions

to be good at math	être bon/fort **en** math
at sea/at peace/at war	**en** mer/**en** paix/**en** guerre

A.T.M.

automatic teller machine	un distributeur automatique/un guichet automatique
an ATM card	une carte bancaire

attend v

to attend a meeting	assister à une réunion
to attend a show/a concert/a performance	assister à un spectacle/un concert/une présentation
to attend a school/a university/a church	aller à une école/une université/une église
to attend a class	suivre un cours

Ø **attendre** means "to wait for."

attentive adj

to be attentive to sb	être attentionné(e) pour qqn
	être prévenant(e) envers qqn
an attentive audience	un public attentif

attractive adj

[*clothes*]	seyant(e)
[*price, idea, plan*]	intéressant(e)
[*objects*]	beau (belle)/joli(e)

a person

She's a very attractive girl.	C'est une très jolie fille.
	Elle a beaucoup d'allure.
	Elle est belle fille.
He's an attractive guy.	Il est beau gars/joli garçon.

17

audience

Ø **attractif**(-ve) is used mainly in physics.

audience   n
[in general]   le public
He disappointed his audience.   Il a déçu son public.
[on the radio/at a concert]   les auditeurs
[in a theater/a sports show]   les spectateurs
[on television]   les téléspectateurs

Ø **audience** [ʃ] means a "hearing."

available   adj
She is not available tonight.   Elle n'est pas libre ce soir.
The manager is not available right now.   Monsieur le directeur n'est pas
                                               disponible pour le moment.
Is this model available in other sizes/   Est-ce que ce modèle existe en d'autres
    colors?   tailles/couleurs?
This book is no longer available.   Ce livre n'est plus disponible.
Butter was not available during the war.   On ne trouvait pas de beurre pendant
                                               la guerre.

average   adj & n
numerical average   la moyenne
to take the average of the prices   faire la moyenne des prix
on the average   en moyenne
[typical]   moyen(-enne)
the average Frenchman   le Français moyen
of average height   de taille moyenne

away   adv
He's away.   Il n'est pas là./Il est parti./Il est en
                                               déplacement.
The lake is ten kilometers away.   Le lac est à dix kilomètres (d'ici).
to go away   partir/s'en aller
Go away!   Va-t'en!/Allez-vous-en!

≡ B ≡

baby-sit *v*/**baby-sitter** *n*

to baby-sit   s'occuper d'enfants/garder des enfants/ faire du baby-sitting

a baby-sitter   un(e) baby-sitter

bachelor *n*

[*unmarried man*]   un célibataire/un vieux garçon [*fam*]

bachelor's degree   une licence

to have a bachelor's degree in arts/ science   être licencié(e) ès lettres/ès sciences

Ø **être bachelier** means to have the secondary school **baccalauréat** diploma.

back *adj & n*

at the back   à l'arrière

We were at the back of the bus.   Nous étions à l'arrière de l'autobus.

the back seat [*of a car*]   le siège arrière

the back tires   les pneus arrière

in the back row   au dernier rang

in back of [*behind*] the wall   derrière le mur

You have your pullover on back to front.   Tu as mis ton pull devant derrière.

Sign the back of the check.   Signez au dos du chèque.

back *adv*

verb + back

to be back   être de retour

to come back   revenir

to come back home   rentrer

to go back   retourner

to give back   rendre

to pay back   rembourser

to phone back   rappeler

It's back-to-school time.   C'est la rentrée.

background *n*

in the background   au fond/à l'arrière-plan

training, experience   la formation (professionnelle)

19

She has a strong background in computer science.	Elle a une formation solide en informatique.

social class

He comes from a working-class/middle-class background.	Il sort d'un milieu ouvrier/bourgeois.

bad *adj*

bad weather	le mauvais temps
a bad mistake	une faute grave
a bad cold	un gros rhume
You're a bad girl!	Tu n'es pas sage!
I feel bad [*sick*].	Je ne me sens pas bien.
I feel bad [*sorry*].	Ça m'ennuie./Je suis désolé(e).
[*see also* **feel**]	

badly *adv*

to dress badly/to eat badly/to speak badly	s'habiller mal/manger mal/parler mal
badly written/badly designed/badly lit	mal écrit(e)/mal conçu(e)/mal éclairé(e)

bake *v*

to bake	faire cuire au four
to bake bread/a cake	faire du pain/un gâteau [*Note: no need to add* **au four**]
to bake [*meats, fish*]	faire rôtir
baked chicken	du poulet rôti
baked potato	une pomme de terre en robe de chambre/en robe des champs

balance *n*

to keep one's balance	garder son équilibre
a balance sheet	un bilan
the balance (of an account)	le solde (d'un compte)
the balance of payments	la balance des paiements

Ø **balance** [*f*] also means "a weighing scale."

balance *v*

to balance the budget	équilibrer le budget
a well-balanced diet	un régime bien équilibré

Ø **balancer** means "to swing."

ball   *n*

[*small ball; e.g., tennis*]	une balle
[*large ball; e.g., basketball*]	un ballon
[*a dance*]	un bal
to have a ball [*enjoy oneself*]	s'amuser follement

band   *n*

a (dance) band	un orchestre (de danse)
the big (50s) bands	les grands orchestres (des années cinquante)
a (marching) band [*in U.S. school*]	un orchestre d'école/une fanfare
a military or town band	une musique/une fanfare
a small band [*a combo*]	un petit groupe de musiciens

Ø **bande** [*f*] has several meanings, including "a strip" or "a gang."

basement   *n*

[*lower floor*]	le sous-sol
The appliance department is in the basement.	L'électroménager est au sous-sol.

French houses do not usually have a basement. They may have a cellar, called **une cave**, for wine, vegetables, etc.

bathroom   [*see* **toilet**]

battery   *n*

[*for radio, flashlight*]	une pile
a car battery	une batterie/les accumulateurs
The battery is dead.	Les accus sont à plat.

Ø **batterie** [*f*] also means "a set of drums."

because   *conj & prep*

because+verb	parce que
because it is foggy	parce qu'il fait du brouillard
because of+noun	à cause de
because of the fog	à cause du brouillard

become v
to become	devenir [*Note: conjugated with* **être**]
They became too important.	Ils sont devenus trop importants.
He became [*was made*] a corporal.	Il est devenu caporal.
What became of the Duvals?	Qu'est-ce qu'ils sont devenus, les Duval?
to become famous/pretty	devenir célèbre/joli(e)
[*see also* **get**]	

bed n
to go to bed	se coucher
to put a child to bed	coucher un(e) enfant

before adv
[*earlier, previously*]	avant/auparavant/plus tôt
three months before	trois mois avant
the day/the night before	la veille
the week before	la semaine précédente
I've heard that song before.	J'ai déjà entendu cette chanson.

before conj
before	avant que [+*subjunctive*]
	avant de [+*infinitive*]
He will be here before I leave.	Il sera là avant que je (ne) parte.
I'll call you before I leave.	Je t'appellerai avant de partir. [*Note:* **avant de** *is used when the subject of both verbs is the same*]

before prep
time / **avant**
before dinner	avant le dîner
before midnight	avant minuit

in front of / **devant**
before the judge	devant le juge

behind [*see* **back**]

believe v
to have faith in / croire à/en
to believe in God	croire en Dieu
to believe in miracles	croire aux miracles

to think / penser/croire

Will he be there? — I believe so. Est-ce qu'il sera là? — Je pense que oui.

belong v
ownership être à/appartenir à
Do these keys belong to you? — No, Ces clés sont à vous? — Non, elles sont
  they belong to the boss.   au patron.

membership faire partie de/être membre de
He belongs to the Young Socialists. Il fait partie des Jeunes Socialistes.

below adv
[*underneath*] en dessous/en bas
She works in the shop below. Elle travaille dans la boutique en
  dessous.
See below. [*in a text*] Voir ci-dessous.

below prep
[*under*] au-dessous de
below average au-dessous de la moyenne

beside prep
[*next to*] à côté de
Put the lamp beside the couch. Mettez la lampe à côté du canapé.
She was sitting beside him. Elle était assise à côté de lui.

besides [*see **addition***]

bet v
to bet parier
I bet it's your friend. Je parie que c'est ton ami.
to bet five to one parier cinq contre un
to bet on a horse miser sur un cheval

better/best adj
better meilleur   meilleurs
  meilleure   meilleures
best le meilleur   les meilleurs
  la meilleure   les meilleures
She got a better grade than you. Elle a obtenu une meilleure note que
  toi.
the better grade (of the two) la meilleure note (des deux)
the best grade (of all) la meilleure note (de toutes)

better/best

	[*Note: **la meilleure note** can mean "the better grade" or "the best grade," depending on the context.*]
the best grade in the class	la meilleure note **de** la classe [*Note: **de** after a superlative*]
much better	**bien** meilleur [*Note: **not beaucoup**]

better/best *adv*

better	mieux
best	le mieux [*invar*]
She writes better than you.	Elle écrit mieux que toi.
She writes the best in the group.	Elle écrit le mieux du groupe. [*Note: **de** after a superlative*]
much better (than)	bien mieux/beaucoup mieux (que)
You had better go now.	Vous feriez mieux de partir tout de suite.
It would be better not to say anything.	Il vaudrait mieux ne rien dire.
Wednesday suits me best.	Mercredi me convient le mieux.

big *adj*

of people	grand(e)/gros (grosse)
a big boy [*tall*]	un grand garçon
a big boy [*fat*]	un gros garçon
his big brother [*older*]	son grand frère

other	
a big city/house/noise	une grande ville/une grande maison/un grand bruit
a big piece/slice/lie	un gros morceau/une grosse tranche/un gros mensonge

In general, **grand** is used for "big [*tall, high, extensive*]" and **gros** for "big [*fat, thick, bulky*]," e.g., **une grande grue** [*crane*], **un gros potiron** [*pumpkin*]. However, in many cases, **grand** and **gros** are interchangeable, e.g., **une grosse fortune, une grande fortune.**

bill *n*

[*hotel, electricity, doctor*]	la note
[*invoice for merchandise*]	la facture
[*restaurant*]	l'addition [*f*]
[*paper money*]	un billet
a 200 franc bill	un billet de 200 francs

billion   n

one billion	un milliard
1,000,000,000	1.000.000.000 [*Note French punctuation*]

Ø **billion** [m] is a US trillion.

birthday   n

a birthday	un anniversaire (de naissance)/une fête
It's my birthday tomorrow.	C'est mon anniversaire demain.

Ø **fête** [*f*] may also mean "a person's name day" (saint's day) or "a party."

blame   v

He is not to blame.	Ce n'est pas de sa faute.
What I blame her for is her laziness.	Ce que je lui reproche, c'est sa paresse.
They blamed the other driver for the accident.	Ils ont rejeté la responsabilité de l'accident sur l'autre conducteur.
I don't blame you.	Tu as raison./Je te comprends./Tu as bien fait.

bless   v

to bless	bénir
Bless you! [*when someone sneezes*]	A tes/vos souhaits!
	A tes/vos amours!

Ø **blesser** means "to hurt."

block   n

It's three blocks away.	C'est à 500 mètres d'ici.
	C'est trois rues plus loin.
Go three blocks and turn left.	Prenez la troisième rue à gauche.
a square [*city*] block	un pâté de maisons

There is no real equivalent in French of "block." In European cities, distances are usually given in meters.

boil   v

to boil	bouillir
The water is boiling.	L'eau bout.
I'm boiling some water.	Je fais bouillir de l'eau.
boiled beef/a boiled egg/boiled potatoes	du boeuf bouilli/un oeuf à la coque/des pommes à l'eau

25

bored *adj*
to be/get bored
I often get bored in class.
They look bored.

s'ennuyer [*Note: not* ***être ennuyé***]
Je m'ennuie souvent en classe.
Elles ont l'air de s'ennuyer.

boring *adj*
boring
Her work is very boring.

ennuyeux(-euse) [*Note: not* ***ennuyant***]
Son travail est très ennuyeux.

born *v*
to be born
Over 100 children are born every day
in that clinic.
She was born in Burgundy.
Where were you born?

naître
Plus de 100 enfants naissent chaque
jour dans cette clinique.
Elle est née en Bourgogne.
Où êtes-vous né?

borrow *v*
to borrow sth from sb
I borrowed this sweater from my
roommate.

emprunter qqch **à** qqn
J'ai emprunté ce tricot à ma camarade
de chambre.

both *adj*
both
to kiss on both cheeks
We need both papers.

les deux
embrasser sur les deux joues
Nous avons besoin des deux journaux.

both *pron*
both
John and his mother both signed.
Both of them signed.
They both signed.
both of us/both of you

tous les deux/toutes les deux
Jean et sa mère ont signé tous les deux.
Tous les deux ont signé.
Ils ont signé tous les deux.
nous deux/vous deux

both . . . and *conj*
I take both milk and sugar.

They are studying both physics and
chemistry.
She could both draw and paint.

Je prends du lait et du sucre. [*Note:
"Both" may be omitted in French.*]
Ils étudient la physique et la chimie.

Elle savait et dessiner et peindre. [*Note:*
et . . . et *is a literary form.*]

bother *v*
to bother sb

ennuyer/déranger/gêner qqn
embêter qqn [*fam*]

I'm sorry to bother you.   Je m'excuse de vous déranger.
The light bothers me in the mornings.   La lumière me gêne le matin.
Please don't bother!   Ne vous dérangez pas!
You're bothering us!   Tu nous embêtes!

bottom (at the) *prep*

at the bottom of	au bas de/en bas de/au fond de
at the bottom of the page/the stairs	au bas de la page/de l'escalier
at the bottom of the sea/the hole/the cupboard	au fond de la mer/du trou/du placard

boyfriend *n*

my boyfriend	mon petit ami/mon copain

brain *n*

[*mind, intelligence*]	le cerveau
animal brains [*cooked*]	la cervelle [*Note: singular*]

brassiere *n*

a brassiere [*a bra*]	un soutien-gorge

Ø **brassière** [*f*] means "a baby's undershirt"; **brasserie** [*f*] means "a brewery" or "a bar."

break *n*

to take a break	faire la pause
the class break	la pause
the coffee break	la pause-café
the lunch break	l'heure du déjeuner

break down *v*/breakdown *n*
of machines, vehicles

to break down	tomber en panne
We had a breakdown right in the middle of the freeway.	Nous sommes tombés en panne en pleine autoroute.
the breakdown truck	la dépanneuse

emotional

to break down crying	fondre en larmes
to have a nervous breakdown	faire une dépression nerveuse

bright *adj*

a bright light	une lumière vive
a bright color	une couleur vive

bring

a bright child [*smart*]	un enfant doué/brillant
a bright room [*well-lit*]	une pièce claire

bring *v*
people, animals, vehicles   amener
Bring your children.   Amenez vos enfants.

things you can carry   apporter
Bring a hot dish.   Apportez un plat chaud.

Amener and **apporter** mean "to bring to the place where you are"; **emmener** and **emporter** mean "to take to another place." [*see* **take**]

brown *adj*
brown	châtain(e)/marron [*invar*]/brun(e)
He has brown hair.	Il a les cheveux châtains.
brown shoes	des chaussures marron [*Note:* **brun** *is not used of clothes*]

building *n*
a building	un bâtiment/un édifice
an apartment/office building	un immeuble
[*the process of building*]	la construction
the building trades	les métiers de construction

bus *n*
a (city) bus	un autobus/un bus
[*a bus going between cities*]	un car/un autocar
a tour bus	un car (de tourisme)

business *n*
in general	les affaires [*f*] [*Note: plural*]
Business is good.	Les affaires marchent bien.
a business lunch/meeting	un déjeuner d'affaires/une réunion d'affaires
a business man/woman	un homme/une femme d'affaires
to travel on business	voyager pour affaires
to do business with sb	traiter avec qqn
Mind your own business!	Mêlez-vous de vos affaires!
	Occupe-toi de tes affaires!
a company	une entreprise/une compagnie/une maison/une société

28

busy n

I'm very busy.	Je suis très occupé(e).
I'm busy tonight.	Je ne suis pas libre ce soir.
	Je suis pris(e) ce soir.
to be busy doing sth	être occupé(e) à faire qqch
The line is busy.	La ligne est occupée.
[of a place, street, town]	animé(e)
The main street is very busy on market days.	La grand-rue est très animée les jours de marché.

by prep
time

by day/by night	**de** jour/**de** nuit
to travel by night	voyager **de** nuit
I need it by Monday/by three o'clock.	J'en ai besoin **pour** lundi/**pour** trois heures.
They should be here by next week.	Ils devraient arriver **avant** la semaine prochaine.

measurement, rate

They are sold by the liter/the meter/the kilogram.	Ils se vendent **au** litre/**au** mètre/**au** kilo.
to rent by the month	louer **au** mois
to be paid by the week	être payé **à la** semaine

place

by the sea/the lake	**au bord de** la mer/du lac
to go by the church	passer **devant** l'église
Come by if you're in the neighborhood.	Passez à la maison si vous vous trouvez dans le quartier.
I'll come by and pick you up around noon.	Je passerai te prendre vers midi.

travel

by boat/by car	**en** bateau/**en** voiture
by motorcycle	**en** moto(cyclette)
by bicycle	**à/en** bicyclette/vélo
by train	**par** le train
People travel by plane.	Les gens voyagent **en** avion.
Letters are sent by plane.	Les lettres sont expédiées **par** avion.

means

made by hand/by machine	fait **à** la main/**à** la machine
I know her by name/by sight.	Je la connais **de** nom/**de** vue.
a novel by Zola	un roman **de** Zola
to do sth all by oneself	faire qqch tout seul/toute seule

by

verb+by+gerund

You learn by studying.

On apprend **en** étudiant.

past participle+by+noun

to be accompanied by/loved by/feared
by/respected by/surprised by/
followed by/surrounded by/preceded
by

être accompagné(e) **de**/aimé **de**/
craint(e) **de**/respecté(e) **de**/surpris(e)
de/suivi(e) **de**/entouré(e) **de**/
précédé(e) **de**

C

cabin *n*
a small (mountain) cabin   un petit chalet (de montagne)

Ø **cabine** [*f*] means "a cubicle" or "a ship's cabin."

camera *n*
a still camera   un appareil (photo)

Ø **caméra** [*f*] means "movie camera."

can *v*

I can [*am able to*] do it.	Je peux le faire.
Can I [*may I*] do it?	Est-ce que je peux le faire?
I can [*know how to*] do it.	Je sais le faire.
Can you swim?	Savez-vous nager?
I can't swim today because of my leg.	Je ne peux pas nager aujourd'hui à cause de ma jambe.

[*see also* **could**]

can *n*

a can of peas	une boîte de petits pois
a can of beer	une canette de bière
a garbage can	une poubelle

cancel *v*

to cancel	annuler/se décommander
to cancel an appointment/a meeting	annuler un rendez-vous/une réunion
They canceled at the last minute.	Ils se sont décommandés à la dernière minute.

car *n*
[*an automobile*]   une auto/une voiture/une bagnole [*fam*]
You can borrow my car.   Tu peux emprunter ma bagnole.

Ø **car** [*m*] (short for **autocar**) means "a bus going between cities."

care *n & v*
to look after

	s'occuper de/se charger de/prendre soin de/soigner
She takes care of three children.	Elle s'occupe de trois enfants.
They take care of all the orders.	Ils se chargent de toutes les commandes.
I'll take care of that.	Je vais m'en charger.
The nurse cares for the patients.	L'infirmière soigne les malades.
Take care of yourself!	Soignez-vous bien!
I take good care of my shoes.	Je prends grand soin de mes chaussures.

to feel interest, concern

to care (a lot) about sb	aimer bien qqn/avoir beaucoup d'affection pour qqn
I really care about that.	C'est vraiment important pour moi.
I don't care.	Ça m'est égal.
I couldn't care less.	Je m'en moque./Je m'en fiche. [*fam*]
Who cares?	Qu'est-ce que ça peut faire?

to like, want something

I don't care for cauliflower.	Je n'aime pas le chou-fleur.
Would you care for some lemon tea?	Voulez-vous du thé au citron?

to pay attention

Take care you don't spill your coffee.	Fais attention à ne pas renverser ton café.
"handle with care"	"fragile"
in care of (c/o)	aux bons soins de (a/s)
Mrs. A. care of Mrs. B.	Mme A. aux bons soins de Mme B.

to have worries

He hasn't a care in the world.	Il n'a pas le moindre souci.
She is carefree.	Elle est sans souci.

careful *adj*
painstaking

	soigneux(-euse)
a careful workman	un ouvrier soigneux

cautious

	prudent(e)
a careful driver	un chauffeur prudent
Be careful!	Sois prudent!/Attention!

carefully *adv*

[*cautiously*]	prudemment
[*painstakingly*]	soigneusement/avec soin

cartoon *n*
[*animated film*]   un dessin animé
[*humorous drawing, e.g., in newspaper*]   un dessin humoristique
[*comic strip*]   une bande dessinée (une B.D.)
[*the comics*]   les bandes dessinées

case *n*
in case
in case of emergency   en cas d'urgence
In case you arrive before her...   Au cas où vous arriveriez avant elle...
                                             [*Note: conditional*]

cash *n*
[*money*]   l'argent [*m*]
[*notes & coins*]   l'argent comptant/l'argent liquide/les
                                             espèces [*f pl*]
I don't have any cash on me.   Je n'ai pas d'argent sur moi.
to pay cash   payer comptant/en liquide/en espèces
Will this be cash or check?   Ce sera en liquide ou par chèque?

cash *v*
to cash a check   encaisser/toucher un chèque
to cash a traveler's check   changer un travellers/un chèque de
                                             voyage

casserole *n*
[*the container*]   un plat à four/un plat allant au four
[*the food*]   un plat (cuisiné) au four [*Note: The U.S.
                                             casserole has no real equivalent in
                                             French cuisine.*]

Ø **casserole** [*f*] means "saucepan."

casual *adj*/**casually** *adv*
casual clothes   des vêtements décontractés [*m*]/des
                                             vêtements sport [*invar*]
a casual atmosphere   une ambiance détendue/une ambiance
                                             décontractée
Dress casually!   Habille-toi décontracté! [*Note:
                                             invariable*]

[*see also* **informal**]

33

catch v
in general
to catch a ball	attraper une balle
to catch [*trap*] an animal	prendre/attraper un animal
He caught three big trout in the stream.	Il a pris trois grosses truites dans le ruisseau.

transportation
You can catch the (number) nine at this stop.	Tu peux prendre le (numéro) neuf à cet arrêt.
I must catch that train.	Il ne faut pas que je manque ce train.
	Il faut absolument que j'attrape ce train.

a disease
The baby caught the measles.	Le bébé a attrapé la rougeole.

caution n
with caution	prudemment/avec prudence

Ø **caution** [*f*] has various meanings, including "a guarantee" and "bail."

cave n
a cave	une caverne/une grotte
cave man	l'homme des cavernes

Ø **cave** [*f*] means "cellar."

challenge n
a challenge	un défi/une gageure
It's a real challenge.	C'est une véritable gageure.
My new job is a challenge [*is challenging*.]	Mon nouvel emploi est motivant/ passionnant/stimulant/absorbant.

chance n
by chance	par hasard
to take a chance	prendre un risque
The chances are/There is a chance that...	Il y a des chances que [+*subjunctive*]
She has a good chance of winning.	Elle a de bonnes chances de gagner.

opportunity
	l'occasion/la possibilité
I have the chance to go to Spain this Fall.	J'ai la possibilité d'aller en Espagne cet automne.
I've never had the chance.	Je n'en ai jamais eu l'occasion.

Ø **chance** [f] also means "luck."

chandelier   n
[*a center hanging light*]   un lustre

Ø **chandelier** [m] means "candleholder."

change   n
[*a modification*]   un changement
[*small change*]   la monnaie

Ø **change** [m] means foreign exchange, e.g., dollars to francs.

change   v
to alter   changer
He has changed a lot.   Il a beaucoup changé.
to change one's mind   changer d'avis/d'idée
I've changed my mind.   J'ai changé d'idée.

to switch
to change doctors/plans/trains   changer de médecin/de projet/de train
                                                 [*Note: singular noun*]
to change shoes/clothes   changer de chaussures/de vêtements
                                                 [*Note: plural noun*]
I have to change (clothes).   Il faut que je me change.

to exchange currency
to change Swiss francs for English   changer des francs suisses en livres
   pounds   anglaises

character   n
temperament, disposition   le caractère/le tempérament
You and I don't have the same   Vous et moi, nous n'avons pas le même
   character.   caractère.
a man of good character   un homme de bonne réputation

a story, film character   un personnage
He's (quite) a character!   C'est un numéro!/Quel type!

Ø **avoir bon caractère** means "to be good-natured"; **avoir mauvais caractère** means "to be ill-natured."

charge

charge *n*

to pay an admission charge	payer l'entrée
There is no charge.	C'est gratuit.
an extra charge	un supplément
The charge will be 50 francs.	Ça va coûter 50 francs.
to be in charge of	se charger de/être responsable de
the person in charge	le/la responsable
I would like to speak with the person in charge.	Je voudrais parler au responsable.

Ø **charge** [ʃ] has various meanings, including "load" and "responsibility."

charge *v*

How much do you charge?	Quels sont vos tarifs?
	Ce sera combien?
He charges 60 francs an hour.	Il prend/demande 60 F de l'heure.
They charged her 10 francs too much.	On lui a fait payer 10 francs de trop.
to charge with a credit card	payer par carte de crédit
Do you wish to charge this?	Ce sera sur votre carte?

Ø **charger** has various meanings, including "to give responsibility" and "to load."

chauvinist *n*

a male chauvinist	un macho/un phallocrate

Ø **chauvin**(e) means "excessively patriotic."

cheap *adj*
inexpensive

	bon marché [*invar*]/pas cher (chère)
Those socks were very cheap.	Ces chaussettes étaient très bon marché.
cheaper [*less expensive*]	meilleur marché/moins cher
It's cheap junk.	C'est de la camelote.

stingy

	radin(e)/pingre/avare
He never pays. He's too cheap.	Il ne paye jamais. Il est trop radin.

cheat *v*

to cheat at cards/in an exam	tricher aux cartes/à un examen
to cheat sb [*swindle*]	escroquer qqn
to cheat on sb [*be unfaithful*]	tromper qqn/être infidèle à qqn

check *n*

a bank check	un chèque

a traveler's check	un chèque (de) voyage/un travellers
[*in a restaurant*]	l'addition [*f*]

check *v*
in general
| to check the date/the oil/the weight/the accounts | vérifier
vérifier la date/l'huile/le poids/les comptes |

other
to check luggage	faire enregistrer des bagages
to check one's coat	laisser son manteau au vestiaire
to check a box [*on a form*]	cocher une case
to check passports/tickets [*e.g., at airport*]	contrôler les passeports/les billets

checkup *n*
| a (medical) checkup | un examen médical/un bilan de santé |
| You ought to get a checkup. | Tu devrais te faire faire un bilan de santé. |

city *n*
| a small city | une petite ville |
| a large city | une grande ville/une ville importante |

Ø cité [*f*] has specific meanings: a medieval walled city, the old part of a town, a student housing complex, a suburban housing development.

class *n*
a course
to take a class	un cours
a class in Greek literature	suivre un cours
the class of '95	un cours de littérature grecque
a classmate [*in elementary or high school*]	la promotion de 1995
We were classmates. [*in university*]	un(e) camarade de classe
a former classmate	Nous avons fait nos études ensemble.
	un ancien camarade d'étude

social class
the working class	la classe ouvrière
the middle class	la bourgeoisie
the upper class	la haute bourgeoisie

clerk [*see **worker**]

climb v

to climb the steps/stairs	monter les marches/l'escalier
They climbed the stairs.	Ils ont monté l'escalier. [*Note:* **monter** *is conjugated with* **avoir** *when it has a direct object.*]
to climb a hill [*a slope*]	monter une pente/une côte
to climb a hill [*a mountain*]	gravir/escalader une colline
to climb a wall/a fence	escalader un mur/une clôture
to climb a tree	grimper dans un arbre

close adj

a close friend	un(e) ami(e) intime
to be close to sb	être proche de qqn/lié(e) avec qqn
We are very close, Jane and I.	Nous sommes très liées, Jeanne et moi.
a close contest/a close election	une lutte serrée/une élection serrée

close prep & adv

I live close to the school.	J'habite près de l'école.
We're getting close to Tours.	Nous approchons de Tours.
I live close by.	J'habite tout près.

closet n

[*a hanging closet*]	une penderie
[*cupboard*]	un placard/une armoire

coed adj

a coed high school/university	un lycée mixte/une université mixte

coffee n

(black) coffee [*small*]	un café
coffee with cream [*small*]	un café crème/un crème
coffee with milk [*large, for breakfast*]	un café au lait
espresso coffee	un café express/un express [*Note: Final "ss" is pronounced.*]

cold adj

It's cold. [*weather*]	Il **fait** froid.
The milk is cold. [*an object*]	Le lait **est** froid.
The child is cold. [*a person*]	L'enfant **a** froid.
My hands are cold.	J'ai froid aux mains.

cold n
temperature

	le froid

I can stand the cold better than the heat.	Je supporte mieux le froid que la chaleur.

infection un rhume (de cerveau)
a bad cold un gros rhume/un sale rhume
to have a cold être enrhumé(e)/avoir un rhume
to catch a cold attraper un rhume/s'enrhumer
She caught a cold. Elle s'est enrhumée.

collect   *v*
to make a collection faire collection de/collectionner
I collect butterflies/water colors. Je collectionne les papillons/les aquarelles.

to pick up ramasser
We collected shells on the beach. Nous avons ramassé des coquillages sur la plage.

telephone
a collect call une communication en PCV [*Note: pronounced **pé cé vé**]

to call collect appeler en PCV

college   *n*
a college une université
to go to/be in college aller/être à l'université

Ø **collège** [*m*] is usually a junior high or high school.

color   *n*
people of color (Blacks, Whites, Asians, Native Americans) les gens de couleur (les Noirs, les Blancs, les Asiatiques, les Indiens d'Amérique)

come   *v*
[*come+adverb*]
to come in/out entrer/sortir
to come back (home) revenir/rentrer
to come up/down monter/descendre
to come up [*to happen*]
He was supposed to be there at three but something came up. Il devait être là à trois heures, mais il a eu un empêchement.

comfortable   *adj*
of things confortable

commencement

a comfortable chair/car/house	un fauteuil/une auto/une maison confortable

of people

[Note: **confortable** is not used of people.]

to be comfortable	être à l'aise
I am/feel comfortable.	Je suis à l'aise.
	Je me sens bien.
Make yourself comfortable!	Mettez-vous à l'aise!
	Faites comme chez vous!
to feel comfortable [in a situation]	se sentir à l'aise
I don't feel comfortable with them.	Je ne me sens pas à l'aise/Je me sens gêné avec eux.
to be comfortably off	être aisé(e)/vivre dans l'aisance

commencement n

[graduation ceremony]   la remise des diplômes

Ø **commencement** [m] means "beginning."

commute n & v

to commute	faire la navette/faire le trajet
He commutes from the suburbs to downtown.	Il fait la navette entre la banlieue et le centre-ville.
the daily commute	le trajet journalier/le trajet régulier
commute time	le temps du trajet
I have a 50 minute commute.	Je mets 50 minutes pour faire le trajet.

commuter n

There is no real equivalent for "commuter" in French. **Un(e) banlieusard(e)**, meaning "a suburbanite," is sometimes used.

compact disk n

a compact disk (CD)	un disque compact/un compact-disque
a compact disk player	un lecteur laser

company n
a business

	une entreprise/une société/une compagnie/une maison
I work for a small business.	Je travaille pour une petite entreprise.

guests

to have company	avoir des invités/de la visite
We expect company tonight.	Nous attendons de la visite ce soir.

competition *n*

a national competition	un concours national
a beauty competition	un concours de beauté
a sports competition	une compétition sportive
competition [*in business*]	la concurrence
unfair competition	la concurrence déloyale

complain *v*
in general

to complain (about)	se plaindre (de)
I can't complain!	Je ne me plains pas!
He's always complaining about his health.	Il se plaint toujours de sa santé.

to make a formal complaint — faire une réclamation/se plaindre
I'm going to complain to the management. — Je vais me plaindre auprès de la direction.

Ø ~~complaindre~~ is not French.

composition *n*

to write a composition — faire une rédaction/une dissertation
[*see also* **paper**]

concentrate *v*

to concentrate (on) — se concentrer/concentrer son attention (sur)

I have trouble concentrating. — J'ai du mal à me concentrer.
He was concentrating on a crossword puzzle. — Il se concentrait sur des mots croisés.

concern *v*
to affect — concerner/regarder
That doesn't concern the other travelers. — Cela ne regarde pas les autres voyageurs.

so far as I'm concerned — en ce qui me concerne

to be worried about — s'inquiéter
I'm concerned about you. — Je m'inquiète pour toi.

condominium *n*

a condominium — une copropriété
a condominium apartment — un appartement en copropriété

Ø **condominium** [*m*] means "joint sovereignty."

41

conductor

conductor *n*
orchestra conductor

Ø **conducteur** [*m*] means "driver."

un chef d'orchestre

conference *n*
[*meeting*]
a medical conference

Ø **conférence** [*f*] means "a lecture."

un congrès/un colloque
un congrès de médecine

confidence *n*
[*trust*]
to have confidence in sb/sth
He has confidence in his employees.

Ø **confidence** [*f*] means "a personal secret."

la confiance
avoir confiance en qqn/qqch
Il a confiance en ses employés.

confident *adj*
self-confident
He looks very confident.

certain
She is confident they will succeed.
We are confident you will be satisfied.

Ø **confident** [*m*] means "a confidant."

Il a l'air très assuré/très sûr de lui.

Elle est sûre qu'ils réussiront.
Nous sommes persuadés que vous
   serez satisfaits.

conflict *n*
a clash, a dispute
That's a conflict of interest.

conflicting engagement
I have a conflict.

un conflit
C'est un conflit d'intérêts.

Je suis déjà pris.
J'ai autre chose de prévu.
J'ai un empêchement.

confuse *v*
[*to mix up*]
I always confuse their names.

confondre
Je confonds toujours leurs noms.

confused adj

I am confused [*don't understand*].

I am completely confused.

Je ne comprends pas très bien.
Je n'y comprends rien.
Je suis complètement perdu.

Ø **confus**(e) means "embarrassed."

confusing adj

It's confusing.

Ce n'est pas clair/net.
Cela prête à confusion.
On s'y perd.

The map is confusing [*hard to read*].
a confusing explanation
I find the whole thing very confusing.

La carte n'est pas du tout claire.
une explication embrouillée
Je ne comprends rien à toute cette
  histoire.

connection n

relation

I don't see any connection between the
  two.
He has excellent (business)
  connections.

Je ne vois aucun rapport entre les deux.

Il a d'excellentes relations (d'affaires).

transit

You have to change planes, but you
  have a good connection.
[*connecting line in the métro*]
To make your connection in the métro,
  follow the "transfer" signs.

Il faut changer d'avion, mais vous avez
  une bonne correspondance.
la correspondance
Pour changer de ligne dans le métro,
  suivez les indications
  "correspondance".

Ø **connexion** [*f*] usually means "an electrical connection."

conservative adj

conservative
conservative opinions
conservative parties

conservateur(-trice)
des opinions conservatrices
les partis de droite/les partis
  conservateurs

considerate adj

to be considerate toward sb

être attentionné(e) pour qqn/
  prévenant(e) envers qqn

consist

consist v
to consist of
What does his job consist of?
The building consists of fourteen
  apartments.

consister en/comprendre
En quoi consiste son travail?
L'immeuble comprend quatorze
  appartements.

contact v
to contact sb

You should contact her when you get
  there.

prendre contact/se mettre en contact
  avec qqn
Vous devriez prendre contact avec elle
  en arrivant.

contents n
the contents of the book/the bottle/the
  drawer
list of contents

le contenu du livre/de la bouteille/du
  tiroir
la table des matières

Ø content(e) means "happy."

controversial adj
controversial
The new law is very controversial.
He's a very controversial writer.

contesté(e)/controversé(e)/discuté(e)
La nouvelle loi est très contestée.
C'est un écrivain très controversé.

Ø controversial is not French.

convenient adj
practical
The new system is not very convenient.

commode/pratique
Le nouveau système n'est pas très
  commode.

suitable
We are looking for a convenient place
  for the picnic.
That date is not convenient for me.

convenable
Nous cherchons un endroit convenable
  pour le pique-nique.
Cette date ne me convient pas.

convention n
[a meeting]
convention center

un congrès
la salle des congrès/le palais des
  congrès

Ø convention [f] has various meanings, e.g., "agreement," "social custom."

cook *v*
in general
At our house, my husband does the
cooking.
to cook sth
Cook the stew slowly.

faire la cuisine/cuisiner
Chez nous, c'est mon mari qui fait la
cuisine.
faire cuire/laisser cuire qqch
Laissez cuire le ragoût à feu doux.

with the name of a meal
to cook dinner/lunch

préparer [*Note: not* **cuire**]
préparer le dîner/le déjeuner

copy *n*
a photocopy

une copie/une photocopie/une
polycopie

[*of a book, a publication*]
Do you have a copy of "Madame
Bovary"?

un exemplaire
Vous avez un exemplaire de «Madame
Bovary»?

corner *n*
the bakery at the corner
at the corner of Broadway and 42nd
street
just around the corner

la boulangerie du coin
à l'angle de Broadway et de la
quarante-deuxième rue
juste après le coin

correct *adj*
[*exact, right*]
the correct change
the correct time
That's correct.
[*see also* **right**]

exact(e)/juste
la monnaie juste
l'heure exacte
C'est exact./C'est juste.

corsage *n*
to wear a corsage

porter une fleur (à la boutonnière)

The American custom of giving or wearing a corsage does not exist in France.
Women do not generally wear flowers, but a man may wear one in his buttonhole.

Ø **corsage** [*m*] means "blouse" or "bodice of a dress."

could *v*
past tense
I could [*was able to*] do it.

J'ai pu/Je pouvais le faire.

conditional
I could [*would be able to*] do it if I tried.

Je pourrais le faire si j'essayais.

I could have done it [*would have been able to do it*] if I had tried. [*see also* **can**]	J'aurais pu le faire si j'avais essayé.

country *n*
[*the nation*] — la nation/la patrie/le pays
[*the countryside*] — la campagne

couple *n*
a few — un(e) ou deux
We have a couple of bottles. — Nous en avons une ou deux bouteilles.
two people together — un couple/un ménage
a young couple — un jeune ménage

course *n*
a class — un cours
to take a French course — suivre un cours de français [*Note: not* **prendre**]

a dish on a menu — un plat
the main course — le plat principal
the first course — l'entrée [*f*] [*Note: not the main course as in the U.S.*]

Ø **course** [*f*] means "a race" or "an errand."

crayon *n*
[*a colored pencil*] — un crayon de couleur

Ø **crayon** [*m*] means "a pencil."

credit *n*
to buy on credit — acheter à crédit
a credit card — une carte de crédit
Will this be on your credit card? — Ce sera sur votre carte?

crowded *adj*
[*of a vehicle, a building*] — bondé(e)/plein(e)
[*of a place, a street*] — plein de monde
The shops are too crowded. — Il y a trop de monde dans les magasins.

cry *v*
[*to shed tears*] — pleurer

46

[*to shout*] crier

curious *adj*
odd
a curious situation — une situation étrange
That's curious! — C'est curieux!

inquisitive
My cat is very curious. — Mon chat est très curieux.
I'm curious. What's the title of that story? — Dites-moi: quel est le titre de ce conte? [*Note: The French do not normally introduce a question with "Je suis curieux." This is an anglicism.*]

bizarre/étrange/curieux(-euse)

curieux(-euse)

cute *adj*
to be cute — être mignon(-onne)
She's really cute. — Elle est vraiment mignonne.
You have a cute dress. — Ta robe est mignonne.
The children were so cute. — Les enfants étaient si mignons.
He's a cute guy. — Il est beau gosse/beau gars.

≡ D ≡

damage *n*
physical damage
The earthquake caused significant damage.

les dommages/les dégâts [*m pl*]
Le tremblement de terre a causé des dégâts importants.

legal damages
to claim damages

les dommages et intérêts
réclamer des dommages et intérêts

damage *v*
to damage sth
Watch you don't damage the furniture.

abîmer/endommager qqch
Fais attention à ne pas abîmer les meubles.

My car was badly damaged.

Ma voiture a été très endommagée.

dance *n*/**dancing** *n*
a dance [*social event*]
an informal dance
to go dancing
ballet/folk dancing

un bal/une soirée dansante
une sauterie [*fam*]
aller danser/aller au bal
la danse classique/folklorique

dark *n*
the dark
I'm afraid of the dark.

le noir
J'ai peur du noir.

dark *adj*
It's dark.
In winter it gets dark at five o'clock.
His room is very dark.
[*of a color*]
a dark green dress

Il fait noir./Il fait nuit.
Il fait noir à cinq heures en hiver.
Sa chambre est très sombre.
foncé [*invar*]
une robe vert foncé

darling [*see dear*]

date *n*
a personal or business date
to have a date
to make a date with sb

un rendez-vous
avoir (un) rendez-vous
prendre rendez-vous avec qqn

the person invited

[*Note: There is no real equivalent for "a date," meaning a person.*]

48

my date	mon invité(e)
	le copain/la copine avec qui je sors
my date for the prom	celui/celle que j'ai invité(e) au bal

date v
They are dating.	Ils sortent ensemble.
She's dating a young French man.	Elle sort avec un jeune Français.
He has started dating.	Il a commencé à sortir avec des filles.

day n
a day	un jour/une journée
What day is it?	Quel jour sommes-nous?
	Quel jour est-ce?
the first day of the month	le premier jour du mois
New Year's Day	le jour de l'An
Come back in two days.	Revenez dans deux jours.
an eventful day	une journée mouvementée
to spend the day at home	passer la journée à la maison
Good day!	Bonjour!
Have a good day!	Bonne journée!

There is a subtle difference in usage between the masculine and the feminine forms. In general, the masculine is used to state WHEN something is done (**le jour de Noël**), and the feminine to describe HOW the time is spent (**une journée à la plage**). The masculine form is always used for "every day" (**tous les jours**), with a number (**dix jours**), and after **par** (**trois fois par jour**). The feminine form is always used for "all day" (**toute la journée**) and when the noun is modified (**une journée passionnante**). In some cases, either form may be used, e.g., **le même jour, la même journée; quelques jours, quelques journées.**

Other pairs that follow the same rules are: **le soir/la soirée, l'an/l'année, le matin/la matinée.**

deal n
a quantity
a good deal (of)	beaucoup (de)
She reads a good deal.	Elle lit beaucoup.
He has a good deal of patience.	Il a beaucoup de patience.
We have completed a good deal of the work.	Nous avons terminé une bonne partie du travail.

a bargain
It's a good deal.	C'est avantageux.
	C'est une (bonne) affaire.

deal

At that price, it's a good deal.	A ce prix-là, c'est une affaire.
She got a good deal.	Elle a fait une bonne affaire.

an agreement — un marché
to make a deal — conclure/faire un marché
to make a good deal — faire un marché avantageux

deal v

to deal with	s'occuper de/se charger de
She deals with the complaints.	Elle s'occupe des réclamations.
He dealt with all the problems.	Il s'est chargé de tous les problèmes.
I'll deal with the late-comers.	Je me charge des retardataires.
A social worker deals with disadvantaged children.	Une assistante sociale s'occupe d'enfants défavorisés.

dear adj & noun

a dear friend	un cher ami/une chère amie
He is very dear to us.	Il nous est très cher.
	Nous avons beaucoup d'affection pour lui.

my dear/my darling — mon chéri/ma chérie

in letters

Dear Sir/Dear Madam/Dear Sirs	Monsieur/Madame/Messieurs [Note: **cher** is omitted.]
Dear Mr. Smith/Mrs. Smith	(Cher) Monsieur/(Chère) Madame [Note: **cher** is optional; no name is stated.]
Dear Paul/Dear Jane	(Mon) cher Paul/(Ma) chère Jeanne [Note: **mon/ma** are optional.]

decision n

to make a decision — prendre une décision [Note: *not* **faire**]

definite adj

certain
Is it definite she'll come? — sûr(e)/certain(e)
C'est sûr qu'elle viendra?

exact, clear — précis(e)/net (nette)
a definite date — une date précise
a definite improvement — une nette amélioration

Ø **défini**(e) is used in grammar for the "definite article," **l'article défini.**

definitely *adv*
[*certainly*]

absolument/certainement/parfaitement/
sans aucun doute

Ø **définitivement** means "permanently" or "for good."

degree *n*
university
to have/get a degree
to have a degree in arts/science/law

to be working towards a degree
a bachelor's degree
a master's degree
a doctoral degree

avoir/obtenir un diplôme
être diplômé(-e) en lettres/en sciences/
 en droit
préparer un diplôme
une licence
une maîtrise
un doctorat

temperature
The freezing point of water is 32
 degrees (Fahrenheit).
Normal body temperature is 98.6
 degrees.
It was 75 degrees in the shade.

un degré
Le point de congélation de l'eau est de
 zéro degré (centigrade).
La température normale du corps est de
 37 degrés.
Il faisait 24 degrés à l'ombre.

Ø **degré** [m] never means a university degree.

demand *v*
to call for
The workers are demanding an
 increase.

réclamer
Les ouvriers réclament une
 augmentation.

to insist on, to require
He demanded an apology from
 everyone.
They demanded that we pay
 immediately.

exiger
Il a exigé des excuses de tout le monde.

Ils ont exigé que nous payions tout de
 suite. [*Note: subjunctive*]

Ø **demander** means "to ask (for)."

demonstration *n*
in general
to give a demonstration of sth

une démonstration
faire la démonstration de qqch

a protest
to hold a demonstration
a violent demonstration

une manifestation
faire une manifestation/manifester
une émeute

deny

deny *v*
to deny
He denied everything.

nier [*Note: not* **dénier**]
Il a tout nié.

depart *v*
to depart
We departed at 6 P.M.

partir/s'en aller
Nous sommes partis à 18 heures. [*Note: conjugated with* **être**]

Ø **départir** is not French.

departure *n*
[*in travel*]
departure time
the departure and arrival board

le départ
l'heure du départ
l'horaire des départs et arrivées

department *n*
in a store
Where is the women's shoe departement?

le rayon
Où se trouve le rayon des chaussures de dames?
Pour les chaussures de dames, s'il vous plaît?

in a business
the maintenance department
the sales department

le service
le service d'entretien
le service des ventes

in a university
the French departement

la section
la section de français [*Note:* **le département** is commonly used in U.S. universities.]

in government
the finance department

le ministère
le ministère des finances

Ø **département** [*m*] is used for the geographic divisions of France, e.g., **le département du Haut-Rhin.**

deposit *n*
down payment
[*on rent, hotel room*]
[*on purchase*]
to pay/leave a deposit

des arrhes
un acompte/des arrhes
verser des arrhes

52

deposit on a container
There's a deposit on that bottle.
no deposit, no return

une consigne
Il y a une consigne sur cette bouteille.
non consigné(e)

depress *v*
to depress [*mentally*]
This weather depresses me.
I often feel depressed.
That's too depressing.

déprimer
Ce temps me déprime.
Je me sens souvent déprimé(e).
C'est trop déprimant.

deserve *v*
to deserve
They deserved better.
That's what she deserves.

mériter
Ils méritaient mieux.
Voilà ce qu'elle mérite.

detour *n*
to make a detour via Amiens
[*rerouting of traffic*]

faire un crochet/un détour par Amiens
une déviation

Ø **détour** [*m*] also means a "bend," e.g., in a road or a river.

development *n*
in general
an unexpected development

le développement
un développement inattendu

a building complex
an industrial development
a housing development
a high-rise development

un complexe industriel
une cité/un grand ensemble
une tour (d'habitation)/un grand
  ensemble

diary *n*
[*a journal*]
to keep a (personal) diary
[*appointment book*]

un journal
tenir un journal (intime)
un agenda

diet *n*
to be on a diet

être au régime/suivre un régime

direction *n*
in the direction of
in the right/wrong direction
in the opposite direction
I don't have much sense of direction.

dans la direction de/en direction de
dans le bon/le mauvais sens
en sens inverse
Je n'ai pas le sens de l'orientation.

director

Could you give me directions to Notre Dame?	Pour aller à Notre Dame, s'il vous plaît?
directions for use	le mode d'emploi/les indications

Ø **direction** [f] also means "the management."

director n

[of a school, a company]	un directeur/une directrice/un administrateur/une administratrice
[of a film]	un réalisateur/un cinéaste
[of a play]	un metteur en scène

disappoint v

to disappoint	décevoir
We were very disappointed by his reaction.	Sa réaction nous a beaucoup déçus.
I'm really disappointed in you.	Tu m'as vraiment déçu.
I was very disappointed to hear he had resigned.	J'ai été très déçu d'apprendre qu'il avait démissionné.
disappointing results	des résultats décevants

disappointment n

The elections were a big disappointment for us.	Les élections ont été une grosse déception pour nous.
	Nous avons été très déçus par les élections.

Ø **désappointement** [m] has limited use.

dish n

a serving dish	un plat
a course or dish on the menu	un plat
a set of dishes	la vaisselle
to do/wash the dishes	faire la vaisselle

dispute [see **argument**]

dissertation n

a dissertation	une thèse/un mémoire
a master's/doctoral dissertation	une thèse de maîtrise/de doctorat

Ø **dissertation** [f] means an "essay" or "composition."

disturb *v*

to bother, interrupt sb
I'm sorry to disturb you.
Please do not disturb.

déranger qqn
Je m'excuse de vous déranger.
Prière de ne pas déranger.

to upset sb
He was deeply disturbed by your
　behavior.

troubler/inquiéter qqn
Il a été profondément troublé par ton
　comportement.
Ton comportement l'a profondément
　troublé.

divorce *n & v*

to divorce/to get a divorce from sb
She is divorced.
She divorced her husband.
She got a divorce two year ago.
They got divorced.
You should ask for a divorce.

divorcer d'avec qqn
Elle est divorcée.
Elle a divorcé d'avec son mari.
Elle a divorcé il y deux ans.
Ils ont divorcé.
Tu devrais demander **le** divorce.

do *v*

for emphasis
I do hope you will come.
If you do go there this year . . .
She does sing very well.

J'espère bien que tu viendras.
Si en fait vous y allez cette année . . .
Elle chante vraiment très bien.
C'est vrai qu'elle chante très bien.

to have finished
Are you done?
I'm not done yet.

avoir fini/terminé
As-tu fini?
Je n'ai pas encore terminé.

in a question, a negative

Do you like spinach?
He doesn't know me.
Did you finish the homework?

[*Note: Do not use **faire** to translate "do,"
　"does," "did."*]
Aimez-vous les épinards?
Il ne me connaît pas.
As-tu vu fini les devoirs?

to do without
I can't do without coffee.
I can't do without it.

se passer (de)
Je ne peux pas me passer de café.
Je ne peux pas m'en passer.

to have to do with
That has nothing to do with what you
　said.

avoir à voir avec
Ça n'a rien à voir avec ce que tu as dit.

doggy bag

doggy bag

Taking left-over food home from a restaurant is not a French custom.

domestic *adj*
domestic work
domestic life
domestic affairs [*as opposed to foreign*]
a domestic flight

les travaux ménagers
la vie de famille/la vie privée
les affaires intérieures
un vol intérieur

dormitory *n*
a student dormitory

un foyer/une résidence universitaire

Ø **dortoir**]m] is a large room with many beds, e.g., in a boarding school.

double *adj*
a double bed
a double room

un grand lit
une chambre pour deux (personnes)
une chambre à un grand lit
une chambre à deux lits

down *adv & prep*
They live down the street/down the hill from us.
His apartment is down below.

Ils habitent plus bas dans la rue/sur la colline.
Son appartement est en bas/en dessous.

verb+down
to come/go down

descendre [*Note: conjugated with* **être** *if there is no object; with* **avoir** *if there is a direct object*]

They haven't come down yet.
She went down the street.
to get down from [*to get off*]
to get off the bus/the train
to take/bring sth down

Ils ne sont pas encore descendus.
Elle a descendu la rue.
descendre (de)
descendre de l'autobus/du train
descendre qqch [*Note: conjugated with* **avoir**]

I brought down the suitcases.
to fall down
to lie down
to lay/put sth down

J'ai descendu les valises.
tomber
se coucher
déposer qqch

downstairs *adv*
to come/go downstairs

descendre

The parents sleep downstairs.	Les parents couchent en bas/en dessous.

dozen *n*
a dozen roses — une douzaine **de** roses

drapes *n*
[*curtains*] — les rideaux

Ø **drap** [*m*] means "a sheet"; **drapeau** [*m*] means "a flag."

dress *n*

casual dress	la tenue détente/la tenue décontractée/ la tenue de sport
formal or evening dress	la tenue de soirée/la grande tenue
street or business clothes	la tenue de ville
We were all in evening dress.	Nous étions tous en tenue de soirée.

dress *v*

to dress/get dressed	s'habiller
to dress well	s'habiller avec goût
to dress up (for an occasion)	s'habiller (pour une occasion)
You don't have to dress up.	Il n'est pas nécessaire de t'habiller.

drink *n*

a drink	une boisson
to have a drink	prendre un verre/un pot [*fam*]
a before-dinner drink [*a cocktail*]	un apéritif
an after-dinner drink	un digestif

drive *v*

to drive a car	conduire une auto
Do you know how to drive?	Sais-tu conduire?
to drive to school/to work	aller à l'école/au travail (en voiture) [*Note: When "to drive" simply means "to go by car," do not use* **conduire**.]
Shall we drive or walk?	On y va en voiture ou à pied?
Did you drive today?	Tu as pris ta voiture aujourd'hui?

driveway *n*
a driveway — une allée/un chemin d'accès

57

drop _v_

to drop sth	laisser tomber qqch
The goalkeeper dropped the ball.	Le gardien de but a laissé tomber le ballon.
to drop out of school	abandonner ses études

drugs _n_

prescription drugs	les médicaments [m]
[_narcotics_]	la drogue/les stupéfiants [m pl]
drug traffic	le trafic de la drogue
to take drugs	se droguer
a drug addict/user	un(e) toxicomane/un(e) drogué(e)

drugstore _n_

a drugstore	une pharmacie

due _adj_

time due

The bill is due on Saturday.	dû (due)/payable
When is the assignment due?	La note est payable samedi.
	Quand faut-il rendre les devoirs?

due to

due to [_because of_] the rain	à cause de la pluie
due to [_thanks to_] my friends	grâce à mes amis

≡ E ≡

each *adj*

each boy/each girl	chaque garçon/chaque fille
each day	chaque jour
each time	chaque fois

[*see also* **every**]

each *pron*

each (one)	chacun(e)
Each of my daughters is different.	Chacune de mes filles est différente.
They gave us each a key.	On nous a donné une clé à chacun.
each (one) of us	chacun d'entre nous
To each his taste.	Chacun (à) son goût.

each other/one another *pron*

each other/one another	nous/vous/se
	[*Note: **l'un(e) l'autre/les un(e)s les autres** may be added for clarity.*]
They have never seen each other.	Elles ne se sont jamais vues.
We write regularly to each other.	Nous nous écrivons régulièrement.
You should help one another. [*more than two people*]	Vous devriez vous aider (les uns les autres).
They live opposite each other. [*two people*]	Elles habitent l'une en face de l'autre.

ear *n*

She has a good ear [*for music, languages*].	Elle a de l'oreille.
I have no ear for languages.	Je n'ai pas d'oreille pour les langues.

early *adj & adv*

for a set time — en avance

She is always early for class.	Elle arrive toujours en avance au cours.
The plane took off five minutes early.	L'avion a décollé cinq minutes en avance/avec cinq minutes d'avance.

in a time period — tôt/de bonne heure

to eat dinner early	dîner tôt
to go to bed early	se coucher de bonne heure
The peach trees bloomed early this year.	Les pêchers ont fleuri tôt cette année.

eat

She's an early riser.	Elle est lève-tôt/matinale.
to take an early flight	prendre un vol tôt le matin
in the early sixties	au début des années soixante

eat *v*

to eat out	manger au restaurant/en ville

with name of a meal
[*Note: Do not use* **manger** *with the name of a meal.*]

to eat breakfast	déjeuner/prendre le petit déjeuner
to eat lunch	déjeuner/prendre le déjeuner
to eat dinner	dîner/prendre le dîner

editor *n*

newspaper editor	le rédacteur/la rédactrice
text editor	le correcteur

Ø **éditeur** [*m*] means "publisher."

educated *adj*

She was educated at the Sorbonne.	Elle a fait ses études à la Sorbonne.
well-educated	instruit(e)/cultivé(e)

Ø **bien éduqué** means "well-bred," "well mannered"; **mal éduqué** means "badly behaved."

education *n*

[*in general*]	l'éducation [*f*]
[*instruction in a school*]	l'enseignement [*m*]/ l'instruction [*f*]
[*vocational training*]	la formation

educational *adj*

educational television	la télévision éducative
I thought the film was very educational.	J'ai trouvé le film très instructif.
educational texts [*for schools*]	les manuels scolaires
educational background	la formation

Ø ~~educationnel~~ is not French.

effective *adj*
of date, time

	en vigueur
effective from 9:00 P.M.	en vigueur à partir de 21 heures

The new law will become effective starting January 1.	La nouvelle loi entrera en vigueur le 1er janvier.

efficient [*of things*]
This method is very effective.

efficace
Cette méthode est très efficace.

efficient [*of people*]
She is a very effective administrator.

capable/efficace
C'est une gérante très capable.

either (one) *adj & pron*

either (one)

l'un(e) ou l'autre
n'importe lequel/laquelle

I can come either day.
Which flavor do you prefer? — I'll take either.
Either one (will do).

Je peux venir l'un ou l'autre jour.
Quel parfum préférez-vous? — Je prendrai l'un ou l'autre.
N'importe lequel (me conviendra).

in the negative
I don't like either.

ni...ni [+*ne with verb*]
Je n'aime ni l'un ni l'autre.

either...or *conj*

either...or

soit...soit
ou (bien)...ou (bien)

You could either write or telephone.
Either you or I

Vous pourriez ou écrire ou téléphoner.
Soit vous, soit moi

in the negative
He doesn't take (either) sugar or milk.
I am not going either.

Il ne prend ni sucre ni lait.
Je n'y vais pas non plus.

elective *n*

an elective course
an elective subject

un cours facultatif
une matière à option

else *adv*

something else
nothing else/not...anything else
I don't need anything else.
somebody else
nobody else/not...anybody else
I didn't see anybody else.
somewhere else
nowhere else
What else, please? [*in a store*]
what else/who else
or else...

quelque chose d'autre
rien d'autre [+ *ne with verb*]
Je n'ai besoin de rien d'autre.
quelqu'un d'autre
personne d'autre [+ *ne with verb*]
Je n'ai vu personne d'autre.
ailleurs
nulle part ailleurs
Et avec ça?/Voulez-vous autre chose?
quoi encore/qui encore
ou bien...

embarrass v

to be embarrassed	être gêné(e)/confus(e)
He looked really embarrassed.	Il avait l'air très gêné.
I'm really embarrassed.	Je suis vraiment confus.
It's an embarrassing situation.	C'est une situation très gênante.

Ø **embarrasser** can mean "to embarrass," but usually means to "burden" or "hamper."

embrace see kiss

emotional adv

of a person	émotif(-ve)/impressionnable/ sensible/ facilement ému(e)
He is too emotional.	Il est trop émotif.

relating to the emotions	émotionnel(-elle)
an emotional shock	un choc émotionnel
an emotional state	un état émotionnel

emphasis n/emphasize v

to accent	mettre l'accent sur/accentuer
In French you put the emphasis on the last syllable.	En français on accentue la dernière syllabe.

to stress the importance	insister sur/souligner
The nurse emphasized the importance of a healthy diet.	L'infirmière a insisté sur l'importance d'un régime sain.
The mother emphasized that the children should stay indoors.	La mère a souligné que les enfants devaient rester à l'intérieur.

enclose v/enclosure n

to enclose sth	joindre qqch
enclosed	ci-joint(e)
I am enclosing a copy of...	Je joins/Veuillez trouver ci-joint une copie de...
enclosures (encl.)	pièces jointes (P.J.)

encore n

to play an encore	jouer un bis
They played an encore of the piece.	Ils ont bissé le morceau.
to shout "encore!"	crier "bis, bis!"

Ø **encore** is an adverb and cannot be used for "an encore" in French.

end *n*
opposite of beginning
the end of the month/the film/the century/the paragraph

of a place
at the end of the street
at the end of the hall

la fin
la fin du mois/du film/du siècle/du paragraphe

le bout/le fond
au bout de la rue
au fond du couloir

energetic *adj*
an energetic person

une personne énergique

Ø **énergétique** is used in physics, e.g., **les ressources énergétiques.**

engaged *adj*/**engagement** *n*
the line is engaged [busy]
to be engaged (to be married)
They got engaged in June.
to announce one's engagement

la ligne est occupée
être fiancé(e)
Ils se sont fiancés en juin.
annoncer ses fiançailles

Ø **être engagé** means "to be committed (to a cause)"; **engagement** [*m*] means "commitment."

engine *n*
[*of a car*]
[*of a train*]

le moteur
la locomotive

Ø **engin** [*m*] means "a tool," "a machine," or a "heavy vehicle."

enough *adv*
He doesn't eat enough.
enough time/patience/money
enough students/cakes
She is big enough to go alone.

I've had enough (to eat).
I've had enough. [*I'm fed up.*]
That's enough.

Il ne mange pas assez.
assez de temps/de patience/d'argent
assez d'étudiants/de gâteaux
Elle est assez grande pour y aller toute seule.

J'ai assez mangé.
J'en ai assez.
Ça suffit.

enroll *v*
to enroll in a course/a club

s'inscrire à un cours/un club

entree *n*

the entree · le plat principal

In a French menu, **l'entrée** [*f*] is the first course, not the main course as in an American menu.

even *adj*

flat, smooth · uni(e)/plat(e)
an even surface · une surface unie

equal · égal(e)
The teams are even. · Les équipes sont égales.

opposite of odd · pair(e)
an even number/day · un nombre pair/un jour pair

even *adv*

even you/even the teacher · même vous/même le professeur
even at night · même la nuit
He even paid for us. · Il a même payé pour nous.
even if · même si
I wouldn't do it, even if I could. · Je ne le ferais pas, même si je pouvais.
even though · bien que [+*subjunctive*]
· quoique [+*subjunctive*]
She's going to play even though she is tired. · Elle va jouer, bien qu'elle soit fatiguée.

evening *n*

the evening · le soir/la soirée [*Note: For difference in usage see* **day**.]

at six o'clock in the evening · à six heures du soir
this evening/yesterday evening/tomorrow evening · ce soir/hier soir/demain soir
every evening · tous les soirs/chaque soir
We are always free in the evening. · Nous sommes toujours libres le soir.
Good evening! · Bonsoir!
Have a good evening! · Bonne soirée!
during the evening · pendant la soirée
all evening/the whole evening · toute la soirée
a musical evening · une soirée musicale

eventually *adv*

[*in time*] · à la fin/finalement/à la longue/tôt ou tard

to do sth eventually
They'll learn eventually.

finir par faire qqch
Ils apprendront à la longue.
Ils finiront par apprendre.

Ø **éventuellement** means "possibly."

ever *adv*
Have you ever been to France?

Avez-vous jamais été en France?

every *adj*
every
every employee
every Monday
every other day
every second day
every five minutes
[*see also* **each**]

chaque/tous les/toutes les
chaque employé/tous les employés
chaque lundi/tous les lundis
un jour sur deux
tous les deux jours
toutes les cinq minutes

everybody/everyone *pron*
everybody
Everybody goes there.

Everyone for himself and God for all.

tout le monde/chacun(e)
Tout le monde y va. [*Note: takes singular verb*]
Chacun pour soi et Dieu pour tous.

everything *pron*
everything
They saw everything.
Everything's fine.

tout
Ils ont tout vu.
Tout va bien.

everything (that)

tout ce qui [subj]
tout ce que [obj]

everything (that's) good
everything (that) you want

tout ce qui est bon
tout ce que tu veux

everywhere *adv*
There are mosquitoes everywhere.
everywhere you look

Il y a des moustiques partout.
partout où vous regardez

exam *n*
in school
a final exam
an oral exam
to take an exam

un examen/une épreuve
un examen de fin d'année
une épreuve orale
passer un examen

exchange

to pass an exam	réussir à un examen/être reçu à un examen [*Note: not* **passer**]
to fail an exam	échouer à un examen/être recalé à un examen [*Note: not* **faillir**]

medical exam
He had a physical exam.

On lui a fait un examen médical/un bilan de santé.

exchange *n & v*

I'd like to exchange this blouse for a bigger size.

Je voudrais échanger ce chemisier contre une taille plus grande.

The exchange rate of the dollar has dropped.

Le taux de change du dollar a baissé.

excited *adj*
enthusiastic

to be excited (about)

être ravi de/enthousiasmé de/ passionné par/emballé par [*fam*]

He's excited about his new hobby.

Il est passionné par son nouveau passe-temps.

She's very excited about the results.

Elle est ravie des résultats.

over-excited

The children are all excited.

Les enfants ne tiennent pas en place/ sont surexcités.

Don't get excited.

Ne t'énerve pas./Ne vous énervez pas.

looking forward to

I'm getting excited about my trip.

Je me réjouis déjà de mon voyage.

I'm excited about going to France.

Je suis emballé à l'idée d'aller en France.

Ø **excité**(e) means "worked up" or "agitated."

excuse *v*
to interrupt, accost sb

Excuse me. Could you please. . .

Pardon, monsieur/madame. Pourriez-vous. . .

to apologize

Excuse me (for disturbing you).

Excusez-moi (de vous déranger). Je m'excuse (de vous déranger).

exercise *n*
to write exercises
to do [*physical*] exercises

écrire des exercices
faire de l'exercice/de la gymnastique

exercise *v*
to exercise [*physically*]

faire/prendre de l'exercice

exhibition *n*
[*a show*]
an exhibition of watercolors
[*an exhibition of sports, animals*]

une exposition
une exposition d'aquarelles
une exhibition

expect *v*
to await
I expect his answer within 24 hours.
She is expecting a baby.

attendre
J'attends sa réponse dans les 24 heures.
Elle attend un bébé.

to anticipate sth
We didn't expect that.
to expect to
She didn't expect to see us so soon.

s'attendre à qqch
On ne s'attendait pas à ça.
s'attendre à [+*infinitive*]
Elle ne s'attendait pas à nous voir si tôt.

That was to be expected.
to expect that . . .
I did not expect that he would refuse.

Il fallait s'y attendre.
s'attendre à ce que [+*subjunctive*]
Je ne m'attendais pas à ce qu'il refuse.

to plan to
I expect to be there early.

avoir l'intention de
J'ai l'intention d'être là de bonne heure.

experience *n*
a good experience
to have experience in sth

une bonne expérience
avoir de l'experience en qqch

Ø **expérience** [*f*] also means "an experiment."

experience *v*
[*to feel, suffer*]
She has never experienced real grief.

éprouver/ressentir
Elle n'a jamais éprouvé de vrai chagrin.

experiment *n*
to do an experiment
He does experiments on mice.

faire une expérience
Il fait des expériences sur des souris.

express *adj*
special delivery
an express package/letter

of transport
an express (train)

exprès [*invar*]
un colis exprès/une lettre exprès

express [*invar*]
un (train) express [*Note: Final "ss" is pronounced.*]

extra *adj*
an extra pillow
some extra blankets
an extra charge

un oreiller supplémentaire
des couvertures supplémentaires
un supplément

Ø **extra** means "fine quality" in foods, e.g., **du boeuf extra.** It is also a slang term meaning "great": **c'est extra.**

extravagant *adj*
in spending
She has always been very extravagant.

dépensier(-ière)
Elle a toujours été très dépensière.

exaggerated
They have extravagant ideas.

extravagant(e)/excentrique/exagéré(e)
Ils ont des idées extravagantes.

F

fabric *n*
[*cloth*]

un tissu/une étoffe

Ø **fabrique** [*f*] means "factory."

face *n*
person's face
clock face
face cloth

le visage/la figure
le cadran
le gant de toilette

face *v*
The house faces east.
a room facing the courtyard
to be sitting facing each other
to face (up to) a problem
I can't face it.

La maison est orientée à l'est.
une chambre qui donne sur la cour
être assis(e) l'un(e) en face de l'autre
faire face à/confronter une difficulté
Je n'en ai pas le courage.

facility *n*
to have a facility for languages
a sports/educational/community facility

avoir de la facilité pour les langues
des équipements sportifs/ scolaires/
   collectifs

fact *n*
to know the facts
It's a fact that...

savoir les faits
C'est un fait que...

in fact (supporting)
He writes to me often; in fact, I
   received a letter today.

de fait/en fait/effectivement
Il m'écrit souvent; en fait, j'ai reçu une
   lettre aujourd'hui.

in fact (contradicting)
He claimed to be an executive, but in
   fact he was a bookkeeper.

en réalité/à vrai dire
Il prétendait être cadre, mais en réalité
   il était comptable.

faculty *n*
[*teachers in a school or university*]

les professeurs/le corps enseignant

Ø **faculté** [*f*] means a "school" or "college" within a French university, e.g., **la
faculté des sciences.**

fail

fail v
to fail an exam

échouer à un examen/être recalé à un examen/rater un examen [*fam*] [*Note: not* **faillir**]

familiar *adj*
well known
That's a familiar problem.
He looks familiar.

bien connu/familier
C'est un problème bien connu.
Je crois l'avoir déjà vu quelque part.

to be familiar with sth
I'm not familiar with this area.

connaître qqch
Je ne connais pas ce quartier.
Ce quartier ne m'est pas familier.

famous *adj*
famous

célèbre/illustre/renommé(e)

Ø **fameux**(-euse), used colloquially, means "excellent"; **pas fameux** means "not all that great."

fan *n*
[*admirer of a star*]
[*supporters of a team*]
[*an enthusiast of an activity, a "buff"*]

l'admirateur(-trice)
les supporters
un(e) enthousiaste/un(e) passionné(e)/ un(e) fana [*slang*]

She's a skating fan.

C'est une passionnée du patinage.
Elle se passionne pour le patinage.

far *adv*
far away/far
not far from the Metro
It's too far to walk.
Keep going as far as the bridge.
How far is it to Fontainebleau?
so far as I'm concerned
so far as I know

loin
pas loin du métro
C'est trop loin pour y aller à pied.
Continuez jusqu'au pont.
C'est à quelle distance, Fontainebleau?
en ce qui me concerne/quant à moi
(pour) autant que je sache

fast *adj*
[*quick*]
a fast train
fast food
[*a quick meal*]
to be fast [*of a clock*]
Your watch is three minutes fast.

rapide [*Note: Do not use* **vite**.]
un (train) rapide
la restauration rapide
un repas rapide
avancer
Votre montre avance de trois minutes.

fast *adv*
[*quickly*]
Run fast!
His car goes fast.

rapidement/vite
Cours vite!
Sa voiture roule vite.

fat *adj*
of a person
to get/grow fat

gros (grosse)/obèse/ corpulent(e)
grossir

of food
The ham is too fat.

gras (grasse)
Le jambon est trop gras.

fat *n*
in food or cooking
There's too much fat in the gravy.

la graisse
Il y a trop de graisse dans la sauce.

in cooked meats
You have to cut off the fat.

le gras
Il faut enlever le gras.

fault *n*
a weakness
We all have our faults.

un défaut
Nous avons tous des défauts.

blame
Whose fault is it?
It wasn't her fault.

A qui la faute?
Ce n'était pas de sa faute.

Ø **faute** [*f*] also means a "mistake."

favorite *adj & n*
favorite
the favorite
This is my favorite beer.

préféré(e)/favori(-ite)
le préféré/la préférée
C'est ma bière préférée.
C'est la bière que je préfère.

This poem is my favorite.
She's her father's favorite.

C'est le poème que j'aime le mieux.
C'est la préférée de son père.

fax *n*
[*the copy*]
[*the machine*]

la télécopie
le télécopieur

fed up *adj*
to be fed up (with sth)
I'm fed up with it/that.
I'm fed up (with) working.

en avoir assez/en avoir marre [*fam*]
J'en ai marre.
J'en ai assez de travailler.

71

feel

feel *v intrans*
health

How do you feel?	se sentir
	Comment vous sentez-vous?
I feel good/bad/better.	Je me sens bien/mal/mieux.
I feel sick/tired	Je me sens malade/fatigué.
[*see also* **sick**]	

physical state

to feel hot/cold	avoir chaud/froid
to feel hungry/thirsty/sleepy	avoir faim/soif/sommeil

inclination

to feel like doing sth	avoir envie de faire qqch
I don't feel like it today.	Je n'en ai pas envie aujourd'hui.

emotional

I feel bad that. . .	Ça m'ennuie que. . .
	Ça me fait de la peine que. . .
	Je suis désolé que [+*subjunctive*]
	Je suis désolé de [+*infinitive*]
I feel bad that she lost her dog.	Ça me fait de la peine qu'elle ait perdu son chien.
I feel bad that I kept you waiting.	Je suis désolé de vous avoir fait attendre.
to feel good that. . .	être content(e)/satisfait(e) que [+*subjunctive*]
I feel good (that) she got a job.	Je suis contente qu'elle ait obtenu un poste.
He feels good about his grades.	Il est satisfait de ses notes.

feel *v trans*
to touch

	tâter/palper
He felt my pulse.	Il m'a tâté le pouls.

to be aware of

	sentir
I felt a few drops of rain.	J'ai senti quelques gouttes de pluie.

to experience

	éprouver/ressentir
We are feeling the effects of the war.	Nous ressentons les effets de la guerre.
to feel affection/regret	éprouver de l'affection/du regret

to have the impression (that)

	avoir l'impression (que)
I felt she was laughing at me.	J'avais l'impression qu'elle se moquait de moi.

to believe

	trouver
I feel she is too young.	Je trouve qu'elle est trop jeune.

A mon avis elle est trop jeune.

few *adj*
not many
He has few friends.

peu (de)
Il a peu d'amis.

some, several
He has a few friends.

quelques
Il a quelques amis.

fewer *adj*
fewer. . .(than)
We have fewer orders this month.

There are fewer tourists than last year.

moins de. . .(que)
Nous avons moins de commandes ce
    mois-ci.
Il y a moins de touristes que l'année
    dernière.

fewest *adj*
the fewest
Margaret makes the fewest mistakes.

le moins de
C'est Marguerite qui fait le moins de
    fautes.

field *n*
[*an open space*]
[*a soccer field*]
a field of interest [*a specialty*]

That's not his field.

un champ
un terrain de football
une spécialité/un domaine/un champ
    d'intérêt
Ce n'est pas de son domaine.

fight *n & v*
to fight physically
to have a fight with sb
He had a fight with his cousin.
The boys were always fighting.

se battre
se battre avec qqn
Il s'est battu avec son cousin.
Les garçons se battaient tout le temps.

to quarrel
She had a fight with her roommate.

se disputer/avoir une dispute
Elle s'est disputée avec sa camarade de
    chambre.

to fight against
to fight against AIDS
the fight against crime

lutter contre
lutter contre le S.I.D.A.
la lutte contre le crime

figure *n*
[*a number*]
to draw a figure

un nombre/un chiffre
dessiner une image/une silhouette

to keep/lose one's figure	garder/perdre la ligne
She has a good figure.	Elle est bien faite.
	Elle est bien balancée. [*slang*]

Ø **figure** [*f*] means a "face."

fill *v*

to fill a glass	remplir un verre
to fill out a form	remplir une fiche/un formulaire

final *adj & n*

[*last*]	dernier(-ière)
in the final analysis	en dernière analyse
the final exam	l'examen de fin de semestre/de fin d'année
the final [*in sports*]	la finale
And that's final!	Un point c'est tout!

finally *adv*

[*at last*]	enfin/finalement/à la fin
They have finally decided.	Ils ont enfin décidé.
	Ils ont fini par décider.

financial aid *n*

[*in general*]	l'aide financière [*f*]
[*a grant*]	une bourse
[*a loan*]	un prêt

finish *v*

to finish	finir
I'm finished./I have finished.	J'**ai** fini. [*Note: not* **je suis**]

fire *n*

a fire	un feu/un incendie
to make/light a fire	faire un feu/du feu
to warm oneself by the fire	se chauffer devant le feu
a forest fire	un incendie de forêt
Five fires were reported in 24 hours.	Cinq incendies ont été signalés en 24 heures.
to be on fire	être en flammes/en feu
to catch fire	prendre feu
the fire department	les pompiers

first *adj*

first	premier(-ière)
the first time	la première fois
to take the first step	faire le premier pas
the first two pages	les deux premières pages [*Note: word order*]
the first of January	le premier janvier [*Note: no preposition*]
Francis I (the first)	François Ier (premier) [*Note: no article*]

first *adv*

(at) first/first of all	d'abord/au début/pour commencer
first. . .then. . .	d'abord. . .ensuite. . .

first *pron*

the first	le premier/la première
They were the first to arrive.	Ils sont arrivés les premiers.

fix *v*

[*to repair sth*]	réparer qqch
to fix dinner	préparer le dîner

Ø **fixer** has various meanings, including "to set," e.g., **fixer une date**, and "to fasten."

flavor *n*

taste

This chocolate has a bitter taste.	Ce chocolat a un goût amer.

le goût/la saveur

ice cream flavor

le parfum

What flavor? - Chocolate, vanilla, strawberry?	Quel parfum? - Chocolat, vanille, fraise?

floor *n*

the floor [*of a structure*]	le plancher
on the floor	par terre/sur le sol
He leaves everything on the floor.	Il laisse tout par terre.

floor level

[*Note: French numbering is different from U.S.*]

the first floor [*ground floor*]	le rez-de-chaussée
the second floor	le premier étage
Our room is on the 22nd (floor).	Notre chambre est au vingt-et-unième (étage).

fly v
of planes, pilots, birds
This plane flies at 500 miles an hour.

voler
Cet avion vole à 800 km à l'heure.

passengers
Will you fly or drive?
First we flew to Marseilles.

[*Note: not* **voler**]
Irez-vous en avion ou en voiture?
D'abord nous avons pris l'avion pour
   Marseille.

food n
nourishment
Children need healthy food.

la nourriture
Les enfants ont besoin d'une nourriture
   saine.

natural food

la nourriture naturelle

something to eat
Is there any food in the fridge?
He enjoys his food.
I need some food.
to give animals/people their food
We have to give the children their food.

Il y a de quoi manger au frigo?
Il aime bien manger.
J'ai besoin de manger./J'ai faim.
donner à manger à/faire manger
Il faut donner à manger aux enfants.

foodstuff

Where do you keep the food?

frozen food
Does that shop sell food?

The price of food has gone up a lot.

les provisions [f]/les aliments [m])/les
   comestibles [m]/ l'alimentation [f]
Où est-ce que vous gardez les
   provisions?
les aliments congelés/surgelés
On vend des comestibles dans ce
   magasin?
Le prix de l'alimentation a beaucoup
   augmenté.

cooking, preparation
Do you like Vietnamese food?
The food's good here.

la cuisine
Aimez-vous la cuisine vietnamienne?
La cuisine est bonne ici.
On mange bien ici.

for prep
destination
to leave for Chartres/Japan/South
   America
the train for Dieppe

partir **pour** Chartres/**pour** le Japon/
   pour l'Amérique du sud
le train **pour** Dieppe/**de** Dieppe/à
   destination de Dieppe

intention, purpose
What's that knife for?

A quoi sert ce couteau?

It's used for cutting vinyl.	Il sert **à** couper le vinyle.
a cure for whooping cough	un remède **contre** la coqueluche
What will you have for dessert?	Qu'est-ce que vous prendrez **comme** dessert?
for sale/for rent	**à** vendre/**à** louer
for example	**par** exemple

reason

the reason for my leaving	la raison **de** mon départ
for joy	**de** joie
for fear of	**de** peur de [+*infinitive*]
for fear that	**de** peur que [+*subjunctive*]
famous for	célèbre **pour**

exchange

in exchange for sth	en échange **de** qqch
to exchange sth for sth else	échanger qqch **contre** qqch d'autre

distance

for miles and miles	**pendant** des kilomètres et des kilomètres

time

He's been living here for two years [*and still is.*]	*Il habite ici* **depuis** *deux ans.*
	Voilà deux ans **qu'**il habite ici.
	Ça fait deux ans **qu'**il habite ici.
He lived here for five months [*but no longer does*].	Il a habité ici **pendant** cinq mois.
I am going away for a month [*in the future*].	Je pars **pour** un mois.
I will be in Norway for part of the time.	Je serai en Norvège **pour** une partie du temps.
I have reserved a room for the first ten days.	J'ai réservé une chambre pour les dix premiers jours.

verb+for

	[*Note: "for" not translated*]
to ask for	demander
to hope for	espérer
to look for	chercher
to pay for	payer
to send for	envoyer chercher
to wait for	attendre

formal *adj*

formal attire	la tenue de soirée/de cérémonie
a formal [*evening dress*]	une robe du soir

former

This suit looks too formal.	Ce tailleur fait trop habillé
a formal reception	une réception officielle
to be formal [in manner]	être cérémonieux(-euse)/être guindé(e) faire des cérémonies/faire des chichis [fam]
She is too formal.	Elle fait trop de cérémonies.
There's no need to be formal.	Ce n'est pas la peine de faire tant de cérémonies.

Ø **formel**(-elle) means "definite," e.g., **une réponse formelle.**

former adj
[past, previous]
the former president

ancien(-enne) [Note: precedes noun]
l'ancien président

former pron
[opposite of the latter]

celui-là/celle-là
le premier/la première

Of the two authors I prefer the former.

Des deux auteurs je préfère celui-là.

fortunate adj
to be fortunate
a fortunate coincidence

avoir de la chance
une heureuse coincidence

Ø **fortuné**(e) means "well off."

fortunately adv
Fortunately, I found my wallet.

Heureusement, j'ai trouvé mon portefeuille.

forward adv
to look forward to sth

attendre qqch avec impatience
se réjouir d'avance/déjà de qqch

The children are looking forward to Easter.

Les enfants attendent Pâques avec impatience.

I'm looking forward to seeing you.

Je me réjouis déjà de vous voir.

fountain n
a drinking fountain

[Note: There is no common French term for drinking fountains, which are rare in France.]

an ornamental fountain

une fontaine

foyer *n*
[entrance hall in public building]   le hall/l'entrée [f]/le foyer

Ø **foyer** [m] also means "home," "family," or "hearth."

free *n*
free of charge   gratuit(e)
free admission   entrée gratuite
a free sample   un échantillon gratuit
a freeway   une autoroute

available   libre
We are not free tonight.   Nous ne sommes pas libres ce soir.
Is this seat free?   Cette place est libre?

independent   libre
the free press   la presse libre
free speech   la liberté de la parole

freeze/frozen *v*
It's freezing. *[weather]*   Il gèle.
We were frozen to the bone.   Nous étions gelés jusqu'aux os.
frozen foods   les aliments congelés/surgelés

French *adj*
French   français(e) *[Note: small "f" when used as an adjective]*

the French flag   le drapeau français
a French actress   une actrice française
French citizens   les citoyens français/les citoyennes françaises

French *n*
the language   le français *[Note: small "f" for the language]*

French is a Latin language.   Le français est une langue latine.
a French book   un livre **de** français
a French class   un cours **de** français
to read/learn/understand French   lire/apprendre/comprendre **le** français
to speak French   parler français *[Note: not **le**]*

friend

the people

French people/the French	les Français [*Note: capital "f" when used as a noun*]
a French man/woman	un Français/une Française
French women are shorter than American women.	Les Françaises sont moins grandes que les Américaines.

friend *n*

a friend	un ami/une amie/un(e) camarade/un copain/une copine [*fam*]
	une connaissance [*Note: always feminine*]
a friend of mine	un de mes amis/une de mes amies/ une de mes connaissances
my boyfriend	mon petit ami
my girlfriend	ma petite amie

from

a place

from the city	**de la** ville
from the church	**de l'**église
from the office	**du** bureau
from the stores	**des** magasins
Where are you from?	**D'**où êtes-vous?/**D'**où venez-vous?
Where have you come from today?	**D'**où arrivez-vous aujourd'hui?

with geographic names

from London	**de** Londres [*a city*]
from Germany	**d'**Allemagne [*a feminine country*]
from Brazil	**du** Brésil [*a masculine country*]
from the Netherlands	**des** Pays-Bas [*plural*]

to take sth from someplace

to take sth from the table/the drawer/ the cupboard	prendre qqch **sur** la table/**dans** le tiroir/**dans** le placard
Go and get the forks from the drawer.	Va chercher les fourchettes **dans** le tiroir.

time

from noon to two P.M.	**de** midi à quatorze heures
from ten o'clock (on)	**à partir de** dix heures
from tomorrow (on)/starting tomorrow	**à partir de** demain/**dès** demain
ten years from now	**dans** dix ans/**d'ici** dix ans
right from the start	**dès** le début

on behalf of

de la part de

a gift from the students
Say hello to them from me.

un cadeau de la part des étudiants
Dites-leur bonjour de ma part.

verb+from
to take sth from sb
to borrow/buy/steal sth from sb
I bought this car from John.
I bought it from him.

prendre qqch **à** qqn
emprunter/acheter/voler qqch **à** qqn
J'ai acheté cette voiture **à** Jean.
Je la **lui** ai achetée.

front   *adj & n*
in front (of)
I was sitting in front of them.
to walk in front (of)
the front [*forward part*]
the front of the dress
You've got your sweater on back to
   front.

devant
J'étais assis devant eux.
marcher devant
le devant
le devant de la robe
Tu as mis ton chandail devant derrière.

in front [*in a vehicle*]
to ride in the front of the bus.
the front seat [*in a car*]
the front wheels
in the front row
on the front page [*of a newspaper*]

à l'avant
être à l'avant de l'autobus
le siège avant
les roues avant
au premier rang
en première page/à la une

Ø **front** [*m*] usually means "forehead."

fruit   *n*
fruit

I'll serve fruit for dessert.
a piece of fruit

des fruits [*Note: normally used in the
   plural*]
Je vais servir des fruits comme dessert.
un fruit

full   *adj*
filled
The cups were not full.
He is full of hope.

plein(e)/rempli(e)
Les tasses n'étaient pas pleines.
Il est plein d'espoir.

no more room
[*in bus, theater, restaurant*]
We are full.
The "full" sign was posted.

complet(-ète)
C'est complet./Nous sommes complet.
C'était affiché "complet".

81

from eating
I'm full.

J'ai assez mangé. [*Note: Do not use* **plein**(e).]

fun *n*/**funny** *adj*
[*strange, odd*]
[*amusing*]

étrange/bizarre/drôle
amusant/drôle/marrant [*fam*]/rigolo [*fam*]

This is very funny/a lot of fun.
to have fun
We had a lot of fun.
to make fun of sb

C'est très amusant.
s'amuser
Nous nous sommes bien amusés.
se moquer de qqn

function *v*
of things
This switch does not function properly.

marcher/fonctionner
Ce commutateur ne marche pas comme il faut.

of people
He doesn't function well under pressure.
I am not functioning well today.

Il ne travaille pas bien sous pression.

Je ne suis pas dans mon assiette aujourd'hui.

fundraiser *n*
to have a fundraiser

faire une collecte de fonds
collecter des fonds

furniture *n*
[*in general*]
They have nice furniture.
a piece of furniture

des meubles [*m pl*]
Ils ont de jolis meubles.
un meuble

future *adj*
[*next*]
the future president
the future (tense)

futur(e)
le futur président
le (temps) futur

future *n*
the future
She has a rosy future.
in the future

l'avenir
Elle a un brillant avenir.
à l'avenir

G

game *n*
in general
the Olympic Games

le jeu
les Jeux Olympiques (les J.O.)

a game with a few players
to have/play a game of cards
a game of tennis/chess

une partie
faire une partie de cartes
une partie de tennis/d'échecs

a team sport
to play a game of football/soccer/ice
   hockey

un match
jouer un match de football/de soccer/
   de hockey sur glace

garbage *n*
household garbage
[*industrial waste*]
[*litter, trash*]
Don't leave litter.

les ordures ménagères [*f pl*]
les déchets industriels [*m pl*]
les détritus [*m pl*]
Ne laissez pas de détritus.
Ne jetez pas de papiers.

a garbage can

une poubelle

gas *n*
a vapor
a gas stove

le gaz
une cuisinière à gaz

gasoline
to fill up with gas
Fill it up.
regular/super/unleaded gas

l'essence [*f*]
faire le plein d'essence
Faites le plein.
l'essence ordinaire/super/sans plomb

gentle *adj*
[*soft, sweet, gradual*]
a gentle voice
a gentle slope

doux/douce
une voix douce
une pente douce

Ø **gentil**(-ille) means "kind" or "nice."

gentleman *n*
the gentleman on my left
Ladies and gentlemen!

le monsieur à ma gauche
Mesdames, Mesdemoiselles, Messieurs!/
   Messieurs-dames!

get

He's a real gentleman.	C'est un vrai gentleman.

get *v*

[*Note: Many meanings of "get" are expressed by reflexive verbs.*]

to get dressed	s'habiller
to get married	se marier
to get well/better	se remettre
to get ready	se préparer

to become

[*Note: When "get" means "become," it can be translated by* **devenir**, *but an alternate form is often preferred.*]

She's getting quite pretty.	Elle devient plutôt jolie.
They got very aggressive.	Ils sont devenus très agressifs. [*Note: conjugated with* **être**]
to get hungry/thirsty/sleepy/hot/cold	commencer à avoir faim/soif/ sommeil/chaud/froid
to get sick	tomber malade
to get fat/thin	grossir/maigrir
to get big/tall	grandir
to get old	vieillir
to get older [*children*]	grandir
to get angry	se fâcher
to get tired	se fatiguer
to get used to	s'accoutumer à/s'habituer à
to get interested in	s'intéresser à
to get bored	s'ennuyer

to obtain

	obtenir/trouver/acheter/avoir/prendre
He got his parents' permission.	Il a obtenu la permission de ses parents.
I got my degree at _____ University.	J'ai eu mon diplôme de l'Université de _____
Try and get the front row.	Essaye d'avoir le premier rang.
He got me this job.	Il m'a trouvé ce poste.
Where did you get your beads?	Où as-tu acheté/trouvé tes perles?
Do we need to get bread?	Il faut acheter/prendre du pain?

to receive

	recevoir
I didn't get any mail.	Je n'ai pas reçu de courrier.
We always get good grades.	Nous recevons toujours de bonnes notes.

to go, to arrive

How do you get to Rouen from here?	Comment fait-on pour aller à Rouen?

Can you get there by train?	On peut y aller par le train?
When will they get here/there?	Quand arriveront-ils?

to fetch

to get sb to come	faire venir qqn/aller chercher qqn
We need to get a plumber.	Il faut faire venir un plombier.
to go and get sth	aller chercher qqch/aller prendre qqch
I'll go and get my glasses from my room.	Je vais chercher mes lunettes dans ma chambre.

to understand

I don't get it.	Je ne comprends pas.
I've got it.	Je comprends./J'y suis.
I didn't get your name.	Je n'ai pas saisi votre nom.

to be able, allowed to

She gets to drive the car.	On la laisse conduire la voiture.
When you're six, you'll get to go to school.	Quand tu auras six ans, tu pourras aller à l'école.
We got to see the fireworks.	C'était chouette, on a vu le feu d'artifice. [*Note: This colloquial use of "got" has no real equivalent in French.*]

to have

	avoir
Have you got their address? — No, I haven't got it with me.	Tu as leur adresse? — Non, je ne l'ai pas sur moi.

impersonal expressions

It's getting hot/cold.	Il commence à faire chaud/froid.
It's getting dark/light.	Il commence à faire noir/jour.
It's getting late.	Il se fait tard.

to get+adverb

to get in/out	entrer/sortir
to get on/off [*a vehicle*]	monter (dans)/descendre (de)
to get up [*from bed, a seat*]	se lever
to get on/along with sb	s'entendre avec qqn
to get back (home)	rentrer
to get sth back	récupérer qqch
to get away [*to leave*]	partir
to get away [*to escape*]	s'échapper

to get+past participle

	se faire [+*infinitive*]
to get arrested/paid/robbed	se faire arrêter/payer/voler
to get knocked down by a car	se faire renverser par une voiture
She got insulted by the other saleswomen.	Elle s'est fait insulter par les autres vendeuses.

girlfriend [n]
my girlfriend [*romantic*]   ma petite amie
[*a woman friend*]   une amie/une copine

gift
a present   un cadeau
It was a wedding gift   C'était un cadeau de noces.

a talent   un don
He has a gift for languages.   Il a le don des langues.
    Il est doué pour les langues.

go   v
to go (somewhere)   aller (quelque part)
Let's go to the movies.   Allons au cinéma.
Shall we go?   On y va?
Go ahead./Go on.   Vas-y./Allez-y.
to go to a city/a country [*see to*]
to go in   entrer
to go up/down   monter/descendre
to go out (of a building)   sortir (d'un immeuble)
Are we going out tonight?   On sort ce soir?
to go out to dinner   dîner en ville/au restaurant
to go away [*to leave*]   partir/s'en aller
Go away!   Va-t'en!/Allez-vous-en!
It's time to go.   C'est le moment de partir.
They're gone (for the summer).   Ils sont partis (pour l'été).

to go+infinitive
I'm not going to buy it.   Je ne vais pas l'acheter.
She wasn't going to tell us.   Elle n'allait pas nous le dire.
Go and see if he's there.   Va voir s'il est là.

goal   n
[*an aim*]   un but/un objectif
[*in sports*]   un but
to score a goal   marquer un but

good   adj
Good morning/Good afternoon/Good day!   Bonjour!
Have a good day!   Bonne journée!
Be good! [*well-behaved*]   Sois sage!/Soyez sage(s)!
a good man/fellow/guy   un brave hommme/un brave type

a good woman	une brave femme [Note: Avoid **un bonhomme** and **une bonne femme** which can be pejorative.]
to be good at math	être fort(e) en maths
She's a good teacher.	Elle est bien comme professeur.
	Elle est bon professeur.
It's good to relax.	Ça fait du bien de se détendre.
to be good [kind] to sb	être bon (bonne) pour qqn
It's very good [nice] of you (to . . .)	C'est très gentil à vous (de . . .)
	Vous êtes très gentil (de . . .)
to have a good time	s'amuser
Have a good time.	Amusez-vous bien.
We had a good time.	Nous nous sommes bien amusés.

verb + good

You look good in that picture.	Vous êtes bien sur cette photo.
You look good today. [well-dressed]	Vous êtes tout beau/toute belle aujourd'hui.
to be good-looking	être bien physiquement/être beau (belle)
He's a good-looking man.	Il est bien./Il est bel homme.
She's a good-looking woman.	Elle est bien./Elle est belle femme.
to look good [health]	avoir bonne mine
to feel good [health]	se sentir bien
to feel good [emotion]	être content(e)/satisfait(e)
She feels good about her work.	Elle est contente de son travail.
to smell good	sentir bon
to taste good	avoir bon goût

good n

good and evil	le bien et le mal
It'll do her good.	Ça lui fera du bien.
It's for your own good.	C'est pour ton bien.
for the good of the country	pour le bien du pays
What's the good (of working)?	A quoi bon (travailler)?
It's no good (trying)!	Ce n'est pas la peine (d'essayer)!
It's no good worrying about it.	Il ne faut pas s'en faire.
for good [for ever]	pour de bon/pour toujours

grade n
year in school

What grade is she in?	la classe
	En quelle classe est-elle?

graduate

to be in sixth grade

être en sixième [*Note: French grades are numbered in reverse order; fifth comes after sixth grade.*]

a score
to get bad grades

une note
obtenir de mauvaises notes

Ø **grade** [*m*] means "rank" (military or administrative).

graduate *v*
to graduate [*from high school*]
to graduate [*from university*]

obtenir son baccalauréat
obtenir son diplôme/sa licence

graduate *n & adj*
to be a graduate of _____
  University
to do graduate studies for a Master's/a
  Doctorate

être diplômé(e)/licencié(e) de
  l'Université de _____
faire des études de deuxième cycle/de
  troisième cycle

graduation *n*
[*the ceremony*]

la remise des diplômes [*Note: The graduation ceremony is not a French custom.*]

grain *n*
[*wheat, barley, etc.*]
Grain grows well in that area.

les céréales [*f pl*]
Les céréales poussent bien dans cette région.

a grain (of salt/sand)

un grain (de sel/de sable)

Ø **graine** [*f*] means "the seed of a plant."

grand *adj*
great, large
the grand ballroom

grand(e)
la grande salle de bal

magnificent

magnifique/splendide/
  impressionnant(e)

a grand banquet

un banquet magnifique

of relatives
grandfather/grandmother
grandparents
grandchildren

le grand-père/la grand-mère
les grands-parents
les petits-enfants [*Note: not **grands-***]

grapes *n*

grapes
a bunch of grapes
one grape
a grape seed
For dessert, I'll have grapes.

le raisin [*Note: singular*]
une grappe de raisin
un grain de raisin
un pépin de raisin
Comme dessert, je prendrai du raisin.

great *adj*
in general
a great man

We are great friends.
a great leader/king/poet
great works of literature
with great care/pleasure

grand(e)
un grand homme [*Note: This also means
"a tall man."*]
Nous sommes de grands amis.
un grand chef/roi/poète
les grandes oeuvres de la littérature
avec grand soin/plaisir

excellent
a great vacation
That's great!

magnifique/merveilleux/formidable
des vacances merveilleuses
C'est formidable/sensationnel/génial!
[*slang*]

relatives
great-grandfather
great-grand-daughter

l'arrière-grand-père [*m*]
l'arrière-petite-fille [*f*]

gross *adj*
[*coarse*]
[*disgusting*]

grossier(-ière)
dégueulasse [*slang*]

Ø **gros** (grosse) means "big" or "fat."

ground *n*
[*earth, soil*]
on the ground
the ground floor

la terre/le sol
par terre/sur le sol
le rez-de-chaussée

grow *v intrans*
of people
to grow in size
to grow up
When I grow up...

grandir
devenir adulte/grandir
Quand je serai grand...

of nails, hair
My beard grows fast.
I'm letting my hair grow.

pousser
Ma barbe pousse vite.
Je me laisse pousser les cheveux.

of plants
Asparagus grows well in this climate.

pousser
Les asperges poussent bien dans ce
   climat.

to increase
Their audience has grown.

grandir/augmenter
Leur public a augmenté.

to grow+adjective: [*see* **get**]

grow *v trans*
to grow plants
In the Southwest they grow a lot of
   wheat.

cultiver/faire pousser
Dans le sud-ouest on cultive beaucoup
   de blé.

guess *v*
to believe, suppose

croire/supposer/avoir l'impression
   (que)

I guess he's pretty important.

J'ai l'impression qu'il est assez
   important.

Are we all going together? — I guess so.

On y va tous ensemble? — Oui, je
   crois.

I guess not.

Je crois que non./Je ne crois pas.

to make a guess
Guess who just phoned!
to guess right

deviner
Devine qui vient de téléphoner!
deviner juste

guest *n*
the person invited
guests
We have guests tonight.
dinner guests
house guests

l'invité(e)
des invités/des visites/de la visite
Nous avons de la visite ce soir.
des invités pour le dîner
des amis de passsage

a paying guest in hotel

un(e) client(e)/un(e) hôte [*Note:* **hôte** *is
seldom used for "guest." It also means
"host," as in* **table d'hôte.**]

guilty *adj*
[*guilty of a wrongdoing*]
to have a guilty conscience
to feel guilty

coupable
avoir mauvaise conscience
avoir des remords

guy *n*
[*colloquial for a male*]

                              un type/un gars/un individu/un mec
                                 [*slang*]

a nice guy   un chic type
a rotten guy   un sale type
you guys   vous autres

≡ H ≡

habit *n*

a habit	une habitude
He has some bad habits.	Il a de mauvaises habitudes.
to be in the habit of doing sth	avoir l'habitude de faire qqch
to get into the habit	prendre l'habitude

Ø **habit** [*m*] means "an article of clothing."

hair *n*

hair [*of the head*]	les cheveux [*m pl*]
a single hair	un cheveu
to have fair/red/brown hair	avoir les cheveux blonds/roux/châtains
She has red hair.	Elle a les cheveux roux.
Her hair was all wet.	Ses cheveux étaient tout mouillés.
She cut her hair.	Elle s'est coupé les cheveux.
She had her hair cut.	Elle s'est fait couper les cheveux.
to do one's hair	se coiffer
a hairstyle	une coiffure
hair [*on chest, arms, etc.*]	les poils [*m pl*]

half *adj*

half-	demi- [*Note: invar before a noun*]
a half-brother	un demi-frère
a half-sister	une demi-soeur
a half-liter jug of red wine	une demi-carafe de (vin) rouge
a half dozen	une demi-douzaine
a half hour	une demi-heure
half past one	une heure et demie [*Note: feminine adjective*]

half *n*

a half	la moitié
Do you want a pear? — Just a half.	Tu veux une poire? — Juste la moitié.
She pays half (of) the rent.	Elle paye la moitié du loyer.

hall *n*

[*a passage, a corridor*]	un couloir
[*entrance in a house*]	un vestibule/une entrée

[*a hotel lobby*]   un hall/une entrée
[*a theater lobby*]   un foyer/une entrée
[*an exhibition or concert hall*]   une salle
[*a market hall*]   une halle

hand   *n*
on the other hand   par contre/en revanche
He is weak in physics; on the other hand, he is good in chemistry.   Il est faible en physique; en revanche, il est fort en chimie.
on one hand...on the other hand   d'un côté...de l'autre côté
   d'une part...d'autre part

handle   *v*
to touch   toucher (à)
Please do not handle the merchandise.   Prière de ne pas toucher à la marchandise.

"Handle with care"   "Fragile"

to take care of, to deal with   s'occuper de/se charger de
She handled everything.   Elle s'est occupée de tout.

to control   s'y prendre avec
She can't handle her children.   Elle ne sait pas s'y prendre avec ses enfants.

to handle oneself   se comporter
He handles himself well under difficult circumstances.   Il se comporte bien dans des situations difficiles.

hang-up   *n*/hang up   *v*
to have a hang-up   avoir un complexe
to hang up [*the phone*]   raccrocher
to hang up the washing   éteindre le linge
to hang sth up on the wall   accrocher qqch au mur

happen   *v*
to happen   se passer/arriver
What happened?   Qu'est-ce qui est arrivé?
   Qu'est-ce qui s'est passé?

That won't happen again.   Cela ne se passera plus.

to a person
What happened to him?   Qu'est-ce qui lui est arrivé? [*Note: not* ***se passer***]

What happened to [*became of*] him?   Qu'est-ce qu'il est devenu?

hard

by chance
if you happen to see him · s'il vous arrive de le voir/si par hasard vous le voyez

hard *adj*
[*of a substance*] · dur(e)/ferme
[*of a person*] · dur(e)/difficile/sévère
[*of a situation*] · dur(e)/difficile/pénible
to have a hard time doing sth · avoir du mal à faire qqch
My children gave me a hard time. · Mes enfants m'en ont fait voir de toutes les couleurs.

hard *adv*
to work hard · travailler dur
to study hard · étudier assidûment/bûcher [*fam*]/ bosser [*fam*]
to try hard to do sth · faire un effort pour faire qqch

hardly *adv*
[*barely, scarcely*] · à peine
I can hardly hear you. · Je vous entends à peine.
hardly ever · presque jamais

hate *v*
to hate · détester/haïr/avoir horreur de
He hates his job/his boss. · Il déteste son travail/son chef.
I hate beans. · J'ai horreur des haricots.
She hates getting up early. · Elle déteste se lever tôt.
He hates doing the housework. · Il a horreur de faire le ménage.

have *v*
to have sth done · faire faire qqch
She has had her hair curled. · Elle s'est fait friser les cheveux.
You should have your shoes repaired. · Tu devrais faire réparer tes chaussures.
I had my car waxed by the man at the garage. · J'ai fait cirer ma voiture par le garagiste.

have to *v*
to have to (do sth) · devoir [+*infinitive*]
il faut que [+*subjunctive*]
il faut [+*infinitive*]

in the present
You have to leave today. · Vous devez partir aujourd'hui.

Il faut que vous partiez aujourd'hui.
Il faut partir aujourd'hui.

in the past (habitually)
When I was your age, I had to milk the cows.
She had to sign every letter herself.

We always had to help him.

Quand j'avais ton âge, je devais traire les vaches.
Il fallait qu'elle signe toutes les lettres elle-même.
Il fallait toujours l'aider.

in the past (a specific occasion)
I had to admit she was right.
They had to be there on Monday.
We had to pay right away.

J'ai dû avouer qu'elle avait raison.
Il a fallu qu'ils soient là lundi.
Il a fallu payer tout de suite.

in the future
They will have to tell me.
I'll have to write to them.
We'll have to get up at dawn.

Ils devront me le dire.
Il faudra que je leur écrive.
Il faudra nous lever à l'aube.

with a negative
You don't have to arrive before noon.
[It's not necessary.]

Il n'est pas nécessaire d'arriver avant midi. [Note: **Il ne faut pas arriver avant midi** would mean "You must not arrive before noon."]

hazard *n*
a health hazard
It's hazardous for your health.

un danger/un risque pour la santé
C'est dangereux pour la santé.

Ø **hasard** [m] means "luck" or "chance."

he *pron*

il [subj]
lui [disj]
He's going alone.
He and his wife are going.

Il y va tout seul.
Lui et sa femme y vont.

healthy *adj*
[of a person]
She is healthy.
[of things]
healthy food

sain(e)/en bonne santé
Elle est en bonne santé.
bon (bonne) pour la santé/sain(e)
une nourriture saine

hear v

to hear	entendre
to hear from sb	avoir/recevoir des nouvelles de qqn
Have you heard from them?	Avez-vous de leurs nouvelles?
to hear of sb/sth	entendre parler de qqn/de qqch
I've never heard of him.	Je n'ai jamais entendu parler de lui.
to hear that...	entendre dire que/apprendre que...
I heard (that) they had gone bankrupt.	J'ai entendu dire qu'ils avaient fait faillite.
We heard he was ill.	Nous avons appris qu'il était malade. Il paraît qu'il est malade.

heat n & v
in general

	la chaleur
The heat is making me sick.	La chaleur me rend malade.

heating

	le chauffage
to turn the (central) heat on	allumer le chauffage (central)

in cooking

on low heat	à feu doux
to heat (up) some soup	faire réchauffer de la soupe

heavy adj
weight

	lourd(e)
The suitcases are heavy.	Les valises sont lourdes.
The weather is heavy.	Il fait lourd.
How heavy are you?	Combien pesez-vous?

other

The traffic is heavy.	Il y a beaucoup de circulation.
a heavy schedule	un emploi du temps chargé

hello excl
[in greeting] — Bonjour!/Salut! [fam]

Ø **allô** is used only on the telephone.

helpful adj

[of a person]	serviable/obligeant(e)/arrangeant(e)
The salesman was very helpful.	Le vendeur était très obligeant.
You have been very helpful.	Vous m'avez vraiment rendu service.
[of a thing]	
That would be very helpful.	Ça m'aiderait beaucoup. Ça me rendrait vraiment service.

a helpful suggestion | une suggestion utile

her *adj*
[*possessive*]
her father and mother

She is at her friend's (house).

son/sa/ses
son père et sa mère [*Note: adjective repeated*]

Elle est chez **son** amie. [*Note:* **son** *is used before a feminine noun beginning with a vowel.*]

her *pron*

la (l') [*dir obj*]
lui [*indir obj*]
elle [*disj*]

I woke her up.
Show her this letter.
Don't leave without her.

Je l'ai réveillée.
Montrez-lui cette lettre.
Ne pars pas sans elle.

here *adv*
Where are you? — Here.
Here I am.
Here! [*in a roll call*]
Here is/here are...
Here are my keys.
Is the teacher here? — No, he's not here today.

Où es-tu? — Ici.
Me voici.
Présent(e)!
Voici...
Voici mes clés.
Est-ce que le professeur est là? — Non, il n'est pas là aujourd'hui. [*Note:* **là** *is often used for "here."*]

hers *pron*
[*possessive*]

le sien   les siens
la sienne   les siennes

She borrowed my gloves; she had forgotten hers.

Elle a emprunté mes gants; elle avait oublié les siens.

herself [*see* **self**]

high *adj*
in general
the highest mountains
The building is 30 meters high.

haut(e)
les plus hautes montagnes
L'immeuble fait 30 mètres/a 30 mètres de haut.

other

a high fever	une grosse fièvre
a high price/a high figure	un prix élevé/un chiffre élevé
a high-rise [*building*]	une tour/un gratte-ciel

hill *n*
a small mountain

We climbed to the top of the hill.

une colline

Nous sommes montés au sommet de la colline.

a hillside, a slope

You have to go up a slight hill to get to the house.

The hill was planted with vines.

une côte/une pente

Il faut monter une légère pente pour arriver à la maison.

La côte était plantée de vignes.

him *pron*

le (l') [*dir obj*]
lui [*indir obj*]
lui [*disj*]

We don't like him.
I'll phone him.
They left without him.

Nous ne l'aimons pas.
Je vais lui téléphoner.
Ils sont partis sans lui.

himself [*see self*]

his *adj*
[*possessive*]
I know his mother.
Do you have his address?

son/sa/ses
Je connais sa mère.
As-tu son adresse? [*Note:* **son** *is used before a feminine noun beginning with a vowel.*]

his *pron*
[*possessive*]

le sien   les siens
la sienne   les siennes

My grades are better than his.

Mes notes sont meilleures que les siennes.

holiday *n*

a public holiday	un jour férié/un jour de congé
a religious holiday	une fête
the Christmas holiday	la fête de Noël
Happy holidays!	Joyeuses fêtes!
[*see also* **vacation**]	

home *adv*

to be at home — être à la maison/être chez soi
Will they be home tonight? — Seront-ils chez eux ce soir?
to come/go home — rentrer (à la maison)
I can take you home. — Je peux vous raccompagner (chez vous).

Is Chantal home? — No, she's not (home). — Est-ce que Chantal est là? — Non, elle n'est pas là.

home *n*

They have a lovely home. — Ils ont une très belle maison.
My home is in Nice. — J'habite Nice./Je viens de Nice.
homework — les devoirs [*m pl*]
a homemaker — une femme au foyer
the homeless — les sans-abri [*invar*]
to be homeless — être sans domicile fixe

honey [see *dear*]

hors d'oeuvres *n*

[*appetizers served before a meal*] — des amuse-gueule [*invar*]

In France, **les hors-d'oeuvre** [*m*] are served at table as the first course of a meal. Note French spelling: no final "s."

hot *adj*

of temperature
chaud(e)
It's very hot. [*weather*] — Il **fait** très chaud.
The coffee is hot. [*a thing*] — Le café **est** chaud.
The baby is too hot. [*a person*] — Le bébé **a** trop chaud.
My feet are hot. — J'ai chaud au pieds.

of spicy food
épicé(e)/piquant(e)/fort(e)
These peppers are too hot. — Ces poivrons sont trop piquants.

house *n*

a house — une maison/une villa
Do you live in a house or an apartment? — Est-ce que vous habitez dans une villa ou dans un appartement?
at/to: my/your/his/her/our/your/their house — chez moi/toi/lui/elle/nous/vous/ eux/elles
Let's go to his house. — Allons chez lui.
Can you come by my house after class? — Tu peux passer chez moi après les cours?

to do the housework — faire le ménage

housing *n*

housing	le logement/l'hébergement [m]
the housing crisis	la crise du logement
workers' housing	des logements ouvriers
I need to find housing.	J'ai besoin de trouver un logement.
student housing [*dorm*]	une résidence/un foyer universitaire
This office handles (student) housing	Ce bureau s'occupe de l'hébergement (des étudiants).
low-income housing	des habitations à loyer modéré (H.L.M.)

how *adv*

How are you?	Comment vas-tu?/Comment allez-vous?
How's it going?	Ça va?/Comment ça va?
How do you say "fish" in French?	Comment dit-on «fish» en français?
How do you spell that?	Comment (est-ce que) ça s'écrit?

an exclamation

How small she is!	Qu'elle est petite!/Comme elle est petite!
How wonderful!	C'est magnifique!/Que c'est magnifique!

a question: how + adjective

How **far** is it to Lille?	Lille, c'est à quelle distance?
How **heavy** is the package?	Combien pèse le colis?
How **high** is the building?	Quelle est la hauteur du bâtiment? Le bâtiment fait combien?
How **long** is the room?	La salle fait/mesure combien? Quelle est la longueur de la salle?
How **long** is the quarter?	Le trimestre dure combien de temps?
How **long** is it since you saw him?	Ça fait combien de temps que vous ne l'avez pas vu?
How **long** did you live in China?	Pendant combien de temps avez-vous habité en Chine?
How **much** is it/is this?	C'est combien?/Ça fait combien?
How **much** is that belt?	Combien coûte/Combien vaut cette ceinture?
How **much** do you weigh?	Combien pesez-vous?
How **much** rice is left?	Combien de riz reste-t-il?
How **many** tickets do you want?	Combien de billets voulez-vous?
How **often** do you go to church?	Vous allez souvent à l'église?
How **often** do the buses run?	Les autobus passent tous les combien? A quel intervalle passent les autobus?
How **old** is she?	Quel âge a-t-elle?

How **tall** is he? | Combien mesure-t-il?
How **well** do you know them? | Vous les connaissez bien?

however *adv*

However I say it, it sounds wrong. | De quelque manière que je le dise, cela sonne faux.

however pretty they may be | quelque jolies qu'elles soient
However hard I try, I never earn enough. | J'ai beau essayer, je ne gagne jamais assez.

however *conj*

[*nevertheless*] | cependant/toutefois/pourtant
She may be right; however, I don't think so. | Elle a peut-être raison; cependant, je ne le pense pas.

hug *n & v*

to hug sb/to give sb a hug | étreindre qqn/serrer qqn (dans ses bras)

She gave me a big hug. | Elle m'a serré très fort.
They hugged each other. | Ils se sont étreints.

humor *n*/**humorous** *adj*

humor | l'humour [*m*]
to have a sense of humor | avoir le sens de l'humour
humorous | amusant(e)/plein(e) d'humour
a humorous story | une histoire amusante
a humorous writer | un écrivain humoristique

Ø **humeur** [*f*] means "temperament" or "mood," as in **être de mauvaise humeur**.

hurt *v*

to hurt sb physically | faire mal à qqn/blesser qqn
You're hurting me. | Tu me fais mal.
The injection won't hurt you. | La piqûre ne te fera pas mal.
Ouch! That hurts! | Aïe! Ça fait mal!
to hurt oneself | se faire mal/se blesser
She hurt her arm. | Elle s'est fait mal au bras.
 | Elle s'est blessé au bras.

to hurt sb mentally | faire de la peine à qqn
Your letter hurt her a lot. | Votre lettre lui a fait beaucoup de peine.

101

hurt

to have pain
Her arm hurts.
[*see also* **pain**]

avoir mal
Elle a mal au bras.

≡ I ≡

I *pron*

je [*subj*]
moi [*disj*]

I love to swim.
Who wants some? — Not I.
They're going but I can't.

J'adore nager.
Qui en veut? — Pas moi.
Eux y vont mais moi, je ne peux pas.

ice *n & v*
[*frozen water*]
ice (on roads)
ice cube
ice cream/an ice
iced tea
icing [*frosting*]

la glace
le verglas (sur les routes)
un glaçon
de la glace/une glace
du thé glacé
le glaçage

ID *n*
identification card
student ID
Could I see your ID?
Your ID, please. [*police*]

une carte/une pièce d'indentité
une carte d'étudiant
Vous avez une pièce d'identité?
Vos papiers, s'il vous plaît.

if *conj*

si [*Note: In sentences with* **si** *meaning "if," the tenses are the same in French as in English.* **Si** *is never followed by a verb in the future or the conditional.*]

Can you come? — If so, leave a
    message.
Come if you can.
Her dog barks if she leaves him alone.
You'll miss the train if you don't hurry.

Tu peux venir? — Si oui, laisse un
    message.
Venez si vous pouvez.
Son chien aboie si elle le laisse seul.
Tu vas manquer le train si tu ne te
    dépêches pas.

If I were younger, I wouldn't hesitate.
You can leave if you have finished.
If I had known you were coming, I'd
    have baked a cake.
(If you) please.

Si j'étais plus jeune, je n'hésiterais pas.
Vous pouvez partir si vous avez fini.
Si j'avais su que vous veniez, j'aurais
    fait un gâteau.
S'il te plaît./S'il vous plaît. [*Note:* **si** *is
    shortened before* **il.**]

[*see also* **whether**]

ignore v

to ignore	faire semblant de ne pas voir/de ne pas entendre
	ne pas faire attention
When I speak, he ignores me.	Quand je parle, il fait semblant de ne pas m'entendre.
Just ignore him.	Ne faites pas attention à lui.

Ø **ignorer** means "not to know."

improve v
to make sth better

	améliorer/perfectionner qqch
to improve the standard of living	améliorer le niveau de vie
I want to improve my French.	Je voudrais me perfectionner en français.

to get better

	s'améliorer
The weather is improving.	Le temps s'améliore.
My French is improving.	Mon français s'améliore.
	Je fais des progrès en français.
His health is improving.	Il se remet./Il va mieux.

in *prep*
with geographic names

in Rome	à Rome [*a city*]
in Sweden	en Suède [*a feminine country*]
in Japan	au Japon [*a masculine country*]
in the United States	aux Etats-Unis [*pl*]

time

in spring/summer/autumn/winter	au printemps/en été/en automne/en hiver
in August	en août
in the month of August	au mois d'août
in the future	à l'avenir
in 1999	en 1999
in the 20th century	au vingtième siècle
in the nineties	dans les années quatre-vingt-dix
Come back in three days.	Revenez dans trois jours.
I finished it in three hours.	Je l'ai fini en trois heures.

time of day

to do sth in the morning/the afternoon/the evening	faire qqch le matin/l'après-midi/le soir
two o'clock in the morning	deux heures du matin

three o'clock in afternoon	trois heures **de** l'après-midi
eight o'clock in the evening	huit heures **du** soir

weather

in all weathers	**par** tous les temps
in the heat	**par** temps chaud
in the rain	**sous** la pluie
in the sun	**au** soleil
in the shade	**à** l'ombre

other expressions

in French	**en** français
in ink/in pencil	**à** l'encre/**au** crayon
in the picture	**sur** la photo/l'image
in fun	pour rire
She is in her fifties.	Elle a une cinquantaine d'années.
one in ten	un **sur** dix
to live in luxury/poverty	vivre **dans** le luxe/la misère
to reply in writing	répondre **par** écrit

inclined *adj*

to be inclined to	avoir tendance à
He's inclined to exaggerate.	Il a tendance à exagérer.

include *v*

to include	comprendre
The test includes three questions on . . .	L'épreuve comprend trois questions sur . . .
The rent includes the heating.	Le chauffage est compris dans le loyer.

including

Everyone is invited, including the children.	y compris [*invar*] Tout le monde est invité, y compris les enfants.

included

service charge included	compris(e) service compris
taxes included	taxes comprises

income *n*

annual income	le revenu annuel
to spend beyond one's income	dépasser ses revenus
income tax	l'impôt sur le revenu

inconvenient *adj*

[*not convenient*]	pas pratique/pas commode
It's very inconvenient.	Ce n'est pas du tout commode.

The schedule is inconvenient. — L'horaire n'est pas pratique.
That time is inconvenient for me. — L'heure ne me convient pas.
if it's not inconvenient for you — si ça ne vous gêne pas

indefinitely adv
to postpone indefinitely — remettre à une date indéterminée

infant n
[a baby] — un bébé [Note: used for a male or female baby]

[a small child] — un petit enfant/une petite enfant
[a new-born] — un nouveau-né/une nouveau-née

Ø enfant [m & f] means "a child."

informal adj
It will be very informal. — Ce sera très simple/sans cérémonie.
an informal lunch — un déjeuner sans cérémonie
She's very informal. — Elle est très simple.
— Elle est sans façon.

informal dress — la tenue décontractée
informal clothes — les vêtements décontractés/les vêtements sport [invar]

information n
information — des renseignements [m pl]/des informations [f pl]

information office — le bureau des renseignements
to ask for information (on) — demander des renseignements (sur)
to get information (about) — se renseigner (sur)
a piece of information — un renseignement
to ask sb for information — demander un renseignement à qqn

injure v/injury n
to injure oneself — se blesser/se faire mal
She injured her ankle. — Elle s'est blessée à la cheville.
to be injured — être blessé(e)/accidenté(e)
Five people were injured in that accident. — Cinq personnes ont été blessées dans cet accident.
an injury — une blessure
[see also hurt]

Ø injurier means "to insult"; injure [f] means "an insult."

in-laws   [see **law**]

inside   *adv*
to stay inside — rester à l'intérieur
to wear sth inside out — porter qqch à l'envers

inside   *prep*
[*inside a place, a thing*] — à l'intérieur de/dans
We arranged to meet inside the theater. — On s'est donné rendez-vous à l'intérieur du théâtre.
Look inside the box. — Regarde dans la boîte.

insist   *v*
to insist on sth — insister sur qqch
to insist on doing sth — insister pour faire qqch
to insist that — insister pour que [+*subjunctive*]
He insisted that we wait for him. — Il a insisté pour que nous l'attendions.

instead   *adv*
We went to Germany instead. — Au lieu de cela nous sommes allés en Allemagne.
He sent his brother instead. — Il a envoyé son frère à sa place.

instead of — au lieu de
He took his car instead of walking. — Il a pris sa voiture au lieu d'y aller à pied.
I stepped on the accelerator instead of the brake. — J'ai appuyé sur l'accélérateur au lieu du frein.

insurance   *n*
to have insurance for — être assuré(e) contre
life insurance — l'assurance-vie
car insurance — l'assurance-automobile
fire insurance — l'assurance-incendie
an insurance policy — une police/un contrat d'assurance
insurance coverage — la couverture
I don't have insurance. — Je ne suis pas assuré(e)/couvert(e). Je n'ai pas d'assurance.

intend   *v*
to intend to do sth — avoir l'intention de faire qqch/compter faire qqch
I intend to finish it tonight. — Je compte le finir ce soir.

107

intentionally adv
He didn't do it intentionally.

Il ne l'a pas fait exprès.

interest v
to interest

intéresser

to be interested in

s'intéresser à

I am not interested in music.

Je ne m'intéresse pas à la musique.

La musique ne m'intéresse pas.

They're not interested in anything.

Rien ne les intéresse.

intermission n
[in a performance]

l'entracte [m]

intoxicated adj
[by alcohol]

ivre/soûl (soûle) [fam]

Ø intoxiqué(e) can mean "intoxicated," but usually means "on drugs" or "poisoned."

introduce v
to introduce sb to sb

présenter qqn à qqn

Madame Lefèvre, I'd like to introduce my cousin Jane.

Madame Lefèvre, je voudrais vous présenter ma cousine, Jeanne.

William, I'd like to introduce James.

Guillaume, je te présente Jacques.

Let me introduce myself.

Je me présente.

He introduced us to his parents.

Il nous a présentés à ses parents.

Ø introduire has various meanings, including "to insert." It is never used for making introductions.

involve v
to concern

concerner

That doesn't involve us.

Ça ne nous concerne pas.

all those involved

tous ceux qui sont concernés

to implicate

impliquer, mêler

They tried to involve him in the plot.

On a essayé de l'impliquer dans le complot.

I was not involved in that.

Je n'étais pas mêlé à cette affaire.

to entail, require

entraîner, nécessiter

That will involve large expenses.

Ça entraînera des frais importants.

Does the job involve overtime?

Est-ce que le travail nécessite des heures supplémentaires?

to get involved
to get involved in sth
Don't get involved in that.
She likes him, but she doesn't want to
get too involved.

se mêler de qqch
Ne t'en mêle pas.
Elle l'aime bien, mais elle ne veut pas
trop s'engager.

involved *adj*
[*complex*]
It's too involved.

compliqué(e)/complexe
C'est trop compliqué.

issue *n*
a question, a topic
a hot issue
the issue of the homeless

une question/un problème/un sujet
une question brûlante
le problème des sans-abri

a copy of a publication
the latest issue of l'Express

un numéro
le dernier numéro de l'Express

Ø **issue** [*f*] means "exit."

it *pron*

il/elle [*subj*]
le/la/l' [*obj*]
ce (c')/cela (ça) [*impersonal*]

a specific object
I don't like this soup. It's too salty.
Have you seen my plant? —It's dying.

The Orsay Museum? — I know it well.

Here's your coffee. Drink it fast.

Je n'aime pas ce potage. Il est trop salé.
Tu as vu ma plante? — Elle est en train
de mourir.
Le musée d'Orsay? — Je le connais
bien.
Voilà ton café. Bois-le vite.

a situation
It wasn't possible.
It's good/funny/fascinating.
It's good for your health.
It would be fun to sing.

Ce n'était pas possible.
C'est bon/amusant/passionnant.
C'est bon pour la santé.
Ce serait amusant de chanter.

to identify
What is it? — It's a picture of
Napoléon.
Who is it? — It's me.
It's the dog barking.
It wasn't the mailman.
It's ours./It's theirs.

Qu'est-ce que c'est? — C'est un portrait
de Napoléon.
Qui est-ce? — C'est moi.
C'est le chien qui aboie.
Ce n'était pas le facteur.
C'est le nôtre./C'est le leur.

its

weather & clock time

It's fine. It's not raining.	Il fait beau. Il ne pleut pas.
What time is it?	Quelle heure est-il?
It's a quarter to four.	Il est quatre heures moins le quart.

impersonal expressions

It's all the same to him.	Cela lui est égal.
It doesn't matter.	Ça ne fait rien.
It's all right.	Ça va.
It's a question of...	Il s'agit de...
It would be better to...	Il vaudrait mieux...

with a preposition

of it/from it/about it	en
Let's not talk about it.	N'en parlons pas.
to it/at it/in it	y
She will not agree to it.	Elle n'y consentira pas.

its *adj·*

[*possessive*]	son/sa/ses
Look at that dog. Its collar is too tight.	Regarde ce chien. Son collier le serre trop.

it's (it is) [*see* **it**]

itself *pron*

[*emphatic*]	lui-même/elle-même
The box itself is not valuable.	La boîte (en) elle-même n'a pas de valeur.

≡ J ≡

jacket *n*

a man's/woman's jacket	une veste
a man's suit jacket	un veston
[*a man's sport coat*]	une veste sport
a casual jacket [*waist-length*]	un blouson
[*a windbreaker*]	un anorak

Ø **jaquette** [*f*] is rarely used for "jacket" and only for specific styles; it also means "a book cover."

jet lag *n*

to have jet lag	souffrir du décalage horaire

job *n*

a job	un poste/un emploi/un travail/un job
a full-time/part-time job	un poste à plein temps/à temps partiel
to look for a job	chercher du travail/un emploi
to do a good job	faire du bon travail
to be laid off (from a job)	être licencié(e)

join *v*

to join two pieces of cloth	joindre deux morceaux d'étoffe
to join a club	devenir membre d'un club
[*to meet someone*]	rejoindre qqn/retrouver qqn
I'll join you at noon.	Je vous rejoindrai à midi.
Do you want to join us?	Voulez-vous être des nôtres?
Join the club!	Tu es en bonne compagnie!

journey *n*

a journey	un voyage

Ø **journée** [*f*] means "day."

junior *adj & n*
in university

the junior year	la troisième année
a junior	un(e) étudiant(e) de troisième année
She is a junior.	Elle est en troisième année.

111

junk

in high school
a junior   [*Note: There is no real equivalent.*]

Ø **junior** [*m & f*] is used only in sports and fashion.

junk *n*

Don't buy that necklace. It's junk.   N'achète pas ce collier. C'est de la
                                          camelote.

to eat junk food   manger des cochonneries
fleamarket junk   du bric-à-brac

just *adv*

just in time   juste à temps
just a little   juste un peu
just over/under three kilometers   un peu plus/moins de trois kilomètres
just past the town hall   tout de suite après l'hôtel de ville
She is just as intelligent as you.   Elle est tout aussi intelligente que toi.
That's just what I said.   C'est exactement ce que j'ai dit.
You will only just get there (on time).   Vous arriverez juste (à l'heure).
He only just missed his plane.   Il a manqué son avion de très peu.
Just tell her.   Vous n'avez qu'à le lui dire.
He was here just now.   Il était là tout à l'heure.

to have just . . .
They have just arrived.   venir de [*+infinitive*]
                                      Ils viennent d'arriver. [*Note: present
                                      tense of* **venir**]

They had just arrived when the phone   Ils venaient d'arriver quand le
   rang.   téléphone a sonné. [*Note: imperfect
                                      tense of* **venir**]

≡ K ≡

keep   *v intrans*
That milk won't keep.

to keep fit
Keep out. [*official sign*]
to keep quiet
Keep quiet!
Keep straight on.
Keep to the left/the right.

to keep warm, cool
Let's go swimming to keep cool.
I'm walking fast to keep warm.

to keep on doing sth
I'll keep on working.
He keeps on interrupting us.

Ce lait ne se gardera pas/ne se
   conservera pas.
se maintenir en forme
Défense d'entrer.
se taire
Tais-toi!/Taisez-vous!
Continuez tout droit.
Gardez votre gauche/votre droite.

Allons nager pour nous rafraîchir.
Je marche vite pour ne pas avoir froid.

continuer à/ne pas cesser de faire qqch
Je vais continuer à travailler.
Il ne cesse pas de nous interrompre.

keep   *v trans*
to keep one's promise/one's word
to keep sb informed about sth
Keep me informed!
to keep sb waiting
I don't like to be kept waiting.
Where do you keep the salt?

to retain
Keep the change!
I'll keep the bones for the dog.

to keep sth hot, cold

Keep the ice cream cold.
I kept the coffee hot.

to keep a person warm
This jacket keeps her warm.

tenir sa promesse/sa parole
tenir qqn au courant de qqch
Tenez-moi au courant!
faire attendre qqn
Je n'aime pas qu'on me fasse attendre.
Où mettez-vous le sel?

garder
Gardez la monnaie!
Je vais garder les os pour le chien.

garder qqch au chaud/au frais [*Note:
   not **au froid**]
Gardez la glace au frais.
J'ai gardé le café au chaud.

Cette veste lui tient chaud.

kid

kid *n*

a kid [*child*]   un(e) gosse/un(e) gamin(e)
She has five kids.   Elle a cinq gosses. [*fam*]
He's just a kid.   Ce n'est qu'un gamin.

kind *adj*

to be kind   être bon (bonne) gentil(-ille)/ aimable
That's very kind of you.   Vous êtes très aimable.
                                                  C'est très gentil à vous.

to be kind to sb   être bon pour/envers qqn
They were very kind to me.   Ils ont été très bons pour moi.

kind *n*

a kind   une sorte/un genre/une espèce
What kind of cheese do you have?   Quelle sorte de fromage avez-vous?
                                                  Qu'est-ce que vous avez comme
                                                      fromage?
that kind of thing   ce genre de chose
that kind of person   ce genre de personne/une personne de
                                                      ce genre
all kinds of people   toutes sortes de gens/des gens de toutes
                                                      sortes
There's a kind of hedge in front of the   Il y a une espèce de haie devant la
  house.   maison.

kiss *n & v*

a kiss   un baiser/une bise [*fam*]
to kiss sb/give sb a kiss   embrasser qqn
                                                  donner un baiser à qqn [*Note: Do not
                                                      use the verb **baiser**, which means "to
                                                      have sex."*]

Give me a kiss.   Embrasse-moi./Donne-moi un baiser.
to kiss on both cheeks   embrasser sur les deux joues/faire la
                                                      bise
They kissed on parting.   Ils se sont embrassés en se quittant.
Love and kisses from . . .   Grosses bises . . .
[*see also* **hug**]

The French normally greet and take leave of friends with an embrace and a kiss
on both cheeks.

114

knock *n & v*
to knock at the door
Did you hear a knock?

frapper à la porte
Tu as entendu frapper?
On a frappé?

know *v*
to be acquainted with
He has known her for five years.
I know him by name/by sight.

connaître
Il la connaît depuis cinq ans.
Je le connais de nom/de vue.

to be familiar with
Do you know the Latin Quarter?
I don't know Molière's plays very well.

He really knows his job.
to know all about sth
He knows all about engines.

connaître
Connaissez-vous le Quartier latin?
Je ne connais pas très bien les pièces de Molière.
Il connaît bien son métier.
s'y connaître en qqch
Il s'y connaît en moteurs.

to know facts, details
Do you know the time?
I don't know his address or his phone number.

savoir
Savez-vous l'heure?
Je ne sais pas son adresse ni son numéro de téléphone.

to know by learning
I know my part by heart.
You know the names of the kings of France.

savoir
Je sais mon rôle par coeur.
Tu sais les noms des rois de France.

to be aware
to know that
Did you know (that) he was a mechanic?
She knows what she wants.
Not so far as I know.
to know why/when/where
Let me know if you are free.

savoir
savoir que
Saviez-vous qu'il était mécanicien?
Elle sait ce qu'elle veut.
Pas que je sache.
savoir pourquoi/quand/où
Faites-moi savoir si vous êtes libre.

to know how to
Does she know how to sew?
I don't know how to play ice hockey.

savoir
Est-ce qu'elle sait coudre?
Je ne sais pas jouer au hockey sur glace.

not to know
What does he do for a living? — I don't know.
I don't know when he's coming.

ignorer/ne pas savoir
Qu'est-ce qu'il fait dans la vie? — Je l'ignore.
J'ignore quand il viendra.

≡ L ≡

label *n*
[*on bottle, garment, etc.*]
une étiquette

lady *n*
a lady
une dame
the ladies' restroom
les toilettes [*f pl*] pour dames
Ladies and gentlemen!
Mesdames, mesdemoiselles, messieurs!/
  Messieurs-dames!

lane *n*
[*small country road*]
un chemin/une petite route
[*small road in a town*]
une petite rue/une ruelle
[*traffic lane*]
une file/une voie
the right-hand lane
la file de droite

language *n*
of a nation or region
la langue
the French language
la langue française/le français
modern languages
les langues vivantes
to be good at languages
être doué(e) pour les langues

means of communication
le langage
body language
le langage du corps
the language of birds
le langage des oiseaux

specialized
le langage
legal/technical language
le langage juridique/technique
bad language
des gros mots/des grossièretés

large *adj*
[*in size*]
grand(e)/gros (grosse)/important(e)
a large room
une grande pièce
a large apple
une grosse pomme
a large sum (of money)
une somme importante
[*see also* **big**]

Ø **large** means "wide."

116

last *adj*
final
Molière's last play
the last Sunday in May
the last two digits

dernier(-ière) [*Note: precedes the noun*]
la dernière pièce de Molière
le dernier dimanche de mai
les deux derniers chiffres [*Note: word order*]

most recent
last year
last Sunday
last night [*evening*]
I had fun last night.
last night [*late night*]
I slept badly last night.

dernier(-ière) [*Note: follows the noun*]
l'année dernière/l'année passée
dimanche dernier
hier soir
Je me suis bien amusé hier soir.
cette nuit/la nuit dernière
J'ai mal dormi cette nuit.

late *adj & adv*
for a set time
to be late [*of a person*]
You're always late!
Sorry I'm late.
[*of means of transportation*]
Flight No. 723 is ten minutes late.

être en retard
Vous arrivez toujours en retard!
Excusez-moi d'être en retard.
avoir du retard
Le vol numéro 723 a dix minutes de retard.

in a time period
to go to bed/get up late
It's getting late.
in the late afternoon

in the late 70's

se coucher/se lever tard
Il se fait tard.
vers la fin de l'après-midi/tard dans l'après-midi
vers la fin des années 70

other expressions
He is in his late forties.
See you later!
at the latest
The homework is to be handed in tomorrow at the latest.
the latest edition/fashion

Il approche de la cinquantaine.
A tout à l'heure!/A bientôt!
au plus tard
Les devoirs sont à remettre demain au plus tard.
la dernière édition/mode

latter *pron*
[*as opposed to former*]
Of the two painters, the latter is better known.

celui-ci/celle-ci
Des deux peintres, celui-ci est plus connu.

laundry *n*

a laundry	une blanchisserie
a laundromat	une laverie automatique
to do the laundry	faire la lessive/laver le linge

law *n*

the law(s) of a country	la loi/les lois d'un pays
a court of law	un tribunal/une cour de justice
to study law	faire son droit
law school	la faculté de droit
the law of gravity	la loi de la pesanteur
in-law	beau-/belle- [*prefix*]
brother-/mother-in-law [*etc.*]	le beau-frère/la belle-mère
son-in-law	le gendre [*Note: exception*]

least *adj, adv & pron*
with an adjective

le moins/la moins/les moins

the least expensive meals — les repas les moins chers

Bridget is the least attentive student in the class. — Brigitte est l'étudiante la moins attentive de la classe. [*Note:* **de** *after a superlative*]

with a noun

le moins de

My family has the least money. — C'est ma famille qui a le moins d'argent.

with a verb or adverb

le moins

the country which exports the least — le pays qui exporte le moins

He's the one who speaks the least fluently. — C'est lui qui parle le moins couramment.

It's the least I can do. — C'est le moins que je puisse faire.

least (at) *adv*
with a quantity

au moins

There were at least 30 people waiting. — Il y avait au moins 30 personnes qui attendaient.

I drank at least as much as you did. — J'ai bu au moins autant que toi.

to qualify a statement

du moins

His train was late; at least, that's what he said. — Son train avait du retard; du moins, c'est ce qu'il a dit.

leave *v*
to go away

partir/s'en aller

We must leave immediately. — Il faut s'en aller tout de suite.

What time does the flight leave?	A quelle heure part le vol?

to leave a place
When do you leave Paris?
I left the house at 8 o'clock.

quitter/partir de
Quand partez-vous de Paris?
J'ai quitté la maison à 8 heures.

to leave sb or sth somewhere
We left the baby at the neighbors'.

I left my suitcase in a locker.

laisser
Nous avons laissé le bébé chez les voisins.
J'ai laissé ma valise à la consigne.

to leave sb or sth for good
He has left his wife.
I left my job.

quitter
Il a quitté sa femme.
J'ai quitté mon poste.

to leave sth unintentionally
I must have left my keys in the classroom.

oublier
J'ai dû oublier mes clés dans la salle de classe.

to leave+adjective
Leave me alone!
Leave the window open.

laisser
Laisse-moi tranquille!
Laisse la fenêtre ouverte.

lecture *n*
[*in general*]
Did you go to the lecture yesterday afternoon?
a lecture course [*university*]

une conférence
As-tu assisté à la conférence hier après-midi?
un cours magistral

Ø **lecture** [*f*] means "reading."

left *adj, adv & n*
opposite of right
my left foot/leg
the left drawer
to turn left
Take the next left.
on the left
on your left

gauche
mon pied gauche/ma jambe gauche
le tiroir de gauche
tourner à gauche
Prenez la première rue à gauche.
à gauche/sur la gauche
à/sur votre gauche

remaining
There are none left.
He has three left.
left-overs [*food*]

Il n'en reste plus.
Il lui en reste trois.
les restes [*m pl*]

Ø **gauche** also means "awkward."

119

lend v

to lend sb sth	prêter qqch à qqn
I can lend him a few francs.	Je peux lui prêter quelques francs.

less adj, adv & n

in comparisons

	moins...que
We spent less than you.	Nous avons dépensé moins que vous.
She was less talkative than usual.	Elle était moins bavarde que d'habitude.
I have less time than you.	J'ai moins de temps que toi.

the less...the less

	moins...moins [Note: no article]
The less you take with you, the less you'll have to carry.	Moins tu emportes, moins tu auras à porter.

less and less

	de moins en moins
He goes out less and less.	Il sort de moins en moins.

let v

to allow

	laisser [+dir obj]
	permettre [+indir obj]
Let me explain.	Laissez-moi expliquer.
The professor let the students leave early.	Le professeur a laissé partir les étudiants avant l'heure.
She doesn't let her son use her car.	Elle ne permet pas à son fils de conduire sa voiture.

in suggestions

Let's go!	Allons-y!/On y va!
Let's hurry!	Dépêchons-nous!

other expressions

Let him in.	Faites-le entrer.
Let me see!	Fais voir!/Faites voir!
Let's see	Voyons...

library n

a library	une bibliothèque

Ø **librairie** [f] means "bookstore."

license n

driver's license	le permis de conduire
license plate [of car]	la plaque minéralogique

Ø **licence** [f] means "a university diploma." It sometimes means "a license" (e.g., import/export), but never "a driver's license."

light *adj & adv*

not heavy	léger(-ère)
a light (weight) coat	un manteau léger
to be a light sleeper	avoir le sommeil léger
to travel light	voyager sans grand bagage

not dark	
It gets light at 6 a.m.	Il fait jour à 6 heures.
a light room	une salle claire
a light color	une couleur claire
light blue	bleu clair [*invar*]
a light blue dress	une robe bleu clair

light *n*

in general	la lumière
sunlight/daylight	la lumière du soleil/du jour
a bright/dazzling light	une lumière vive/éblouissante
the city lights	les lumières de la ville

lighting	l'éclairage/la lumière
soft light	un éclairage doux
to turn on/off the light	allumer/éteindre la lumière
There's not enough light in this room.	Cette pièce est mal éclairée.

traffic lights	les feux (de signalisation)
to stop at the red light	s'arrêter au feu rouge
to go through a red light	brûler un feu rouge

of a car	
headlights	les phares
rear lights	les feux arrière

other	
Do you have a light? [*for a cigarette*]	Vous avez du feu, s'il vous plaît?

light *v*

to light the gas	allumer le gaz
to light a fire	faire du feu
to light a match	frotter une allumette

like *v*

I like Peter.	J'aime bien Pierre. [*Note:* **aimer bien** is *less strong than* **aimer**; *see also* **love**.]

likely

I like Peter very much.	J'aime beaucoup Pierre.
	Pierre me plaît beaucoup.
Do you like cheese/pasta?	Tu aimes le fromage/les pâtes?
Did you like the movie?	Ça t'a plu, le film?
Do you like it here?	Vous vous plaisez ici?

likely *adj*

likely	probable
It's not likely.	C'est peu probable.

line *n*

a straight line	une ligne droite
on the first line [*of a page*]	à la première ligne
to draw a line	tirer un trait
a line of poetry	un vers
to learn one's lines in a play	apprendre son rôle
to stand/wait in line	faire la queue

liquor *n*

[*alcohol*]	l'alcool
He never drinks liquor.	Il ne boit jamais d'alcool.

Ø **liqueur** [*f*] is used only for a sweet alcoholic beverage served after meals (e.g., **Cointreau, Grand Marnier**).

listen *v*

to listen to	écouter [*Note: no preposition*]
to listen to a piece of music	écouter un morceau de musique
Listen to your father!	Ecoute ton père!

litter [*see **garbage***]

little *adj, adv & n*
small

I know a nice little hotel.	petit(e)
	Je connais un bon petit hôtel.

not much

She eats very little.	peu (de)
We have very little hope.	Elle mange très peu.
	Nous avons très peu d'espoir.

a small quantity

Do you take sugar in your tea? — Just a little.	un peu (de)
	Vous prenez du sucre dans votre thé? — Juste un peu.

I'll have a little time this weekend.	J'aurai un peu de temps ce weekend.
a little bit (of)	un petit peu (de)
little by little	peu à peu/petit à petit

live v
to be alive

He will live to be 100.	Il vivra jusqu'à l'âge de 100 ans.
Are your parents still living?	Vos parents sont encore en vie?

to reside

	habiter/demeurer/vivre
to live at [*specific address*]	habiter/demeurer
They live at No. 28.	Ils habitent au 28.
I lived in Brazil for 20 years.	J'ai vécu 20 ans au Brésil.
to live together [*a couple*]	cohabiter/vivre en ménage
Paul and Lucile live together.	Paul et Lucile cohabitent.

living n

to make a living doing sth	gagner sa vie à faire qqch
What does he do for a living?	Qu'est-ce qu'il fait dans la vie?
the cost of living	le coût de la vie

loan n

a loan	un prêt/un emprunt [*Note: depending on the point of view*]
a loan [**to** *someone*]	un prêt
a loan [**from** *someone*]	un emprunt
The bank gave him a loan.	La banque lui a accordé un prêt.
He got a loan from the bank. [*see also* **borrow** & **lend**]	Il a fait un emprunt à la banque.

lobby n [*see* **hall**]

locate v

to locate a place on a map	repérer un endroit sur une carte
Where is your house located?	Où se trouve votre maison?

location n

[*a site*]	un emplacement
to look for a location for a factory	chercher un emplacement pour une usine
It's in a good location.	C'est bien situé.

Ø **location** [*f*] means "rental" or "renting."

lock *n & v*
to lock — fermer à clé
Is the door locked? — La porte est fermée à clé?
to lock sb/sth in — enfermer qqn/qqch
a lock — une serrure

lonely *adj*
to feel lonely — se sentir seul(e)
to lead a lonely life — mener une vie solitaire

long *adj*
long — long (longue)
She has long hair. — Elle a les cheveux longs.
a long trip — un long voyage
a long story — une longue histoire

long *adv*
[*for a long time*] — longtemps [*Note: one word*]
Have you been waiting long? — Il y a longtemps que vous attendez?
Will you be long? — Tu en as pour longtemps?
a long time ago — il y a longtemps
Let's wait a bit longer. — Attendons encore un peu.

how long. . .? — Depuis/pendant combien de temps. . .?
How long have you lived in France? [*i.e., you still do*] — Depuis combien de temps habitez-vous en France? [*Note: present tense*]
How long did you live in France? [*i.e., in the past*] — Pendant combien de temps avez-vous habité en France?

as long as
Stay as long as you like. — Restez aussi longtemps que vous voudrez.

[*provided that*] — pourvu que [*+subjunctive*]
You can take the car as long as you bring it back before 6. — Tu peux prendre la voiture pourvu que tu la ramènes avant 6 heures.

long *v*
to long to do sth — avoir hâte de/avoir très envie de faire qqch
I'm longing to see my brother. — J'ai hâte de voir mon frère.
Il me tarde de voir mon frère.

look *v*
to seem — avoir l'air/paraître
You look tired. — Vous avez l'air fatigué.

That looks good! [to eat]	Ça a l'air bon!

to look like sb
He looks like his mother.
Her children look like her.

ressembler **à** qqn
Il ressemble à sa mère.
Ses enfants lui ressemblent.

to look at
to look at a picture
to look out of the window
to have/take a look (at sth)

regarder [*Note: no preposition*]
regarder un tableau
regarder par la fenêtre
jeter un coup d'œil (sur qqch)

to look forward to [*see* **forward**]

lost *adj*
to get lost
We got lost on our way here.

se perdre
Nous nous sommes perdus en venant ici.

I think we are lost.

Je crois que nous sommes perdus/que nous avons perdu notre chemin.

the lost and found department

le bureau des objets trouvés

lot *adv*
[*a great deal*]
I liked that play a lot.

beaucoup
Cette pièce m'a beaucoup plu.

lot(s) *n*
[*many*]
a lot of friends
lots of problems

beaucoup/des tas [*fam*]
beaucoup d'amis
des tas de problèmes

love *v & n*
I love my parents.
to fall/be in love with sb
Are you in love with him?
to make love (to sb)
Love from . . . [*at end of letter*]
I love champagne!
[*see also* **like**]

J'aime mes parents.
tomber/être amoureux de qqn
Tu l'aimes?/Tu es amoureuse de lui?
faire l'amour (avec qqn)
Grosses bises./Je t'embrasse (bien fort).
J'adore le champagne!

lovely *adj*
of appearance
Isn't she lovely!
You have a lovely dress.
They have a lovely home.

beau (belle)/joli(e)/ravissant(e)
Comme elle est belle!
Vous avez une robe ravissante.
Ils ont une très belle maison.

pleasant   charmant(e)/très agréable
We had a lovely evening.   Nous avons passé une soirée
                                  charmante.

lover   *n*
to be lovers   avoir une liaison
They've been lovers for a year.   Leur liaison dure depuis un an.
                                  Ils sont ensemble depuis un an.

a lover   un amant/une amante
a live-in lover   un concubin/une concubine
He's a wonderful lover.   Il fait bien l'amour.
to be a music/art lover   être amateur de musique/d'art

lucky   *adj*
You're a lucky guy.   Tu as de la chance.
That was lucky!   Quelle chance!
a lucky charm   un porte-bonheur

luggage   *n*
luggage   les bagages [*m pl*]
Where did you put your luggage?   Où avez-vous mis vos bagages?
a piece of luggage   une valise/un sac
to buy luggage   acheter des valises
left luggage (office)   la consigne des bagages
luggage locker   une consigne automatique

luxury   *adj & n*
to live in luxury   vivre dans le luxe
a luxury hotel   un hôtel de luxe
I can't afford luxuries.   Je ne peux pas me payer de produits
                                  de luxe.

a block of luxury apartments   un immeuble de grand standing

≡ M ≡

mad *adj*
angry
He'll be mad when he finds out.
to be mad at sb
I'm still mad at her.

fâché(e)/furieux(-euse)/en colère
Il sera furieux quand il le saura.
être fâché contre qqn/en vouloir à qqn
Je lui en veux toujours.

crazy
She's quite mad!

fou (folle)
Elle est complètement folle.

magazine *n*
a magazine
[*monthly*]
[*weekly*]

une revue/un magazine
une revue mensuelle
une revue hebdomadaire/un
   hebdomadaire

Ø **magasin** [*m*] means "store" or "shop."

major *n*
field of study
What is your major?

to change one's major

la matière principale/la spécialité
Quelle est ta spécialité?
En quoi te spécialises-tu?
s'orienter vers une autre spécialité

person studying
He is a chemistry major.

Il fait des études de chimie.
Il se spécialise en chimie.
Il est étudiant en chimie.

major *v*
to major in [*a subject at university*]
I am majoring in languages.

My father majored in math.

se spécialiser en/faire des études de
Je me spécialise en langues.
Je fais des études de langues.
Mon père a fait des maths.

make *v*
to make a mistake/a cake/a dress/a trip

to make friends
to make an appointment

faire une erreur/un gâteau/une robe/un
   voyage
se faire des amis
prendre rendez-vous

127

manage

to make a decision	**prendre** une décision
to make good grades	**obtenir** de bonnes notes
to make money	**gagner** de l'argent
How much does he make?	Combien gagne-t-il?
to make a meal	**préparer** un repas
"Made in France."	"Fabriqué en France."

to make sb do sth
to make sb work	faire travailler qqn
The mother made the children go outside.	La mère a fait sortir les enfants.
I couldn't make him understand.	Je n'ai pas pu le faire comprendre.
Don't make me laugh!	Ne me fais pas rire!

to cause to be
to make sb sad/ill	rendre qqn triste/malade
to make sth difficult	rendre qqch difficile
Your letter made her happy.	Ta lettre l'a rendue heureuse.
to make sb hungry/thirsty	donner faim/soif à qqn
Physical exercise makes you thirsty.	L'exercice physique donne soif.

to make out
I can't make out his handwriting.	Je n'arrive pas à déchiffrer son écriture.
I can't make him out.	Je ne le comprends pas.

to make up
[with cosmetics]	se maquiller
[after a quarrel]	se réconcilier (avec qqn)
Have you two made it up?	Vous vous êtes réconciliés, vous deux?
to make up for lost time	rattraper le temps perdu
to make up a story	inventer une histoire

manage v
to run (a business)
He manages three restaurants.	Il gère trois restaurants.

to succeed in doing sth
	réussir à faire qqch
	arriver à faire qqch
	pouvoir faire qqch
I can't manage to thread this needle.	Je n'arrive pas à enfiler cette aiguille.
He managed to persuade us.	Il a réussi à nous persuader.
I didn't manage to finish.	Je n'ai pas pu terminer.
Did you manage to reach her?	Avez-vous pu la joindre?

to handle a tricky situation
	se débrouiller
We managed very well at the station.	Nous nous sommes très bien débrouillés à la gare.

128

Will you be able to manage?   Tu sauras te débrouiller?

manager *n*
[*of a company*]
    le directeur/la directrice
    le gérant/la gérante/le chef
[*owner, boss of small business*]
    le patron/la patronne

Ø **ménagère** [*f*] means "housewife."

manners *n*
good/bad manners   les bonnes/mauvaises manières
He has good manners.   Il a du savoir-vivre.
Children have to learn good table manners.   Les enfants doivent apprendre à se tenir à table.

many *adj & pron*
She has many friends.   Elle a beaucoup d'amis.
many of them/of us/of you   beaucoup d'entre eux/d'entre nous/d'entre vous

many times   souvent
I have thought about it many times.   J'y ai souvent pensé.
many years ago   il y a bien longtemps
    il y a bien des années [*Note: not* **beaucoup**]

as many as   autant que
He has as many as you.   Il en a autant que toi.
as many . . . as   autant de . . . que
He has as many problems as you.   Il a autant d'ennuis que toi.

map *n*
[*of the world/a country/a region*]   une carte
the map of France   la carte de la France
[*of a town or transport system*]   un plan
the map of Paris/of the Metro   le plan de Paris/du Métro

market *n*
[*open-air*]   le marché (en plein air)
[*supermarket*]   le supermarché
[*big supermarket*]   l'hypermarché [*m*]/la grande surface
[*small grocery store*]   l'épicerie [*f*]
the corner market   l'épicerie du coin/l'épicerie de dépannage

maroon *adj*

maroon (color)	(couleur) bordeaux [*invar*]
a maroon jacket	une veste bordeaux

Ø **marron** means "brown," specifically "chestnut brown."

marry *v*
to marry/to get married

	se marier avec/épouser
X. is going to marry Y.	X. va se marier avec Y.
	X. va épouser Y.
They got married in June.	Ils se sont mariés au mois de juin.

to be married

	être marié(e)
She's not married.	Elle n'est pas mariée.
They have been married for two years.	Ils sont mariés depuis deux ans.

master's [*see* **degree**]

match *v*
to go well together

	aller (bien) ensemble
These colors match well.	Ces couleurs vont bien ensemble.

to be of the same shade

	être assorti(e)
Her shoes matched her blouse.	Ses chaussures étaient assorties à son chemisier.

material *n*

[*fabric*]	le tissu/l'étoffe (f)
I bought some material for a dress.	J'ai acheté du tissu pour faire une robe.
raw material(s)	les matières premières
building materials	les matériaux de construction
He is looking for some material for his article.	Il cherche des matériaux/de la documentation pour son article.

Ø **matériel** usually means "equipment."

matter *n & v*

as a matter of fact	à vrai dire/en réalité
What's the matter?	Qu'est-ce que tu as?
	Qu'est-ce qui ne va pas?
Nothing's the matter.	Je n'ai rien./Il n'y a rien.
It doesn't matter.	Ça n'a pas d'importance.
	Cela n'a aucune importance.

130

	Ça ne fait rien.
No matter what I do, he's never satisfied.	Quoi que je fasse, il n'est jamais content.
It's a matter of opinion.	C'est une question/une affaire d'opinion.

mature *adj*
[*of a person*]
a mature woman
[*for a young person*]
She isn't mature enough to decide.

to become mature
She has become much more mature in the last year.

mûr(e)
une femme mûre
mûr(e) pour son âge
Elle n'est pas assez mûre pour prendre cette décision.

mûrir
Elle a beaucoup mûri depuis un an.

may *v*
permission
You may leave.
May I borrow this book?
May I come in?

pouvoir
Vous pouvez partir.
Est-ce que je peux emprunter ce livre?
Est-ce que je peux entrer?
Puis-je entrer? [*formal*]

possibility
I may have his address.
She may have left already.

Il est possible que j'aie son adresse.
Elle est peut-être déjà partie.

me *pron*

me [*dir obj*]
me [*ind obj*]
moi [*disj*]

He knows me.
He gave them to me.
Do it for me.
Look at me!

Il me connaît.
Il me les a donnés.
Fais-le pour moi!
Regarde-moi!

mean *adj*
cruel
a mean stepmother
to play a mean trick on sb

méchant(e)/vilain(e)
une belle-mère méchante
jouer un vilain tour à qqn

stingy
He's too mean to take her out to dinner.

radin(e)/pingre/avare
Il est trop radin pour l'inviter à dîner.

131

mean

mean *v*
to signify
What does this mean?
It doesn't mean anything.

to imply
That's not what I meant!

medicine *n*
field of study
He is studying medicine.

medication
medicine for an illness

Ø **médecin** [*m*] means "doctor."

vouloir dire/signifier
Qu'est-ce que ça veut dire?
Ça ne signifie rien./Ça ne veut rien
    dire.

vouloir dire
Ce n'est pas ce que je voulais dire!

la médecine
Il fait sa médecine.

le médicament/le remède
un remède contre une maladie

meet *v*
to make sb's acquaintance

I met her two years ago.

They met in high school.
Dad, I'd like you to meet Bill.
I'm very pleased to meet you.

by arrangement
I am going to meet my mother at noon.
to meet (each other)
Let's meet outside the library.
to go and meet sb [*at the airport,
    station, etc.*]

by chance
I met an old friend on the way here.

faire la connaissance de qqn/connaître
    qqn/rencontrer qqn
J'ai fait sa connaissance il y a deux ans.
Je l'ai connue il y a deux ans.
Ils se sont connus au lycée.
Papa, je te présente Bill.
Très heureux de vous connaître.

retrouver qqn/rejoindre qqn
Je vais retrouver ma mère à midi.
se retrouver
On se retrouve devant la bibliothèque?
aller à la rencontre de qqn/aller
    attendre qqn

rencontrer/tomber sur
Je suis tombé sur un vieil ami en
    venant ici.

The expression "It's been nice meeting you," used by Americans on parting, has
no real equivalent. A French person simply says "Au revoir, Monsieur (Madame),"
and shakes hands.

meeting *n*
a meeting
to have/to hold a meeting

une réunion/un meeting/un entretien
tenir une réunion

memory *n*
the mental faculty
He has an excellent memory.

la mémoire
Il a une excellente mémoire.

an experience remembered
This brings back memories.

le souvenir
Cela me rappelle des souvenirs.

menu *n*
the menu
May we look at the menu?
The menu was excellent.
What's on the menu tonight?

la carte/le menu
On peut voir la carte, s'il vous plaît?
Le menu était excellent.
Qu'est-ce qu'il y a au menu ce soir?

Carte [*f*] is more usual for the printed menu. **Menu** [*m*] has come to mean "a meal at a fixed price," e.g., **un menu touristique, un menu à 100 francs.**

Mexico *n*
[*the country*]
in or to Mexico
from Mexico
Mexico City
in or to Mexico City
from Mexico City

le Mexique [*Note: masculine country*]
au Mexique
du Mexique
Mexico
à Mexico
de Mexico

middle *n*
in the middle of
in the middle of the square
right in the middle of Paris
in the middle of the night

au milieu de/en plein(e)
au milieu de la place
en plein Paris
en pleine nuit/au milieu de la nuit

to be busy doing sth
I was in the middle of fixing dinner
    when he called.

être en train de faire qqch
J'étais en train de préparer le dîner
    quand il a téléphoné.

mileage *n*
total distance covered
This car has a low mileage.

le kilométrage
Cette voiture a peu de kilomètres/a peu
    roulé.

distance per gallon
I get good mileage with my car.

la consommation
Ma voiture consomme peu.

mind *n*
to have a logical mind.
to change one's mind
to go out of one's mind

avoir l'esprit logique
changer d'avis
perdre la tête/la raison

mind

mind *v*

Do you mind if I smoke? — No, I don't mind.

What do you want to do this evening? — I don't mind.

If you don't mind...

Ça vous gêne si je fume? — Non, ça ne me gêne pas.

Qu'est-ce que tu veux faire ce soir? — Ça m'est égal.

Si vous n'y voyez pas d'inconvénient ...

mine *pron*

[*possessive*]

Your mother is younger than mine.
a friend of mine

le mien　　les miens
la mienne　les miennes
Ta mère est plus jeune que la mienne.
un de mes amis/une de mes amies

minister *n*

[*religious title*]
[*in government*]

le pasteur
le ministre

miserable *adj*

[*of a person*]
[*of a situation*]

triste/malheureux
pénible

Ø **misérable** means "impoverished."

miss *v*
to fail to catch
We missed our bus.
You missed your chance!

manquer/rater
Nous avons manqué notre autobus.
Tu as raté l'occasion!

to be absent
You missed the meeting this morning.

Two people are missing.

There's a button missing on my pajamas.
a missing [*lost*] child

to feel the absence of
I miss you.

manquer
Vous avez manqué à la réunion ce matin.
Il manque deux personnes. [*Note: impersonal verb*]
Il manque un bouton à mon pyjama.

un enfant perdu

Tu me manques. [*Note: different construction in French; literally, "you are lacking to me"*]

134

My parents miss me. | Je manque à mes parents.
I miss my parents. | Mes parents me manquent.

mistake *n*

a mistake | une erreur/une faute
a grammar mistake | une faute de grammaire
I made lots of mistakes in that dictation. | J'ai fait beaucoup de fautes dans cette dictée.
to make a mistake | se tromper
Everyone makes mistakes! | Tout le monde peut se tromper!

mistake *v*

to mistake sb for sb else | prendre qqn pour qqn d'autre
He mistook me for my brother. | Il m'a pris pour mon frère.

mix *v*

to mix drinks | préparer des boissons
a mixed salad | une salade composée
to mix easily [*of a person*] | être sociable

mixed up

I get these two verbs mixed up. | Je confonds ces deux verbes.
I'm all mixed up. | Je suis tout embrouillé.
He's a mixed-up kid. | C'est un gosse à problèmes.

money *n*

[*in general*] | l'argent [*m*]
They don't have much money. | Ils n'ont pas beaucoup d'argent.
Time is money. | Le temps, c'est de l'argent.

Ø **monnaie** [*f*] means "change."

mood *n*

to be in a good/bad mood | être de bonne/mauvaise humeur
I'm not in the mood to go out. | Je n'ai pas envie de sortir.
 | Ça ne me dit rien de sortir.

more *adj, adv & pron*

in comparisons | plus . . . que
I work more than she does. | Je travaille plus qu'elle.
He is more patient than I am. | Il est plus patient que moi.
He has more friends/money than we do. | Il a plus (d'amis/d'argent) que nous.

before a number
more than twenty
more than half/a third/a quarter

plus de
plus de vingt
plus de la moitié/du tiers/du quart

additional
(Would you like) some more coffee?
A little more sugar?
one more/two more
I have one more favor to ask you.
a few more
a few more days

encore
(Voulez-vous) encore du café?
Un peu plus de sucre?
encore un(e)/encore deux
J'ai encore une faveur à vous demander.
encore quelques-uns(-unes)
encore quelques jours

remaining
Is there any more pie?

Il reste de la tarte?
Il y a encore de la tarte?

in negative sentences
We have no more bananas.
I don't go there any more.

ne . . . plus
Nous n'avons plus de bananes.
Je n'y vais plus.

more and more
I am more and more certain he is
    innocent.
There are more and more of them.

de plus en plus
Je suis de plus en plus sûr de son
    innocence.
Ils sont de plus en plus nombreux.

the more . . . the more
The more I see him, the more I like
    him.

plus . . . plus
Plus je le vois, plus il me plaît.

morning *n*
a morning

un matin/une matinée [*Note: For
    difference in usage, see* **day**.]

in the morning [*habitually*]
I go jogging in the morning.
this morning/tomorrow morning/
    yesterday morning
the next morning
seven o'clock in the morning
every morning
during the morning
I spent the whole morning in the
    museum.
I have a very busy morning.

le matin
Je fais du jogging le matin.
ce matin/demain matin/hier matin

le lendemain matin
sept heures du matin
tous les matins/chaque matin
pendant/dans la matinée
J'ai passé toute la matinée au musée.

J'ai une matinée très chargée.

most *adj, adv & n*
with an adjective
the most famous film stars
the most beautiful parks in the city

le plus/la plus/les plus
les vedettes les plus célèbres
les plus beaux parcs de la ville [*Note:* ***de*** *after a superlative*]

with a noun
Jean buys the most clothes.

le plus de
C'est Jeanne qui achète le plus de vêtements.

with a verb or adverb
He laughed the most.
The foreign students worked the most diligently of all.

le plus
C'est lui qui a ri le plus.
Les étudiants étrangers ont travaillé le plus diligemment de tous.

most (of) *n*
followed by a plural noun
Most of the students agree.
Most of my friends are here.

la plupart
La plupart des étudiants sont d'accord.
La plupart de mes amis sont ici.

followed by a singular noun
We ate most of the bread.

la plus grande partie
On a mangé la plus grande partie du pain.
On a mangé presque tout le pain.

most of the time

la plupart du temps [*Note: exception to rule*]

mostly *adv*
for the most part
They are mostly English-speaking.

pour la plupart/surtout
Ils sont pour la plupart anglophones.

mainly
I read mostly detective novels.

surtout
Je lis surtout des romans policiers.

mountain *n*
a mountain
a chain of mountains
to go to the mountains

une montagne
une chaîne de montagnes
aller à la montagne [*Note: singular*]

move *v trans*
physical
to move a piece of furniture

déplacer/bouger
déplacer un meuble

emotions
His story moved me (to tears).

émouvoir
Son histoire m'a ému (jusqu'aux larmes).

137

move

His story is very moving. | Son histoire est très émouvante.

move *v intrans*
Don't move! | Ne bouge pas!
to move away [*to change residence*] | déménager
They have moved. | Ils ont déménagé.
They have moved to New York. | Ils sont allés s'installer à New York.
They have moved in next door (to us). | Ils ont emménagé à côté (de chez nous).

movie *n*
a movie | un film
a movie theater | un cinéma
to go to the movies | aller au cinéma
a movie star | une vedette [*Note: always feminine*]

much *adj, adv & pron*
He doesn't talk much. | Il ne parle pas beaucoup.
I don't know much about this subject. | Je ne sais pas grand'chose à ce sujet.
There isn't much butter left. | Il ne reste pas beaucoup de beurre.
How much does this cost? | C'est combien?

in comparisons
as much as | autant **que**
We don't travel as much as we used to. | Nous ne voyageons pas autant qu'avant.
as much . . . as | autant **de** . . . **que**
He has as much money as I do. | Il a autant d'argent que moi.

so much | tant (de)/tellement (de)
I miss you so much! | Tu me manques tellement!
There was so much snow that the door was stuck. | Il y avait tant de neige que la porte était coincée.

too much | trop [*Note: do not add* **beaucoup**]
I have eaten too much! | J'ai trop mangé!

musical *adj*
a musical instrument | un instrument de musique
[*of a person*] | musicien/musicienne
My son is very musical. | Mon fils est très musicien.
a musical (show) | une comédie musicale

must *v*
obligation | devoir/falloir
We must leave immediately. | On doit partir tout de suite.

| | Il faut partir/Il faut qu'on parte tout de suite. |
| You mustn't say that! | Il ne faut pas dire cela! |

probability
He must be over 50.
They must have lost their way.
You must be joking!

devoir
Il doit avoir plus de 50 ans.
Ils ont dû se tromper de route.
Tu plaisantes!

my *adj*
[*possessive*]
my friend [*male*]
my friend [*female*]

mon/ma/mes
mon ami
mon amie [*Note:* **mon** *is used with a feminine noun beginning with a vowel sound.*]

myself [*see* **self**]

≡ N ≡

name *n*
first name | le prénom/le petit nom
family name | le nom (de famille)
maiden name | le nom de jeune fille
nickname | le surnom
What is your name? | Comment vous appelez-vous?
 | Comment t'appelles-tu?
My name is. . . | Je m'appelle. . .

native *adj*
native country | le pays natal/la patrie
native language | la langue maternelle

native *n*
the natives (of a country) | les indigènes
He is a native of France. | Il est français de naissance.
 | Il est originaire de France.
He is a native of Chicago. | Il est né à Chicago.
She speaks French like a native. | Elle parle français comme si c'était sa langue maternelle.
French nationals [*living abroad*] | les ressortissants français

near *adj & prep*
of places | près de
Is the hotel near the Metro? | L'hôtel est près du Métro?
near here | près d'ici/à côté
other
in the near future | dans un proche avenir
a near relative | un parent proche

nearby *adv*
[*close by*] | à côté/tout près (d'ici)
He lives nearby. | Il habite à côté.

nearly [see *almost*]

neat *adj*
[*of room, desk, etc.*]
[*of person's dress or general appearance*]
neat handwriting
Neat! [*slang*]

bien rangé(e)/ordonné(e)
soigné(e)/net (nette)
une écriture nette
Chouette!/Super!/Génial!

necessary *adj*
it is necessary
Is it necessary to reserve?

It is necessary for you to be present.

if necessary

il faut/il est nécessaire
Il est nécessaire de réserver?
Il faut réserver?
Il faut/Il est nécessaire que vous soyez
    là. [*Note: subjunctive*]
s'il le faut

in the negative
It's not necessary to reserve.
It's not necessary that you be present.

Il n'est pas nécessaire de réserver.
Il n'est pas nécessaire que vous soyez
    là. [*Note:* **Il ne faut pas que vous
    soyez là** *would mean "you are not
    allowed to be present."*]

need *v*
to need sth

avoir besoin de qqch

an unspecified quantity
I need air/money/clothes.
Everyone needs friends.
We need (some) wine and cheese.
He needs help.

J'ai besoin **d**'air/**d**'argent/**de** vêtements.
Tout le monde a besoin **d**'amis.
On a besoin de vin et **de** fromage.
Il a besoin **d**'aide.

a specific item
He needs a car.
He needs the car.
I need the scissors I lent you.

He needs our help.

Il a besoin **d**'une voiture.
Il a besoin de **la** voiture.
J'ai besoin **des** ciseaux que je t'ai
    prêtés.
Il a besoin de **notre** aide.

followed by a verb
I need to talk to my teacher. [*see also*
    have to *and* **must**]

J'ai besoin de parler à mon professeur.
Il faut que je parle à mon professeur.

neighborhood *n*
[*district*]
We like our neighborhood.
a neighborhood movie theater

le quartier
Nous aimons bien notre quartier.
un cinéma de quartier

neither (one)

neither (one) *adj & pron*

Which one do you want? — Neither.
Neither book is available.

Lequel veux-tu? — Ni l'un ni l'autre.
Aucun des deux livres n'est disponible.
[*Note:* **ne** *before verb*]

neither . . . nor *conj*

ni . . . ni [+**ne** *with verb*]
He drinks neither beer nor wine.
I have neither the time nor the money.
Neither my father nor my mother can
come with us.
Me neither!/Neither do I!

Il ne boit ni bière ni vin.
Je n'ai ni le temps ni l'argent.
Ni mon père ni ma mère ne peuvent
nous accompagner.
Moi non plus!

nervous *adj*
apprehensive
I was too nervous to speak.
He makes me nervous.
I'm always nervous before an exam.

Don't be nervous, it will be all right.

J'étais trop intimidé pour parler.
Il m'intimide.
J'ai toujours le trac [*fam*] avant les
examens.
N'aie pas peur, tout ira bien.

tense
We were all nervous because of the
storm.

tendu(e)/énervé(e)
Nous étions tous énervés à cause de
l'orage.

medical
to have a nervous breakdown

nerveux(-euse)
faire une dépression nerveuse

Ø **nerveux**(-se) also means "highly strung" or "irritable."

nevertheless *adv*
[*however*]
I don't agree; nevertheless, I respect
your opinion.

néanmoins/cependant
Je ne suis pas d'accord; néanmoins, je
respecte ton point de vue.

new *adj*
brand-new
She has a new car.

neuf (neuve)
Elle a une voiture neuve.

newly acquired, different
Do you like my new hairstyle?
We have a new apartment.
What's new?
There's nothing new.

nouveau/nouvel (nouvelle)
Tu aimes ma nouvelle coiffure?
Nous avons un nouvel appartement.
Quoi de neuf?/Quoi de nouveau?
Il n'y a rien de neuf/de nouveau.

142

news *n*

Have you any news from your son?	Vous avez des nouvelles de votre fils?
a piece of news	une nouvelle
I have some good news for you.	J'ai une bonne nouvelle à t'annoncer.
radio/TV news	les actualités/les informations

next *adj*
of future time prochain(e)

next Monday	lundi prochain
next week/month/year	la semaine prochaine/le mois prochain/l'année prochaine
next time I see you	la prochaine fois que je te verrai

of past time suivant(e)

The next [*the following*] Monday I left Paris.	Le lundi suivant j'ai quitté Paris.
the next day	le lendemain
the next week	la semaine suivante

next *adv*
[*then, after that*] puis/ensuite

I washed the dishes, next I fed the cat.	J'ai fait la vaisselle, puis j'ai donné à manger au chat.
What happened next?	Qu'est-ce qui s'est passé ensuite?

next *prep*

next to	à côté de
The church is next to the school.	L'église est à côté de l'école.
Go and sit next to the others.	Va te mettre à côté des autres.
next to nothing	presque rien

nice *adj*

He is very nice.	Il est très gentil/sympathique.
a nice guy	un type sympa [*fam*]
Their apartment is very nice.	Ils ont un très bel appartement.
That was a nice dinner!	Le repas était délicieux!
to have a nice time	s'amuser

night *n*
as opposed to day la nuit

to spend the night at a friend's	passer la nuit chez un(e) ami(e)
to work nights/at night	travailler la nuit

late night la nuit

It was cold last night.	Il a fait froid cette nuit.
I couldn't sleep last night.	J'ai passé une nuit blanche.

no

evening
We had some friends over last night.
ten o'clock at night
I'm a "night owl."

le soir
Nous avons invité des amis hier soir.
dix heures du soir
Je suis du soir./Je suis noctambule.

no *adj*
[*not any*]

I have no money.
She has no friends.
No problem.
You have no excuse.
No Frenchman would dress like that.

(ne)...pas de
(ne)...aucun(e)

Je n'ai pas d'argent.
Elle n'a pas d'amis.
(Il n'y a) pas de problème.
Vous n'avez aucune excuse.
Aucun Français ne s'habillerait de la sorte.

in public notices
No parking/smoking.

Défense de stationner/de fumer.

nobody (no one) *pron*
nobody
Who's absent today? — Nobody.

Nobody spoke.
I saw no one.
There is nobody interesting here.

personne [+*ne with verb*]
Qui est absent aujourd'hui? — Personne.

Personne n'a parlé.
Je n'ai vu personne.
Il n'y a personne d'intéressant ici.
[*Note: When* **personne** *is followed by an adjective,* **de** (*d'*) *must be inserted; the adjective is always masculine.*]

Be careful to distinguish the negative, **personne**, from **une personne**, "a person."

none *pron*
not any
There are none in the shops.
I have none left.

Il n'y en a pas dans les magasins.
Il ne m'en reste plus.

not one
I asked three policemen, but none could tell me.
Do you have any grandchildren? — No, none.
None of my friends speaks Russian.
none of them
none of us

aucun(e) [+*ne with verb*]
J'ai demandé à trois agents, mais aucun n'a pu me le dire.
Vous avez des petits-enfants? — Non, aucun.
Aucun de mes amis ne parle russe.
aucun d'entre eux/aucune d'entre elles
aucun(e) d'entre nous

144

note *n*

I took notes during the speech.	J'ai pris des notes pendant le discours.
I'll leave him a note [*a message*].	Je vais lui laisser un mot.
a bank note/a 100 franc note	un billet de banque/un billet de 100 francs

Ø **note** [*f*] also means "a bill" or "a grade (in school)."

note *v*

[*to note down*]	noter qqch/prendre note de qqch
[*to notice*]	remarquer/constater

nothing *pron*

nothing	rien [*+ne with verb*]
Nothing interests him.	Rien ne l'intéresse.
We have nothing to do.	Nous n'avons rien à faire.
nothing at all	rien du tout
nothing good/bad	rien de bon/mauvais
nothing else	rien d'autre
What are you doing this weekend? — Nothing special.	Qu'est-ce que tu fais ce weekend? — Rien de spécial. [*Note: When* **rien** *is followed by an adjective,* **de** *must be inserted; the adjective is always masculine.*]

notice *n*

[*a sign*]	un écriteau
"Notice to passengers."	"Avis aux voyageurs."
until further notice	jusqu'à nouvel ordre
to give notice [*to quit work*]	démissionner/donner sa démission
to give notice [*to an employee*]	licencier/renvoyer
to give notice [*to a tenant*]	donner congé à
a month's notice	un mois de préavis
to take notice (of)	faire attention (à)
Don't take any notice of him!	Ne fais pas attention à lui!

notice *v*

to notice sth	s'apercevoir de qqch/remarquer qqch
I noticed that the window was open.	Je me suis aperçu que la fenêtre était ouverte.
Did you notice her hairstyle?	As-tu remarqué sa coiffure?
Was his car there? — I didn't notice.	Est-ce que sa voiture était là? — Je n'ai pas fait attention.

notify *v*
to notify sb of sth .... avertir qqn de qqch

I was not notified of the change of date.   Je n'ai pas été averti du changement de
date.

novel *n*
[*literary genre*]   un roman

Ø **nouvelle** [*f*] means "short story."

now *adv*
at the present time   maintenant/en ce moment/à présent
Where are you living now?   Où est-ce que tu habites en ce
moment?

Now that everyone is here, we can   Maintenant que tout le monde est
begin.   arrivé, nous pouvons commencer.
now and then   de temps en temps

right now   tout de suite
Let's do it now [*not later*].   Faisons-le tout de suite.

nowadays *adv*
nowadays   de nos jours/ces temps-ci/ces derniers
temps

nowhere *adv*
[*no place*]   nulle part [+*ne with verb*]
Where did you go — Nowhere.   Où es-tu allé? — Nulle part.
She is nowhere to be found.   On ne la trouve nulle part.

nuisance *n*
of a situation or occurrence   un ennui/un embêtement
That's a real nuisance!   C'est vraiment ennuyeux/embêtant!
[*fam*]/Quelle plaie! [*fam*]

of a person   une peste
What a nuisance that child is!   Quelle peste que cet enfant!
to make a nuisance of oneself   être embêtant/embêter tout le monde

Ø **nuisances** [*f pl*] means "pollution."

number *n*
in mathematics   un nombre
even/odd number   un nombre pair/impair
cardinal/ordinal number   un nombre cardinal/ordinal

digit, figure
the numbers on a clock face
Roman/Arabic numerals
an exact number
Six million (6,000,000) is a large
  number.

un chiffre
les chiffres d'un cadran
des chiffres romains/arabes
un chiffre exact
Six millions (6.000.000), c'est un
  chiffre important. [*Note French
  punctuation*]

for house, telephone, etc.
What is your phone number?

un numéro
Quel est ton numéro de téléphone?

a quantity or amount
a large number of people

un nombre/une quantité
un grand nombre de gens

nuts   *n*

[*Note: There is no general word for "nuts"
  in French.*]

hazelnut
peanut
walnut
You're nuts! [*slang*]

une noisette
une cacahuète
une noix
T'es cinglé!/Ça va pas? [*fam*]

O

obey *v*

to obey sb

A child must obey his parents.

I obeyed him.

obéir **à** qqn

Un enfant doit obéir **à** ses parents.

Je **lui** ai obéi.

object *n*

a thing

an art object

un objet/une chose

un objet d'art

an aim

his sole object in life

un but/un objectif

son seul but dans la vie

grammar term

a direct object

un complément d'objet direct

object *v*

to object to sth

protester contre qqch/désapprouver
  qqch

obvious *adj*

It's quite obvious.

an obvious error

C'est évident.

une erreur évidente

obviously *adv*

obviously

Obviously you haven't understood.

évidemment/de toute évidence

De toute évidence, tu n'as rien compris.

occasion *n*

time

on that occasion

on the occasion of her visit

on several occasions

à cette occasion

à l'occasion de sa visite

plusieurs fois/à plusieurs reprises

special function

It was a big occasion.

un événement

C'était un grand événement.

occasionally *adv*

[*sometimes*]

He is occasionally late.

parfois/quelquefois

Il arrive parfois en retard.

odd *adj*
strange
He is very odd.
How odd!

bizarre/curieux
Il est très bizarre.
Comme c'est curieux!

other
an odd number
odd socks
to do odd jobs around the house

un nombre impair
des chaussettes dépareillées
bricoler

of *prep*
the 1st of May
the 15th of November
two of them
several of us
There are five of us.
nine (times) out of ten
Of the twelve, only one returned.
That's very nice of you.
a friend of yours
Of course!
to think of [see **think**]

le premier mai
le 15 novembre [*Note: no **de**]*
deux **d'entre** eux
plusieurs **d'entre** nous
Nous sommes cinq.
neuf (fois) **sur** dix
Sur les douze, un seul est revenu.
C'est très gentil **à** vous.
un de vos amis
Bien sûr!

off *adj & adv*
light, stove, radio, etc
The light is off./The gas is off.
to turn off
Turn the light off!

éteint(e)/fermé(e)
La lumière est éteinte./Le gaz est fermé.
éteindre/fermer
Eteins la lumière!

other
I'm off!
to take a day off
I have the afternoon off.
The party's off.

Je m'en vais./Je pars.
prendre un jour de congé
J'ai congé cet après-midi.
La soirée est annulée.

off *prep*
to jump off the wall
to get off the bus/the train
to take a dish off the sideboard
to eat off a dirty plate
Keep off the grass. [*official sign*]

sauter **du** mur
descendre **de** l'autobus/**du** train
prendre un plat **sur** le buffet
manger **dans** une assiette sale
Défense de marcher sur la pelouse./
  Pelouse interdite.

[*see also* **take off**]

149

offend

offend v
I didn't mean to offend you.   Je ne voulais pas vous vexer.
He was really offended.   Il a été réellement vexé.

offense n
to take offense (at sth)   se formaliser (de qqch)

offer v
to offer (to)   proposer (de)
He offered to give me a ride.   Il a proposé de m'emmener en voiture.

Ø **offrir** can mean "to offer," but more usually means "to give," as in **offrir des fleurs à son hôtesse**. In a store the question: **C'est pour offrir?** is the equivalent of "Would you like it gift-wrapped?"

office n
place of work   le bureau
Come and see me in my office tomorrow.   Venez me voir demain à mon bureau.

He's at the office.   Il est au bureau.
an office worker   un(e) employé(e) (de bureau)
the post office   la poste/le bureau de poste
the information office   le bureau de renseignements
a doctor's office   un cabinet médical
a lawyer's office   une étude de notaire
the box office   le bureau de location
an office building   un immeuble de bureaux

official post
to take office/to go out of office   entrer en fonction/quitter ses fonctions
He took office last month.   Il est entré en fonction le mois dernier.

Ø **office** [m] is used for **bureau** in specific cases, e.g., **Office du tourisme.** It also means "church service." **Office** [f] means "pantry."

official adj
official   officiel(-elle)
the official version   la version officielle
unofficial   officieux(-euse)/non officiel(-elle)

official n
[*person in charge*]   le/la responsable
[*government employee*]   le/la fonctionnaire/l'employé(e)

150

officially *adv*
officially advised
unofficially

officiellement informé(e)
officieusement

often *adv*
often

souvent [*Note: never placed before the verb*]

I often come here.
We have often talked about it.

Je viens souvent ici.
Nous en avons souvent parlé.

oil *n*
olive/peanut oil
an oil painting
to check the oil [*in a car*]
the oil crisis

l'huile [*f*] d'olive/d'arachide
une peinture à l'huile
vérifier l'huile
la crise du pétrole

okay (O.K.) *adj & excl*
to express agreement
Shall we go? — O.K.!

D'accord!/D'acc! [*fam*]
On y va? — D'accord!

in response to an apology
Sorry to have bothered you. — It's O.K.

Excusez-moi de vous avoir dérangé. — Ce n'est pas grave./Il n'y a pas de mal.

acceptable
Is Monday O.K. with you?
Is it O.K. if I use the phone?

Lundi, ça te va?
Ça ne vous ennuie pas que je téléphone?

not hurt
Are you O.K.?
Luckily he's O.K.

Ça va?/Vous n'êtes pas blessé?
Heureusement il n'a rien.

in order
Everything is O.K.

Tout est dans l'ordre./Tout va bien.

not great
What do you think of this dress? — It's O.K.

pas mal
Comment trouves-tu cette robe? — Pas mal.

old *adj*
age
an old man
an old lady
We are old friends.

vieux (vieil)/vieille
un vieil homme/un vieillard
une vieille dame/une vieille
Nous sommes de vieux amis.

151

on

| to grow old | vieillir |
| How old are you? | Quel âge as-tu? |

former
| our old house | notre ancienne maison |
| in the old days | autrefois |

ancien(-enne) [Note: *precedes noun*]

on *prep*
means of travel
to get/be on the train/bus	monter/être **dans** le train/**dans** l'autobus
to go somewhere on the train	aller quelque part **en** train/**par** le train
on foot/on a bike	**à** pied/**à/en** vélo

place
on the second floor	**au** premier étage [Note: see **floor**]
to live on Lafayette street	habiter rue Lafayette [Note: *no preposition with the verb* **habiter**]
The drugstore is on Lafayette street.	La pharmacie est **dans** la rue Lafayette.
on page 39	à la page 39
on the last line	à la dernière ligne
on the other side (of the street, of the building)	**de** l'autre côté (de la rue, du bâtiment)

time
on Saturday	samedi [Note: *no preposition*]
Come and see me on Saturday.	Viens me voir samedi.
on Saturdays	**le** samedi
I like to sleep in on Saturdays.	J'aime faire la grasse matinée le samedi.
on the 12th of May	le 12 mai [Note: *no preposition*]
on time	à l'heure

other
on the radio/TV	à la radio/**à** la télé
on the telephone	**au** téléphone
to be on a team	faire partie d'une équipe
on the one hand/on the other hand	**d'**un côté/**d'**un autre côté
on one condition	à une seule condition
The light is on.	La lumière est allumée.
There's a good film on tonight [*at the movie theater*].	On passe/On joue un bon film ce soir.
What time is that (TV) show on?	A quelle heure passe cette émission?

verb+on
to go on	continuer
to put on/try on (an article of clothing)	mettre/essayer (un vêtement)
to spend money on sth	dépenser de l'argent **pour** qqch

152

to congratulate sb on sth · féliciter qqn **de** qqch
to turn on [*appliance, light*] · allumer/ouvrir
to live on bread and cheese · vivre **de** pain et **de** fromage
to live on 5,000 francs a month · vivre **avec** 5.000 f par mois

once *adv*
on one occasion · une fois
I have only been there once. · Je n'y suis allé qu'une fois.

in the past · autrefois
Once there were dinosaurs here. · Autrefois il y avait des dinosaures ici.
Once upon a time there was a prince... · Il y avait une fois un prince...

at once
[*immediately*] · tout de suite
I recognized him at once. · Je l'ai reconnu tout de suite.
[*at the same time*] · à la fois
Don't all speak at once! · Ne parlez pas tous à la fois!
all at once [*suddenly*] · tout à coup

one *pron*
One must help those in need. · On doit aider ceux qui sont dans le besoin.

one of my friends · un(e) de mes ami(e)s
one of them · l'un(e) d'entre eux (elles)
Would you like one? · En voulez-vous un(e)?
the one I want [*see also* **the one**] · celui/celle que je veux
this/that one [*see* **this one**]
which one(s)? [*see* **which one**]

one another [*see* **each other**]

only *adj*
only · seul(e)/unique
my only mistake · ma seule erreur
the only way to do something · la seule façon de faire qqch
the only two foreigners in the class · les deux seuls étrangers de la classe
  [*Note: word order*]
an only child · un enfant unique

the only one(s) · le seul/la seule/les seul(e)s
It's the only one we have. · C'est le seul/la seule que nous ayons.
  [*Note: takes the subjunctive*]

only

You're the only one who understands me.	Tu es le seul/la seule à me comprendre. Il n'y a que toi qui me comprennes.

only *adv*

only	seulement/ne. . .que
He has only one brother.	Il n'a qu'un frère.
There is only one solution.	Il n'y a qu'une solution.
You have only to say yes.	Tu n'as qu'à dire oui.
If only I had known!	Si seulement j'avais su!

operation *n*

[*surgical*]	une opération/une intervention chirurgicale
an open-heart operation	une opération à coeur ouvert
to have an operation	se faire opérer
He had a gall bladder operation.	Il s'est fait opérer de la vésicule biliaire.

opinion *n*

in my opinion	à mon avis

opportunity *n*
the chance

If I have the opportunity, I'll ask him.	l'occasion [*f*]
	Si j'en ai l'occasion, je lui demanderai.
to take the opportunity (of doing sth)	profiter de l'occasion (pour faire qqch)

job opportunity

There are not many job opportunities at the moment.	un débouché Il y a peu de débouchés en ce moment.

Ø **opportunité** means "timeliness," but is now also used with the meaning "opportunity."

opposite *adj & n*

in the opposite direction	en sens inverse
the opposite opinion	l'opinion contraire
He always says the opposite of what he thinks.	Il dit toujours le contraire de ce qu'il pense.

opposite *adv & prep*

We were sitting opposite each other.	Nous étions assis l'un en face de l'autre.
The pharmacy is opposite the park.	La pharmacie est en face du jardin public.
the house opposite	la maison d'en face

154

order *n*
business transaction   une commande
to place an order   passer une commande
made to order   fait(e) sur commande

a command   un ordre
to be under the orders of sb   être sous les ordres de qqn

out of order   en dérangement/en panne
The elevator is out of order.   L'ascenseur est en panne.

in order to   afin de/pour [+*infinitive*]
In order to succeed, you have to work hard.   Pour réussir, tu dois travailler dur.

in order that   afin que/pour que [+*subjunctive*]
I will speak slowly in order that you may understand better.   Je parlerai lentement pour que vous compreniez mieux.

order *v*
to order the soldiers to advance   ordonner aux soldats d'avancer
to order a sherbet   commander un sorbet

other *adj & pron*
the other student   l'autre étudiant(e)
the others   les autres
the other two   les deux autres [*Note: word order*]
others/other people   d'autres [*Note: shortened article*]
Some are standing; others are sitting.   Certains sont debout, d'autres sont assis.

I have other fish to fry.   J'ai d'autres chats à fouetter.

otherwise *conj*
[*if not*]   sinon/autrement
You must arrive promptly, otherwise they won't let you in.   Il faut arriver à l'heure, sinon on ne vous laissera pas entrer.

ouch *excl*
Ouch!   Aïe!/Ouille!

ought *v*
ought to   devoir
You ought to pay your taxes.   Vous devriez payer vos impôts. [*Note: conditional*]

You ought to have told me.   Vous auriez dû me le dire. [*Note: past conditional*]

our

[see also **should**]

our adj
[possessive]

our son-in-law

notre/nos

notre gendre

our grandparents

nos grands-parents

ours pron
[possessive]

le nôtre/la nôtre/les nôtres [Note: circumflex accent]

Their country is older than ours.

Leur pays est plus ancien que le nôtre.

He is a cousin of ours.

C'est un de nos cousins.

ourselves [see **self**]

out adv
He is out.

Il est sorti./Il n'est pas là.

out of prep

to take sth out of a drawer/ one's pocket

prendre qch **dans** un tiroir/**dans** sa poche

to look out of a window

regarder **par** la fenêtre

nine (times) out of ten

neuf (fois) **sur** dix

We are out of that item.

Nous **n'**avons **plus** cet article.

to run out (of the house)

sortir (de la maison) en courant

outdoor(s) adj & adv

an outdoor concert

un concert en plein air

outdoors

dehors

to eat outdoors

manger en plein air/dehors

Go and play outdoors!

Va jouer dehors!

outside prep

outside (of)

hors de/à l'extérieur de/en dehors de

outside the city limits

hors de la ville

outside adv
[outdoors]

dehors

Let's go outside.

Allons dehors.

over adv

to be over [finished]

être fini(e)

When the war is over...

Quand la guerre sera finie...

over here/over there	ici/là-bas
to invite somebody over	inviter qqn à la maison
Can you come over?	Peux-tu venir chez moi/nous?
all over (the place)	partout
to do something over (again)	refaire/recommencer qqch
You'll have to do it over.	Il faudra que tu le refasses.

over *prep*
place

to look over a hedge	regarder **par-dessus** une haie
to jump over a puddle	sauter **par-dessus** une flaque d'eau
to wear a jacket over a shirt	porter une veste **par-dessus** sa chemise
They live over the store.	Ils habitent **au-dessus** du magasin.
over the mountains/the river/the border	**de l'autre côté** des montagnes/ du fleuve/de la frontière
to go over a bridge/a hill	traverser un pont/une colline
We flew over the Great Lakes.	Nous avons survolé les Grands Lacs.
all over France	**dans** toute la France
all over the world	**dans** le monde entier
You have mud all over your shoes!	Tes chaussures sont couvertes de boue!

number

over 100 francs/3 meters/5 minutes	**plus de** 100 francs/3 mètres/5 minutes
to be over 21	avoir **plus de** 21 ans
a number over fifty	un chiffre **au dessus de** 50

time

| over the weekend | **pendant** le weekend |
| over the last ten years | **pendant** les dix dernières années/**au cours des** dix dernières années |

own *adj & pron*

[one's own]	propre [Note: before noun]
She has her own car.	Elle a sa propre voiture.
I saw it with my own eyes.	Je l'ai vu de mes propres yeux.
He did it on his own.	Il l'a fait tout seul.

When **propre** comes before a noun, it means "own"; when it follows the noun, it means "clean," e.g., **J'ai les mains propres.**

own *v*
in general

| She owns two fur coats. | possséder/avoir |
| | Elle possède/elle a deux manteaux de fourrure. |

own

real estate
He owns two apartment buildings.
It's better to own than to rent.

être propriétaire de
Il est propriétaire de deux immeubles.
Il vaut mieux être propriétaire que
    locataire.

P

pack *v*

to pack (one's suitcases)	faire ses valises
I am packed and ready to go.	J'ai fait mes valises et je suis prêt(e) à partir.
to unpack (one's suitcase)	défaire sa valise

pain *n*
physical pain

	la douleur/la souffrance
to be in pain	souffrir
He is in great pain.	Il souffre beaucoup.
He is out of pain.	Il ne souffre plus.
I have a pain in my leg.	J'ai mal à la jambe.

other

to take pains (doing sth)	se donner du mal (pour faire qqch)
What a pain!	Quelle plaie! [*fam*]

[*see also* **ache**]

painful *adj*

painful	douloureux(-euse)/pénible
a painful illness	une maladie douloureuse
a painful subject	un sujet pénible
a painful conversation	une conversation pénible
My leg is painful.	Ma jambe me fait mal.

pair *n*

a pair of gloves/scissors	une paire de gants/de ciseaux
a pair of pants/jeans/shorts	**un** pantalon/**un** jean/**un** short [*Note: singular*]
[*two people*]	un couple
They're an odd pair.	C'est un drôle de couple.

paper *n*

made of paper	en papier
a sheet of paper	une feuille de papier
a newspaper	un journal
[*a written composition*]	une rédaction/une dissertation/une composition
[*a paper done in class*]	une copie/une épreuve

park

Hand in your papers, please.	Remettez vos copies, s'il vous plaît.

park *v*
to park the car	garer la voiture/stationner/se garer
Where did you park?	Où est-ce que tu t'es garé?

parking *adj & n*
I couldn't find a parking place.	Je n'ai pas pu trouver de place pour stationner.
No parking.	Défense de stationner./Stationnement interdit.
a parking lot/garage/car park	un parking
a parking meter	un parcmètre/un parcomètre
a parking ticket	un P.-V. [*procès-verbal*]

part *n*
part of the house/the work/the rent	une partie de la maison/du travail/du loyer
to be a part of sth	faire partie de qqch
to take part in sth	participer à qqch
in part	en partie
a spare part [*e.g., for a car*]	une pièce détachée
a part [*e.g., in a play*]	un rôle
to play a part	jouer un rôle

Ø **part** [*f*] has various meanings, including "a share."

part *v*
to part from sb	se séparer de qqn/quitter qqn

Ø **partir** means "to depart."

partner *n*
[*in business*]	un(e) associé(e)
[*in sport, dancing*]	un(e) partenaire
[*husband or wife*]	l'époux/l'épouse
	le conjoint/la conjointe

party *n & v*
a social event
	une fête/une soirée [*formal*]
to give/have a party	organiser une fête/inviter des amis
to "party"	faire la fête
It's a pot-luck party.	Tout le monde apporte un plat.

other

a party of five	un groupe de cinq
a political party	un parti politique

pass *v*

to pass an exam	réussir à un examen/être reçu à un examen [*Note: not **passer***]
to get a passing grade	recevoir la mention "passable"
to pass by a building	passer devant un bâtiment

to overtake a vehicle

	dépasser/doubler
No passing.	Défense de doubler.

to pass sb/sth going in the opposite direction

	croiser
I passed her in the street.	Je l'ai croisée dans la rue.
They passed each other.	Ils se sont croisés.

patron *n*
customer

	un client
Patrons are requested to . . .	Nous demandons à notre aimable clientèle de . . .

benefactor

	un bienfaiteur/une bienfaitrice
a patron of the arts	un protecteur/une protectrice des arts
patron saint	un saint patron/une sainte patronne

Ø **patron** [*m*] also means "boss" or "employer."

pay *n*

[*salary*]	le salaire/la paie
to ask for a pay raise	demander une augmentation de salaire
take-home pay	le salaire net
pay day	le jour de paie
The pay is good.	C'est bien payé.
minimum pay/wage	le S.M.I.C. (Salaire minimum interprofessionnel de croissance)

pay *v*

to pay for sth	payer qqch [*Note: no preposition*]
to pay sb	payer qqn
to pay sb for sth	payer qqch à qqn
How much did you pay for it?	Combien l'as-tu payé?
to pay a bill/invoice	régler une note/une facture
to pay back	rembourser

peaceful

He paid back all he owed.	Il a remboursé tout ce qu'il devait.
to pay attention (to)	faire attention (à)

peaceful *adj*
quiet — tranquille/calme/paisible
How peaceful it is here! — Comme c'est tranquille ici!

not warlike — pacifique
peaceful co-existence — la coexistence pacifique

peas *n*
green peas — les petits pois
split peas — les pois cassés

people *n*
a precise or countable number — les personnes
How many people are there in the waiting room? — Il y a combien de personnes dans la salle d'attente?
several people — plusieurs (personnes)
some people — quelques-uns/quelques personnes/ certains

an uncountable number — les gens
There are people who don't know this. — Il y a des gens qui ne savent pas cela.
many people — beaucoup de gens/bien des gens
few people — peu de gens

a crowd
There are a lot of people in the stores on Christmas eve. — Il y a beaucoup de monde dans les magasins la veille de Noël.
There were fewer people at the show tonight than last night. — Il y avait moins de monde au spectacle ce soir qu'hier.

people in general — on
What will people think? — Qu'est-ce qu'on va penser?

inhabitants — les habitants
There are thirty thousand people in this town. — Cette ville compte trente mille habitants.

a nation, the masses, the proletariat — le peuple [*Note: takes singular verb*]
The French people suffered a great deal during the war. — Le peuple français a beaucoup souffert pendant la guerre.
The people have taken the Bastille! — Le peuple a pris la Bastille!

performance *n*
at the movies — la séance

162

| The next performance is at 8:00 P.M. | La prochaine séance est à 20 heures. |

at the theater, ballet, etc.
There will be three performances.

la représentation
Il y aura trois représentations.

manner of acting, singing, etc.
The critics didn't like the performance.

l'interprétation
Les critiques n'ont pas aimé cette interprétation.

It was a good performance.

C'était bien joué.

of sports, machines, vehicles

la performance

perhaps adv
[maybe]
Perhaps he is sick.

peut-être
Il est peut-être malade.
Peut-être qu'il est malade.

The normal position of **peut-être** is after the verb; if it is placed at the beginning of a sentence, **que** must be inserted. (Formal or literary style: **Peut-être est-il malade.**)

person n
a person
Your uncle is a very interesting person.

une personne [Note: always feminine]
Votre oncle est une personne très interéssante. [Note: When used without an article, **personne** means "nobody." See **nobody**]

pet n
Have you any pets?
She has a pet.

As-tu des animaux chez toi?
Elle a un chien/un chat. [Note: Specific animal is stated.]

50% of French homes have a pet.

50% des ménages français ont un animal domestique.

No pets allowed.
the teacher's pet

Les animaux sont interdits.
le chouchou du prof

phone v
to phone sb
Let's phone him tonight.
You should phone the bookstore.

téléphoner **à** qqn
Téléphonons-lui ce soir.
Tu devrais téléphoner à la librairie.

photograph n & v
a photograph
to photograph/take a photograph

une photographie/une photo
photographier/faire une photo

Ø **photographe** [*m & f*] means "a photographer."

phrase *n*
[*a saying*]   une expression
[*in grammar*]   une locution

Ø **phrase** [*f*] means "a sentence."

physical   [*see checkup*]

physician   *n*
[*medical doctor*]   un médecin, une femme médecin
She is a physician.   Elle est médecin.

Ø **physicien** [*m*] means "a physicist."

physics   *n*
[*field of study*]   la physique [*Note: singular*]

pick   *v*
to gather   cueillir
to pick flowers/fruit   cueillir des fleurs/des fruits

to choose   choisir
You can pick whatever you want.   Tu peux choisir ce que tu veux.

pick up   *v*
to pick up an object from the floor   ramasser un objet par terre
to go and pick up clothes from the   passer prendre des vêtements chez le
  cleaner's   teinturier
I'll pick you up at 6 o'clock.   Je passerai te prendre/Je viendrai te
                                                 chercher à 6 heures.

to pick up the phone   décrocher

to tidy   ranger
Pick up your things!   Range tes affaires!

to learn   apprendre
I picked that up as a child.   J'ai appris ça quand j'étais enfant.

picture   *n*
art work   un tableau/une peinture
a picture by Matisse   un tableau de Matisse

a portrait	un portrait
a picture of Louis XIV	un portrait de Louis XIV
a photograph	une photo
We took lots of pictures.	Nous avons fait beaucoup de photos.
illustration in a book	une image
Children love picture books.	Les enfants adorent les livres d'images.
on TV	l'image
The picture is fuzzy.	L'image est floue.

piece   *n*

a piece of bread/cheese, etc.	un morceau de pain/de fromage
a piece of paper	une feuille de papier
a piece of string	un bout de ficelle
a piece of music	un morceau de musique
a piece of land	un terrain
a piece of advice	un conseil
a piece of information	un renseignement
a piece of news	une nouvelle
a piece of furniture	un meuble

Ø **pièce** [*f*] has several meanings, including "a room," "a coin," "a play"; it rarely means "a piece."

pill   *n*

to take a pill	prendre un cachet/un comprimé

Ø **pilule** [*f*] usually means "contraceptive pill."

pitfall   *n*

[*a trap*]	un piège
This book will help you to avoid pitfalls in French.	Ce livre vous aidera à éviter les pièges du français.

place   *n*
in general

a quiet place for a picnic	un endroit/un lieu
	un endroit tranquille pour faire un pique-nique
That's a place I would like to visit.	C'est un endroit que j'aimerais visiter.
a public place	un lieu public
premises	un local

plain

We are looking for a place for our club.	Nous cherchons un local pour notre club.

residence

I left my glasses at your place.	J'ai oublié mes lunettes chez vous.
I'm going to my uncle's place.	Je vais chez mon oncle.
to come/go by sb's place	passer chez qqn

in a competition, race

to be in first/second place	terminer premier/deuxième

to take place — avoir lieu

The summit will take place in May.	Le sommet aura lieu en mai.

other

in place of [see **instead of**]
some place [see **somewhere**]
any place [see **anywhere**]
no place [see **nowhere**]

Ø **place** [f] has various meanings, including "a square," "a seat," and "room" or "space."

plain adj
obvious — clair(e)/évident(e)

It's plain to everyone.	C'est clair pour tout le monde.

simple — simple

She was wearing a very plain dress.	Elle portait une robe très simple.

in a solid color — uni(e)

I need a plain fabric.	J'ai besoin d'un tissu uni.

plan n
drawing or map — un plan

Can I see the plans of the building?	Est-ce que je peux voir les plans du bâtiment?

projected activity — un projet/un programme

to make plans for a vacation	faire des projets de vacances
a change of plan	un changement de programme
I've changed my plans.	J'ai changé de programme.

plan v
to intend — compter/avoir l'intention de/projeter de [+infinitive]

How long do you plan to stay?	Combien de temps comptez-vous rester?
I don't plan to tell him about it.	Je n'ai pas l'intention de lui en parler.

to make preparations
We are planning a party for Friday.

organiser/prévoir
Nous organisons une fête pour vendredi.

I have nothing planned for tonight.

Je n'ai rien de prévu pour ce soir.

plant *n*
[*vegetation*]	une plante
[*a factory*]	une fabrique/une usine
a nuclear plant	une centrale nucléaire

plate *n*
[*for eating*]	une assiette

Ø **plat** [*m*] means "a serving dish" or "a course in a menu."

play *v*
a game or sport
We played cards.
Do you play tennis?

jouer **à**
Nous avons joué **aux** cartes.
Est-ce que tu joues **au** tennis?

a musical instrument
She plays the piano and the clarinet.

jouer **de**
Elle joue **du** piano et **de** la clarinette.

other
What's playing at the movie theater this week?

Qu'est-ce qu'on joue/Qu'est-ce qu'on passe au cinéma cette semaine?

plus *adv, n & prep*
two plus two

deux plus deux

in addition
Plus, he's a liar.

d'ailleurs/en plus
En plus, il est menteur.
Il est menteur par-dessus le marché.

an advantage
Knowing a foreign language is a plus.

un atout
Savoir une langue étrangère est un atout.

P.M.
three o'clock P.M.	trois heures de l'après-midi/15 heures
10 P.M.	dix heures du soir/22 heures

point

point *n*
a dot
a decimal point
6.5% of the population

un point
une virgule décimale
6,5% de la population [*Note French punctuation*]

sharp end
the point of a pencil/a knife

la pointe
la pointe d'un crayon/d'un couteau

in time
at this point
at that point
to be on the point of doing sth

à ce stade/en ce moment
à ce moment-là
être sur le point de faire qqch

a characteristic
We all have good points and bad points.

Nous avons tous des qualités et des défauts.

in discussion
to make a point
That's a good point!
That's not the point.
That's beside the point.

faire une remarque
C'est juste!
Il ne s'agit pas de cela.
Là n'est pas la question.

purpose
What's the point?
There's no point (in trying).

A quoi bon?
Cela ne sert à rien (d'essayer).

other
the points of a star
the point of departure

les branches d'une étoile
le point de départ

point *v*
to point at sb or sth

montrer/indiquer qqn ou qqch du doigt

He pointed at the church.
to point sth out to sb

Il a montré l'église du doigt.
faire remarquer qqch à qqn/signaler qqch à qqn

I would like to point out to you that . . .

J'aimerais vous faire remarquer que . . .

poisonous *adj*
[*gas, chemical substance*]
[*snake, insect*]
[*plant*]

toxique
venimeux(-euse)
vénéneux(-euse)

police *n*

the police force	la police
the police station	le commissariat de police
to have a police record	avoir un casier judiciaire
The police have arrested three suspects.	La police a arrêté trois suspects. [*Note: singular verb*]

police officer *n*

[*city*]	un agent de police/un policier
[*national and highway*]	un gendarme

policy *n*

government policy	la politique du gouvernement
foreign policy	la politique étrangère/extérieure
Our usual policy is to . . .	Nous avons pour règle de . . .
an insurance policy	une police d'assurance

politician *n*

politician	un homme/une femme politique
De Gaulle was a very famous French politician.	De Gaulle était un homme politique français très célèbre.

politics *n*

politics	la politique [*Note: singular*]
She's not interested in politics.	Elle ne s'intéresse pas à la politique.

poor *adj*

unfortunate

Poor man!	Le pauvre homme! [*Note: precedes noun*]

impoverished

a poor man	un homme pauvre [*Note: follows noun*]
poor people	les pauvres

positive *adj*

opposite of negative

	positif(-ve)
The results of the tests were positive.	Les résultats des analyses étaient positifs.

certain

	sûr(e), certain(e)
Are you positive of that?	Tu 'en es sûr?

possibility *n*

outcome

	l'éventualité
to foresee all possibilities	envisager toutes les éventualités

possible

chance

There is a good possibility that. . .	Il est possible que/Il y a des chances que [+*subjunctive*]
That's a possibility.	C'est possible.

possible *adj*

possible	possible/eventuel(-elle)
It's possible.	C'est possible.
It's possible that I'll be there.	Il est possible que je sois là.
the possible consequences	les conséquences éventuelles
as soon/as quickly/as often as possible	le plus tôt/le plus vite/le plus souvent possible

possibly *adv*

[*perhaps*]	peut-être
Will you be there? — Possibly.	Tu seras là? — Peut-être.
I can't possibly finish that before tomorrow.	Il m'est impossible de finir ça avant demain.
We did all we possibly could.	Nous avons fait tout notre possible.

Ø ~~possiblement~~ is not French.

postpone *v*

[*to put off*]	remettre/reporter
The meeting has been postponed till April 10th.	On a remis la réunion au 10 avril.

power *n*

ability or capacity

	le pouvoir/la capacité/la faculté
It's not in my power to grant that.	Il n'est pas en mon pouvoir d'accorder cela.
mental powers	les facultés mentales

authority

the power of the President	le pouvoir/l'autorité
	le pouvoir du président

strength

the power of an engine	la puissance
Victor Hugo had great powers of imagination.	la puissance d'un moteur
	Victor Hugo avait une grande puissance d'imagination.

energy

electric power	l'énergie électrique/l'électricité

a power station	une centrale électrique
a power failure	une panne d'électricité
nuclear power	l'énergie nucléaire

other

the world powers	les puissances mondiales
power brakes	des freins assistés
power steering	la direction assistée

powerful *adj*
[*strong*]   puissant(e)
a powerful voice   une voix puissante

practice *v*

to practice [*a sport or a skill*]	s'entraîner à/s'exercer à
I have to practice my French.	Il faut que je m'exerce à parler français.
to practice a musical instrument	faire des exercices/travailler un instrument
to practice a religion	pratiquer une religion
to be a practicing Catholic, Jew, etc.	être pratiquant(e)
to practice a part in a play	répéter un rôle
to practice a profession	exercer une profession

prejudice *n*/**prejudiced** *adj*

a prejudice	un préjugé/un parti pris
There is a lot of prejudice in this society.	Il y a beaucoup de préjugés dans cette société.
to be prejudiced/unprejudiced	avoir des préjugés/être sans préjugés
a prejudiced person	une personne pleine de préjugés
to be prejudiced against sb	être prévenu(e) contre qqn

Ø **préjudice** means "loss" or "damage," e.g., in insurance.

presently *adv*
[*at the present moment*]   actuellement/maintenant/à présent
[*in the near future*]   tout à l'heure/bientôt

preservative *n*
[*in food products*]   un agent de conservation

Ø **préservatif** [*m*] means "a condom."

171

pressure *n & v*

to put pressure on sb or sth	faire pression/exercer une pression sur qqn ou qqch
pressurized [*draft*] beer	une bière à la pression/une bière pression
the pressures of modern life	le stress de la vie moderne

pretend *v*

to pretend (to)	faire semblant (de)
The child was pretending to be asleep.	L'enfant faisait semblant de dormir.

Ø **prétendre** means "to claim" or "to assert."

prevent *v*

to prevent sb from doing sth	empêcher qqn de faire qqch
to prevent an accident	éviter/empêcher/prévenir un accident

Ø **prévenir** also means "to warn."

primary *adj*

primary school	l'école primaire
primary color	une couleur fondamentale
primary cause	la cause première
the primary reason	la raison principale
of primary importance	d'une importance primordiale

privacy *n*

I need some privacy.	J'ai besoin de solitude.
	J'ai besoin d'être seul.
in the privacy of one's home	dans l'intimité de son foyer
to tell sb sth in privacy	dire qqch à qqn dans le plus grand secret
Film stars have no privacy.	Les vedettes de cinéma n'ont pas de vie privée.

private *adj*

not public	privé(e)
private property	la propriété privée
"Private" [*sign posted*]	"Interdit au public"
a private school	une école privée/une école libre
private life	la vie privée
confidential	confidentiel(-elle)

172

This matter is strictly private.	Cette affaire est strictement confidentielle.

personal — particulier(-ière)/privé(e)/personnel(elle)/

room with a private bathroom	chambre avec salle de bain particulière
private lessons	des leçons particulières
for private reasons	pour des raisons personnelles

other

a private citizen	un particulier

probably *adv*

probably	probablement/sans doute
We will probably arrive before nine.	Nous arriverons probablement avant 9 heures.
He probably guessed.	Il l'a sans doute deviné.

problem *n*

un ennui/un problème/une difficulté/du mal

to have health/financial problems	avoir des ennuis de santé/d'argent
They are having problems with their son.	Ils ont des difficultés avec leur fils.
a problem child	un enfant difficile (à élever)
I had a problem finding your house.	J'ai eu du mal à trouver ta maison.
What's the problem?	Qu'est-ce qui ne va pas?
No problem!	(Il n'y a) pas de problème!/Il n'y a aucun problème!
It's not my problem.	Ça ne me concerne pas.
That's a problem for me.	Cela me pose un problème.
I have a problem [*disagree*] with that.	Je ne sais pas si je suis d'accord. Je n'aime pas beaucoup ça.

process *n*
a progression or development

a slow/natural/chemical process	un processus lent/naturel/chimique

a method or procedure

They've invented a new process.	On a inventé un nouveau procédé.

to be in the process of doing sth — être en train de faire qqch

We are in the process of painting the house.	Nous sommes en train de repeindre la maison.

Ø **procès** [m] usually means "a trial" or "a lawsuit."

program

program *n*
[*printed program, list of events*]   le programme
TV program [*the listing*]   le programme
TV program [*the show*]   une émission

progress *n*
to make progress [*e.g.,in school, on a*   faire des progrès [*Note: usually plural*]
   job]
He has made great progress.   Il a fait de grands progrès.
the work in progress   les travaux en cours

health
The patient is making progress.   Le malade va mieux.
    L'état du malade s'améliore.

prohibit *v*
to prohibit sb from doing sth   interdire à/défendre à qqn de faire
      qqch
Smoking prohibited.   Défense de fumer.
Walking on the grass is prohibited.   Il est interdit de marcher sur la
  [*official sign*]   pelouse./Pelouse interdite.

proper *adj*
socially acceptable   bienséant(e)/convenable
proper dress   une tenue convenable
proper behavior   une conduite bienséante
That's not the proper way to behave.   Ça ne se fait pas.

well-mannered   comme il faut
She's always very proper.   Elle est toujours très comme il faut.

suitable, correct [*see* **right**]

public *adj*
[*in general*]   public/publique
public holiday   un jour férié/une fête légale
public transport   les transports en commun
public library   une bibliothèque municipale
public spirit   le civisme
public school   une école laïque/une école d'état

publish *v*
to publish a book   éditer/publier un livre
This book was published by. . .   Ce livre a été édité par. . .
    Ce livre a paru chez. . .

Her book has just been published.	Son livre vient de paraître.
This magazine is published every month.	Cette revue paraît tous les mois.

publisher *n*

a publisher	une maison d'édition
the publishers of a book	les éditeurs d'un livre

purple *adj*

[*purple color*]	violet(-ette)
to turn purple (in the face)	devenir cramoisi(e)/pourpre

Ø **pourpre** usually means "scarlet" or "crimson," rather than "purple."

purpose *n*

the purpose of the meeting	l'objet/le but de la réunion

on purpose

I didn't do it on purpose!	Je ne l'ai pas fait exprès!
	exprès

put *v*

to put	mettre

put + adverb

to put away [*tidy*]	ranger
to put sth back	remettre qqch (à sa place)
to put down	poser/déposer
to put off [*postpone*]	remettre/reporter
to put on [*clothes*]	mettre
to put on weight	prendre du poids/grossir
I've put on ten pounds.	J'ai pris cinq kilos.
to put out [*light, cigarette*]	éteindre
to put up with	supporter/tolérer
I can't put up with it any longer.	Je ne peux plus le supporter.
to put sb up for the night	recevoir qqn pour la nuit
Can you put me up for the night?	Est-ce que je peux passer la nuit chez toi?

≡ Q ≡

qualified *adj*

He's not qualified for the job.

Il n'a pas les qualifications requises
pour le poste.

a qualified teacher

un professeur diplômé

quarrel [*see* **argument**]

quarter *n*

[*fraction*] un quart
a quarter liter of wine un quart de vin
the first quarter of the moon le premier quartier de la lune
a quarter of an hour un quart d'heure
a quarter past five cinq heures et quart
a quarter to six six heures moins le quart
[*division of academic year*] le trimestre

Quebec *n*

in or to Quebec [*province*] au Québec
in or to Quebec [*City*] à Québec
from Quebec [*province*] du Québec
from Quebec [*City*] de Québec

question *n*

to ask a question poser une question: [*Note: not*
  demander]
without question sans aucun doute
It's a question of understanding the Il s'agit de comprendre les règles.
  rules.
It's not a question of money. Il ne s'agit pas d'argent.
That's not the question. Il ne s'agit pas de ça!
It's out of the question. Il n'en est pas question.

question *v*

to question sb poser des questions à qqn
  interroger/questionner qqn
to question sth [*put in doubt*] douter de qch
I question his honesty. Je doute de son honnêteté.

176

questionable *adj*
[*open to doubt*]
a questionable statement

douteux/discutable
une affirmation douteuse

quick *adj*
[*fast*]
a quick reflex

rapide [*Note: not* **vite**]
un rèflexe rapide

quickly *adv*
[*fast*]
Come quickly!

rapidement/vite
Viens vite!

quiet *adj*
a quiet spot
a quiet room
a quiet child
to keep quiet
Be quiet! [*stop talking*]

un endroit tranquille
une chambre tranquille
un enfant calme
se taire/garder le silence
Tais-toi!/Taisez-vous!

quit *v*
to resign from
I am going to quit my job.

Je vais quitter ma place.
Je vais donner ma démission.
Je vais démissionner.

to stop
He has quit smoking.
Quit saying that!
I quit!

(s')arrêter de faire qqch
Il s'est arrêté de fumer.
Arrête de dire ça!
J'abandonne!

quite *adv*
completely
You are quite right.

tout à fait
Vous avez tout à fait raison.

rather
He is quite intelligent.

assez
Il est assez intelligent.

quiz *n*
[*in school*]
[*see also* **test**]

un contrôle/une interrogation

quotation *n*
[*passage or sentence cited*]   une citation
quotation marks   les guillemets [*m pl*]
in quotation marks   entre guillemets
to open/close quotation marks   ouvrir/fermer les guillemets

quote *v*
to cite exactly   citer
to quote (from) Voltaire   citer Voltaire
You can quote me.   Vous pouvez me citer.
Don't quote me!   Ne dites pas que c'est moi qui l'ai dit.

to name a price   indiquer/établir/proposer un prix
The price you quoted is too high.   Le prix que vous avez indiqué est trop
                                                   élevé.
This is the best price we can quote   C'est le meilleur prix que nous
  you.   puissions vous proposer.

R

race *n*

[*in sports*]	une course
to run a race with sb	faire la course avec qqn
the 100 meters race	le 100 mètres
the human race	la race/l'espèce humaine
the black race/the white race	les Noirs, les Blancs

raise *n & v*

Raise your hands if you want to speak.	Levez la main si vous avez quelque chose à dire.
to raise children	élever des enfants
I was raised in the country.	J'ai grandi à la campagne.
to raise prices	augmenter les prix
to get a raise (in salary)	recevoir une augmentation (de salaire)

rate *n*

[*price charged*]	le tarif
What are your rates?	Quels sont vos tarifs?
the exchange rate	le taux du change
the birth rate	le taux de natalité
at any rate	en tout cas/de toute façon

rather *adv*

before an adjective

I am rather tired.	Je suis un peu fatigué.
He is rather shy.	Il est plutôt timide.

to express preference

I would rather not go out tonight.	J'aimerais mieux/Je préférerais ne pas sortir ce soir.

to correct a statement

	plutôt
She came in her car, or rather in her parents' car.	Elle est venue dans sa voiture, ou plutôt dans la voiture de ses parents.

rayon *n*

[*fabric*]	la rayonne/la soie artificielle

Ø **rayon** [*m*] has several meanings, including "ray" (of light), "department" (in a store), and "shelf."

179

reach n

within easy reach of the park	à proximité du jardin public
out of reach	hors de portée
within (arm's) reach	à portée (de la main)

reach v

When do we reach Paris?	Quand arriverons-nous à Paris?
I haven't been able to reach him [i.e., by phone].	Je n'ai pas pu le joindre.
Your letter reached me yesterday.	Votre lettre m'est parvenue hier.
to reach one's goal	atteindre son but

reading n

reading	la lecture
I have a lot of reading to do for tomorrow.	J'ai beaucoup de lecture à faire pour demain.
She likes reading.	Elle aime lire./Elle aime la lecture.

ready adj

to be ready	être prêt(e)
We aren't ready yet.	Nous ne sommes pas encore prêts.
to get ready	se préparer
Get ready to leave.	Préparez-vous à partir.

realize v

[to become aware]	se rendre compte que/de
I realized he was not listening to me.	Je me suis rendu compte **qu'**il ne m'écoutait pas.
He realized his mistake.	Il s'est rendu compte **de** son erreur.
I hadn't realized that.	Je ne m'**en** étais pas rendu compte.

Ø **réaliser** means "to achieve" or "to carry out," but is now also used with the meaning "to become aware."

really adv

[truly, very]	vraiment/réellement
He looked really ill.	Il avait l'air vraiment malade.
Really? [surprise, delight]	C'est vrai?/Vraiment?/Sans blague!
Really? [mild interest]	Ah, bon?
Yes, really! [affirmation]	Oui, absolument!

reason n

the reason for my absence	la raison **de** mon absence

That's the reason (why) I got here so late. — C'est la raison **pour laquelle** je suis arrivé si tard.

Do you know the reason why? — Tu sais pourquoi?

It stands to reason. — Cela va sans dire.

There is reason to believe that... — Il y a lieu de croire que...

receipt n
[for a purchase]

Do you need a receipt? — un reçu/un récépissé

a cash register receipt — Il vous faut un reçu?

un ticket de caisse

receiver n
[addressee of a letter] — le/la destinataire

telephone receiver — le combiné/le récepteur

to pick up/replace the receiver — décrocher/raccrocher

recipe n
a recipe [in cooking] — une recette (de cuisine)

record n
in music

to put on/play a record — mettre/jouer un disque

a stereo record player — une chaîne stéréo

in sports — un record

to break/hold the record — battre/détenir le record

record v
to record music — enregistrer de la musique

to record on tape — enregistrer sur bande

a recorded message — un message enregistré

recover v intrans
to recover from an illness — guérir/se rétablir/se remettre d'une maladie

The patient is recovering slowly. — Le/La malade se remet petit à petit.

I have completely recovered. — Je suis tout à fait rétabli.

to recover from a shock — se remettre d'un choc

recover v trans
to recover one's appetite — retrouver l'appétit

to recover one's strength — reprendre des forces

to recover a lost article — récupérer un objet perdu

181

red *adj*

to have red hair	avoir les cheveux roux
He/She has red hair.	Il est roux./Elle est rousse.
a redhead	un rouquin/une rouquine

refer *v*

He never refers to it.	Il n'en parle jamais.
What are you referring to?	A quoi faites-vous allusion?
Please refer to page 90.	Prière de se reporter/se référer à la page 90.

regard(s) *n*

I have a high regard for him.	J'ai beaucoup d'estime pour lui.
Give my regards to your wife.	Mes amitiés à votre femme.
Give her/him my regards.	Faites-lui mes amitiés./Dites-lui bien des choses de ma part.
Best regards [*at end of letter*]	amicalement/cordialement
with regard to...	quant à/en ce qui concerne...
With regard to your raise...	En ce qui concerne votre augmentation de salaire...

register *v*

to register for a class	s'inscrire à un cours
to send a letter by registered mail	envoyer une lettre recommandée
to register for the draft	se faire recenser

Ø **enregistrer** means "to record."

registration *n*

registration fee [*university*]	les droits d'inscription
registration number [*for a vehicle*]	le numéro minéralogique/le numéro d'immatriculation

regular *adj*
steady, at regular intervals

	régulier
a regular job	un emploi régulier
There is a regular bus service.	Il y a un service régulier d'autobus.
to keep regular hours	mener une vie réglée

usual, ordinary

	habituel(-elle)/normal(e)/ordinaire
in the regular meaning of the word	au sens habituel du mot
a regular day	un jour ordinaire
the regular customers	les habitués/les bons clients
"regular" gas [*as opposed to "super"*]	de l'essence ordinaire/de l'ordinaire

182

regular size [*not small or large*]   la taille normale/la taille moyenne

rehearse *v*/**rehearsal** *n*
to rehearse a play/a part   répéter une pièce/un rôle
a rehearsal   une répétition
a dress rehearsal   une (répétition) générale

relation/relationship *n*
to have a good relationship with sb   avoir de bons rapports avec qqn
to be in a relationship with sb   être avec qqn
Their relationship has lasted for two years.   Ils se fréquentent/Ils sont ensemble depuis deux ans.
There is no relation between these two matters.   Il n'y a aucun rapport entre ces deux affaires.
[*family member: see* **relative**]
What is your relationship to her?   Quels sont vos liens de parenté avec elle?

relative *n*
my relatives   mes parents
Is he a relative of yours?   Est-il de vos parents?/Y a-t-il une parenté entre vous?

Ø **parents** also means "father and mother."

relax *v*
to rest   se détendre/se délasser
I am going to the country to relax.   Je vais à la campagne pour me détendre.

to calm down   se calmer
Relax!   Calme-toi!/Ne t'énerve pas! Calmez-vous!/Ne vous énervez pas!

rely *v*
to rely on   compter sur/avoir confiance en
You can rely on me.   Vous pouvez compter sur moi.

Ø **relier** means "to join" or "to bind."

remark *n & v*
to make a remark   faire une observation/une réflexion/une remarque

remember

to remark to sb that . . .	faire remarquer à qqn que . . .
He remarked to me that the box had been opened.	Il m'a fait remarquer qu'on avait ouvert la boîte.
"It's getting late," he remarked.	«Il se fait tard»- dit-il.

Ø **remarquer** usually means "to notice."

remember v

to remember sth	se souvenir de/se rappeler qqch
I don't remember his name.	Je ne me souviens pas de son nom.
	Je ne me rappelle pas son nom.
Did you remember to go to the post office?	As-tu pensé à aller à la poste?

remind v

to remind sb to do sth	faire penser à qqn à faire qqch
Remind me to buy some stamps.	Fais-moi penser à acheter des timbres.
to remind sb that . . .	rappeler à qqn que . . .
He reminded us that it was Sunday.	Il nous a rappelé que c'était dimanche.
You remind me of my cousin.	Tu me rappelles ma cousine.
That reminds me! . . .	A propos! . . .

rent n & v

to rent a house/a car	louer une maison/une voiture
to pay the rent	payer le loyer
"Apartment for rent"	"Appartement à louer"
Do you own your house, or are you renting it?	Etes-vous propriétaire ou locataire?

rental n

car rental	la location d'une voiture
to pay the rental	payer la location
the rental charge/cost	le prix de location

report n

to write a report	écrire un rapport/un compte-rendu
a school report [grades]	un bulletin de notes/un bulletin scolaire
the weather report	le bulletin météorologique/la météo

representative n

[elected]	un député
[salesperson]	un représentant (de commerce)

require *v*
to demand
The law requires that . . .

exiger
La loi exige que [+*subjunctive*]

to need
Do you require anything else?

avoir besoin de
Avez-vous besoin d'autre chose?

required *adj*
[*necessary*]

exigé(e)/requis(e)/de rigueur/
    obligatoire

Evening dress required.
the required degrees
a required course [*in school*]
Helmets are required.
Reservations are not required.

Tenue de soirée de rigueur.
les diplômes requis
un cours obligatoire
Le port du casque est obligatoire.
Les réservations ne sont pas
    nécessaires.

resign *v*
to resign oneself to a situation
to resign from a job

se résigner à une situation
démissionner d'un poste/donner sa
    démission

resort *n*
a seaside resort
a ski resort
as a last resort

une station balnéaire
une station de ski
en dernier ressort

resort *v*
to resort to violence

avoir recours à la violence

rest *n & v*
the remainder
the rest of the time
the rest of the money
the rest of the books

le reste/le restant/ce qui reste
le reste du temps
le restant de l'argent/l'argent qui reste
les autres livres/les livres qui restent

relaxation
to rest
Have a good rest!
I need rest.

le repos
se reposer
Repose-toi bien!
J'ai besoin de repos.
J'ai besoin de me reposer.

Ø **rester** means "to stay" or "to remain."

restroom

restroom [see *toilet*]

resumé *n*
[*summary of work experience*]
I enclose my resumé [*with a letter of
  application*].

le curriculum vitae/le C.V.
Je joins mon curriculum vitae.
Ci-joint mon curriculum vitae.

Ø **résumé** [*m*] means "a summary."

resume *v*
[*to start again*]
to resume work
Classes will resume on Monday.

recommencer/reprendre
reprendre le travail
Les cours reprendront lundi.

Ø **résumer** means "to sum up" or "to summarize."

retire *v*/**retirement** *n*
to retire [*from work*]
He retired last year.
He is retired.
retirement age

prendre sa retraite
Il a pris sa retraite l'année dernière.
Il est retraité/à la retraite.
l'âge de la retraite/le troisième âge

return *v intrans*
[*to go back*]
[*to come back*]
[*to come or go home*]
I hope to return to France some day.
When will he return?

retourner
revenir
rentrer
J'espère retourner en France un jour.
Quand reviendra-t-il?/Quand
  rentrera-t-il?

return *v trans*
to give back
I forgot to return my books to the
  library.

rendre
J'ai oublié de rendre mes livres à la
  bibliothèque.

to pay back
I want to return the money I borrowed.

rembourser
Je veux rembourser l'argent que j'ai
  emprunté.

to take back
You can return it if it's too big.

rapporter
Vous pouvez le rapporter si c'est trop
  grand.

to send back

renvoyer/retourner

"Return to sender." "Retour à l'expéditeur."

reverse *adj, n & v*
to drive in reverse | faire marche arrière
to reverse (the car) down the street | descendre la rue en marche arrière
in reverse order | dans l'ordre inverse
It's just the reverse. | C'est tout le contraire.

Ø **revers** [m] means "lapel"; **renverser** means "to overturn."

review *n & v*
to write a review of a play | faire la critique/le compte-rendu d'une pièce
to review for an exam | réviser/faire des révisions
to review [*reconsider*] a situation | réexaminer une situation

ride *n & v*
to give sb a ride | emmener qqn en voiture
Do you need a ride? | Vous avez une voiture?/Je peux vous emmener?
Do you have a ride to the picnic? | Est-ce qu'on vient te prendre pour aller au pique-nique?
I have a ride. | Quelqu'un m'emmène.
It's just a short ride. | Ce n'est pas loin.
to go for a ride in the car | (aller) faire un tour/se promener en voiture
to take a bike/boat ride | faire un tour à vélo/en bateau
I rode my bike to the park. | Je suis allé au parc à vélo.
to go (horseback) riding | faire du cheval/monter à cheval/faire de l'équitation

right *adj, adv & n*
opposite of left | droit(e)
my right arm/my right hand | mon bras droit/ma main droite
the right side | le côté droit
on the right side (of the street) | du côté droit (de la rue)
on/to the right | sur la droite/à droite
on your right | à/sur votre droite
Turn right at the (traffic) light. | Tournez à droite au feu.
the right-hand lane | la file de droite
the [*political*] right | la droite

correct | exact(e)/correct(e)/juste/bon (bonne)
the right answer | la bonne réponse/la réponse correcte

Is this the right number/address? — Est-ce que c'est le bon numéro/la bonne adresse?

the right spelling of a word — l'orthographe correcte d'un mot
the right word — le mot juste
That's right. — C'est juste./C'est exact./C'est ça.
You are right. — Vous avez raison.
That clock is not right. — Cette horloge n'est pas à l'heure.
to guess right — deviner juste

appropriate, suitable
approprié/convenable/qu'il faut/ qui convient/bon (bonne)

to wear the right clothes — mettre les vêtements appropriés
the right tool — l'outil qui convient/l'outil approprié
the right size — la taille qu'il faut/la bonne taille
It's the right job for me. — C'est le poste qu'il me faut.
You've come at the right time! — Tu arrives au bon moment!

moral
bien
It's not right to cheat. — Ce n'est pas bien de tricher.
to know right from wrong — savoir distinguer le bien du mal
He has no right to... — Il n'a pas le droit de...
What right have you to do that? — De quel droit faites-vous cela?
civil rights/women's rights — les droits civiques/les droits de la femme

other
right in front of you — droit devant vous
right now/right away — tout de suite
right here — ici même
Right on! — C'est ça!
all right [see okay]

ring n
to wear a ring — porter un anneau/une bague
engagement ring — une bague de fiançailles
wedding ring — une alliance

river n
a major river — un fleuve
The Loire river is the longest in France. — La Loire est le plus long fleuve de France.

a lesser river or a tributary — une rivière

road n
[in cities] — une rue

[*between cities*]
Is this the road to Bordeaux?

une route
C'est la route de Bordeaux?

robe *n*
bathrobe/dressing-gown
magistrate's robe

un peignoir/une robe de chambre
une robe/une toge

Ø **robe** [ʃ] usually means "a woman's dress."

roman *adj & n*
a Roman
the ancient Romans
a Roman temple

Roman ruins

un(e) Romain(e)
les Romains de l'antiquité
un temple romain [*Note: small "r" for adjective*]

des ruines romaines

Ø **roman** as a noun means "a novel"; as an adjective it means "romanesque," e.g., **l'art roman.**

room *n*
in a residence
How many rooms are there in the apartment?
dining room
living room
bathroom
bedroom
I'm looking for a room to rent.
a hotel room
a roommate

une pièce
Il y a combien de pièces dans l'appartement?
la salle à manger
la salle de séjour/le living/le séjour
la salle de bain(s)
la chambre (à coucher)
Je cherche une chambre à louer.
une chambre d'hôtel
un(e) camarade de chambre

in a public building
classroom/waiting room
We need a room for our meeting.

une salle
une salle de classe/d'attente
Nous avons besoin d'une salle pour notre réunion.

space
There is no more room.
Do you have room for me?

de la place
Il n'y a plus de place.
Il y a de la place pour moi?

round [*see* **around**]

rude *adj*
[*impolite*]

impoli/grossier

rudely

He was very rude to us.	Il a été très impoli envers nous.
a rude word	un gros mot
a rude gesture	un geste obscène

Ø **rude** means "rough", "harsh."

rudely *adv*
[*impolitely*] impoliment/insolemment/ grossièrement

Ø **rudement** can mean "harshly," but is most often used like the colloquial English "awfully" or "terribly": e.g., **rudement difficile, rudement bon.**

ruin *v*
to ruin one's health/hopes/reputation — ruiner sa santé/ses espoirs/sa réputation

to spoil an event — gâter
He ruined our evening. — Il a gâté notre soirée.

to spoil an object — abîmer/esquinter
My shoes are ruined. — Mes chaussures sont complètement abîmées.

run *v*
[*of a person*] — courir
[*of a machine*] — marcher
[*of a vehicle*] — rouler
The car runs well. — La voiture roule bien.
The engine is running. — Le moteur est en marche.
The bus runs every half-hour. — L'autobus passe toutes les demi-heures.
Do the trains run on Sundays? — Est-ce que les trains sont en service le dimanche?

to run a business — tenir un commerce
to run out of sth — ne plus avoir de qqch
We've run out (of it). — Nous n'en avons plus.

≡ S ≡

's/s'
[*possessive*]
John's address
the workers' union
Your father is younger than Robert's.

The boys' hair is longer than the girls'.

[*Note: Possession is expressed by **de**.*]
l'adresse de Jean
le syndicat des ouvriers
Ton père est plus jeune que celui de Robert.

Les cheveux des garçons sont plus longs que ceux des filles.

safe *adj*
not in danger
We will be safe here.
to arrive safely
They arrived home safely.
Have a safe journey!
safe and sound

en sécurité/hors de danger
Ici nous serons en sécurité.
bien arriver
Ils sont bien arrivés.
Bon voyage!
saine et sauf (saine et sauve)

not dangerous
a safe place/part of town
Is it safe?
This toy is safe for infants.

He is a safe driver.

sans danger/sûr(e)
un endroit sûr/un quartier sûr
Il n'y a pas de danger?
Ce jouet ne présente aucun danger pour les tout petits.
C'est un conducteur prudent.

sale *n*
for sale
car for sale
for sale in all the stores
on sale [*a special*]
on sale [*a markdown*]
There are sales in all the stores in January.

à vendre/en vente
voiture à vendre
en vente dans tous les magasins
en promotion/en réclame
en solde
Il y a des soldes dans tous les magasins en janvier.

same *adj & pron*
at the same time
all the same
It's all the same to me.
I'll have the same as yesterday.
He is just the same (as ever).
The same to you!

en même temps
quand même/tout de même
Ça m'est égal.
Je prendrai la même chose qu'hier.
Il n'a pas changé.
A vous de même!/A vous aussi!

save *v*
from death, destruction
You saved my life!
They were able to save a wing of the building.

sauver
Tu m'as sauvé la vie!
On a pu sauver une aile du bâtiment.

from a danger
to save sb from an enemy

protéger
protéger qqn contre un ennemi

to store
Let's save some bread for tonight.

garder/mettre de côté
On va garder du pain pour ce soir.

money

You should save your money.
I am saving up for a new car.

économiser/faire des économies/mettre de côté
Tu devrais économiser ton argent.
Je fais des économies pour m'acheter une nouvelle voiture.

[*in a bank*]
a savings account

épargner
un compte d'épargne

time
You will save time by taking the bus.

The Yellow Pages save you time.

gagner/faire gagner
Vous gagnerez du temps en prenant le bus.
Les pages jaunes vous font gagner du temps.

say *v*
to say sth
How do you say "butterfly" in French?
to say that...
They say (that) they're hungry.

dire qqch
Comment dit-on «butterfly» en français?
dire que...
Ils disent qu'ils ont faim. [*Note:* **que** *may not be omitted.*]

scary *adj*
a scary movie
It's scary.

un film d'épouvante
Ça fait peur.

schedule *n*
[*in general*]

I have a heavy schedule.
to make out a schedule

un horaire/un programme/un emploi du temps
J'ai un emploi du temps chargé.
établir un horaire/un programme

transportation
a train/plane schedule
The train is on schedule.

un horaire
Le train est à l'heure.

The train is ahead of schedule/behind schedule.

Le train a de l'avance/du retard.

schedule v
to schedule a meeting
You are scheduled to leave on Tuesday.
the scheduled date

organiser une réunion
Votre départ est fixé pour mardi.
la date prévue

school n
primary school
secondary school
to go to school

l'école primaire
l'école secondaire/le lycée
aller à l'école

college or university

l'université/la fac [Note: short for **faculté**]

to go to school
Is she working? — No, she's going to school.
Where do you want to go to school?
to finish school

faire des études
Elle travaille? — Non, elle est à l'université.
A quelle université veux-tu aller?
finir ses études

scientist n
a scientist

un(e) scientifique/un chercheur

Ø **scientiste** [m & f] is a believer in Christian Science.

seat n
to reserve a seat [for a performance]
There are no more seats.
Is this seat taken?
Have a seat!

réserver une place
Il n'y a plus de places.
Cette place est occupée?
Asseyez-vous donc!

second adj
[second of many]
[second of two]
every second Monday
second-hand
a second-hand car

deuxième
second(e)
un lundi sur deux
d'occasion
une voiture d'occasion

seed n
[in general]
to sow seeds
an apple/grape seed

la graine
semer des graines
un pépin de pomme/de raisin

seem v
to appear

She seems honest.

You don't seem to understand.

It seems easy.

I can't seem to open this can.

avoir l'air/sembler/paraître

Elle a l'air honnête.

Vous n'avez pas l'air de comprendre.

Ça paraît facile.

Je n'arrive pas à ouvrir cette boîte.

impersonal

It seems that. . .

It seems to me that. . .

Il paraît que [+*indicative*]

Il semble que [+*subjunctive*]

Il me semble que [+*indicative*]

self *pron*
in a reflexive verb

myself/yourself/himself/herself /
  ourselves/yourselves/themselves/
  oneself

me/te/se/nous/vous/se

to see oneself

I can see myself in the mirror.

He cut himself shaving.

se voir

Je me vois dans la glace.

Il s'est coupé en se rasant.

in an imperative

Help yourself!

Don't hurt yourself!

Sers-toi!/Servez-vous!

Ne te fais pas mal!

emphatic

moi-même/toi-même/lui-même/
  elle-même/nous-mêmes/
  vous-même(s)/eux-mêmes/
  elles-mêmes/soi-même

She said so herself.

One must do it oneself.

Elle l'a dit elle-même.

Il faut le faire soi-même.

(all) by oneself

by myself/yourself

He did it (all) by himself.

tout(e) seul(e)

Il l'a fait tout seul.

self-service *n*

It's a self-service store.

C'est un libre-service.

senior *adj & n*

a senior in high school

a senior in university

senior year

un(e) élève de dernière année

un(e) étudiant(e) de dernière année

la dernière année d'études

senior citizens	les personnes âgées, les gens du troisième âge, les retraité(e)s
a senior citizen	un(e) retraité(e)

sense *n*

the five senses	les cinq sens
the sense of hearing/of smell/of sight/of taste/of touch	l'ouïe/l'odorat/la vue/le goût/le toucher
common sense	le bon sens
sense of humour	le sens de l'humour
You have a good sense of direction.	Vous avez le sens de l'orientation.
This doesn't make sense.	Ça n'a aucun sens.
	Ça ne tient pas debout.
	Ce n'est pas logique.
That makes sense.	C'est logique.
What's the sense (of doing that)?	A quoi bon (faire cela?)

sensible *adj*

a sensible girl	une fille raisonnable/sage
sensible advice	des conseils raisonnables/sensés

Ø **sensible** means "sensitive."

sensitive *adj*

a sensitive child	un enfant sensible/émotif/impressionnable
sensitive to the cold	sensible au froid
[*easily offended*]	susceptible
You are too sensitive.	Tu es trop susceptible.

Ø **sensitif** (-ive) is currently used only in physiology.

sentence *n*

[*in grammar*]	une phrase

Ø **sentence** [*f*] means "verdict."

serious *adj*

serious	sérieux(-euse)/grave
a serious tone of voice	un ton de voix sérieux
to take a serious interest in sth	s'intéresser sérieusement à qqch
I'm serious! [*not joking*]	Je ne plaisante pas.

servant

a serious illness

Je parle sérieusement.
une maladie grave

servant *n*
[*in general*]
[*female maid*]
[*male servant*]

un/une domestique
une bonne/une servante
un serviteur

several *adj & pron*
several
Several customers are waiting.
several of them/of us

plusieurs
Plusieurs clients attendent.
plusieurs d'entre eux/d'entre elles/
    d'entre nous

sew *v*
to sew
She likes to sew.
I have to sew this hem.
She sews her dresses herself.

coudre/faire de la couture
Elle aime la couture.
Je dois coudre cet ourlet.
Elle fait ses robes elle-même.

share *n*
a share
Give him his share.
shares in a corporation

une part
Donne-lui sa part.
des actions [*f pl*]

share *v*
to share a piece of fruit
to share someone's joy
I have sth to "share" with you.

partager un fruit
prendre part à la joie de qqn
J'ai qqch à vous raconter.

she *pron*
she
Is she French?
She's the one who will do it.

elle
Est-ce qu'elle est française?
C'est elle qui le fera.

shoot *v*
to shoot at sb or sth
"Shoot the Piano Player" [*title of film by Truffaut*]
A man has been shot [*wounded*].
A man has been shot [*killed*].
He was shot [*executed by a firing squad*].
to shoot a film

tirer sur qqn ou qqch
«Tirez sur le pianiste.»
Un homme a été atteint d'une balle.
Un homme a été abattu.
Il a été fusillé.
tourner un film

shop *n*
a store
a workshop

une boutique/un magasin
un atelier

shopping *n & v*
to go shopping
to go grocery shopping

I'll put the shopping away.

faire des achats/des courses
faire les courses/acheter des
   provisions/faire le marché
Je vais ranger les provisions.

short *adj*
short
a short break
a short story
a short man

court(e)/bref (brève)
une courte interruption
une nouvelle
un petit homme [*Note:* **court** *is not used*
   of people.]

should *v*

We should leave today.

We should have left yesterday.

You shouldn't do that.
You shouldn't have said that.

[**devoir** *or* **falloir** *in the conditional*]
On devrait partir aujourd'hui.
Il faudrait partir aujourd'hui.
Il faudrait qu'on parte aujourd'hui.
On aurait dû partir hier.
Il aurait fallu partir hier.
Il aurait fallu qu'on parte hier.
Vous ne devriez pas faire ça.
Vous n'auriez pas dû dire ça.

show *n*
a show
the two o'clock show [*theater*]
the two o'clock show [*movie*]
TV show

un spectacle
la représentation de 2 heures
la séance de 2 heures
une émission

show *v*
to show sb sth

He showed it to her.
Show me!

montrer qqch à qqn/faire voir qqch à
   qqn
Il le lui a fait voir.
Fais voir!

sick *adj*
ill
to get/be sick
I feel sick.

tomber/être malade
Je ne me sens pas bien.

side

to be sick to one's stomach	avoir mal au coeur/avoir la nausée
to be seasick/airsick/homesick	avoir le mal de mer/le mal de l'air/le mal du pays

disgusted — dégoûté(e)/écœuré(e)

That makes me sick! — Ça me rend malade.

Ça me dégoûte.

tired

I am sick of waiting. — J'en ai marre d'attendre.

side n

a side	un côté
on the other side (of)	de l'autre côté (de)
on both sides	des deux côtés
by the side of the lake/the road	au bord du lac/de la route

sign n
an indication — un signe

It's a good/bad sign. — C'est bon/mauvais signe.

There are no signs of life. — Il n'y a aucun signe de vie.

with the hand — un signe/un geste

to make a sign — faire signe/faire un geste

to make a sign to sb to do sth. — faire signe à qqn de faire qqch

printed, official sign

[*small*] — un écriteau

[*large*] — une pancarte

a road sign — un panneau indicateur/un panneau de signalisation

significant adj
sizeable — considérable/important(e)

a significant amount — une quantité considérable

important — important(e)/significatif(-ive)

a significant event — un événement important

silence n/silent adj
silent [*person, place*] — silencieux(-euse)

Silence, please! — Silence, s'il vous plaît!

to be silent [*not to talk*] — se taire/garder le silence

a silent movie — un film muet

198

since   *conj & prep*
time

She's been living in Rouen since August.

No one has phoned since I've been here.

depuis [+*noun*]
depuis que [+*verb*]
Elle habite à Rouen depuis le mois d'août. [*Note: present tense.*]
Personne n'a téléphoné depuis que je suis là. [*Note: present tense*]

reason
Since he had lost his pen, I lent him mine.

puisque
Puisqu'il avait perdu son stylo, je lui ai prêté le mien.

sincerely   [*see **yours sincerely***]

single   *adj*
She is single [*unmarried*].
a single mother
a single room

He hasn't a single friend.

Elle est célibataire.
une mère célibataire
une chambre particulière/une chambre à un lit/une chambre pour une personne
Il n'a pas un seul ami.

sit/sitting   *v*
to sit down
Please sit down!
Everyone sat down.

s'asseoir
Asseyez-vous donc!
Tout le monde s'est assis.

to be seated
She was sitting in front of me.

être assis
Elle était assise devant moi.

size   *n*
clothes
What size [*clothes*] do you wear?

I wear size 12 [*women*].
I wear size 38 [*men*].
We have all sizes.

la taille
Quelle est votre taille?/Quelle taille faites-vous?
Je fais du 42.
Je fais du 48.
Nous avons toutes les tailles.

shoes
What size [*shoes*] do you wear?

I wear size 8 [*women*].
I wear size 10 [*men*].

la pointure
Quelle est votre pointure?/Vous chaussez du combien?
Je chausse/je fais du 39.
Je chausse/je fais du 45.

building, car, etc.
What size is the table?

les dimensions
Quelles sont les dimensions de la table?

sleep v/asleep adj

to sleep/to be asleep	dormir
I slept well last night.	J'ai bien dormi cette nuit.
You can't see him now; he's asleep.	Vous ne pouvez pas le voir maintenant; il dort.
to fall asleep/to go to sleep	s'endormir

to spend the night — coucher

The children sleep in another room.	Les enfants couchent dans une autre chambre.
You can sleep at my place.	Tu peux coucher chez moi.

slip n

[half slip]	un jupon
[full slip]	un fond de robe

Ø slip [m] means "briefs" (for either men or women).

slow adj

slow	lent(e)
a slow waltz	une valse lente
a slow train	un train omnibus
He's a slow worker.	Il travaille lentement.
My watch is slow.	Ma montre retarde.

smart adj

elegant, fashionable — élégant(e)/chic [invar]

You're very smart today!	Tu es très élégant aujourd'hui.
a smart restaurant	un restaurant à la mode

intelligent — intelligent(e)

Her daughter is really smart.	Sa fille est très intelligente.
That's the smart thing to do.	C'est la chose intelligente à faire.

smell n

[in general]	l'odeur [f]
[pleasant fragrance]	le parfum
a bad smell	une mauvaise odeur
the sense of smell	l'odorat
He has no sense of smell.	Il n'a pas de nez.

smell v

to smell (sth)	sentir (qqch)
I smell something burning.	Je sens quelque chose qui brûle.

to smell good/bad
That smells good!

sentir bon/mauvais
Ça sent bon!

so *adv*
This is so difficult!
so much/so many
There is so much to do!
I think so.
I don't think so.
I hope so.
I told you so!

C'est si difficile!/C'est tellement difficile!
tant (de)
Il y a tant (de choses) à faire!
Oui, je pense.
Je ne crois pas.
Je l'espère (bien).
Je te l'avais bien dit!

so *conj*
[*as a result*]
I woke up late, so I didn't have time to
  eat breakfast.
so that
Come closer so that everyone can hear.

alors/par conséquent
Je me suis réveillé tard, alors je n'ai pas
  eu le temps de déjeuner.
afin que/pour que
Approchez-vous pour que tout le
  monde puisse entendre.

solid *adj*
solid food
solid gold/oak, etc.
on solid ground
a solid color

des aliments solides
de l'or massif/du chêne massif
sur la terre ferme
une couleur unie

some *adj*
a quantity

We have some bread and cheese.
Would you like some mustard?
some distance away
There are some magazines in the
  waiting room.

du/de la/de l'/quelque [*sing*]
des/quelques [*plural*]
Nous avons du pain et du fromage.
Voulez-vous de la moutarde?
à quelque distance
Il y a quelques revues dans la salle
  d'attente.

as opposed to others
Some people don't think that.

certain(e)s
Certaines personnes ne sont pas de
  cette opinion.

other expressions
Some day you'll understand.
He's coming home some time today/
  this week.
Some man wants to see you.
That was some cake!

Un jour tu comprendras.
Il rentre dans la journée/dans la
  semaine.
Un monsieur veut te voir.
Quel gâteau!

some

some *pron*
a quantity
There's no more milk; I'll buy some tomorrow.

en
Il n'y a plus de lait; j'en achèterai demain.

a few things, people
Do you have any stamps? I'll take some.

Some of the guests have already left.

quelques-uns/quelques-unes
Vous avez des timbres? Je vais en prendre quelques-uns.
Quelques-uns des invités sont déjà partis.

somebody/someone *pron*
somebody
Somebody wants to see you.
somebody else
I think someone knocked.

quelqu'un
Quelqu'un veut vous voir.
quelqu'un d'autre
Il me semble qu'on a frappé (à la porte).

somehow *adv*
[*one way or another*]
[*for some reason*]

d'une façon ou d'une autre
pour une raison ou pour une autre

someplace [*see somewhere*]

something *pron*
something
Is there something to eat?
something good

quelque chose
Il y a quelque chose à manger?
quelque chose de bon [*Note: When **quelque chose** is followed by an adjective, **de** must be inserted; the adjective is always masculine.*]

sometimes *adv*
sometimes
She is sometimes forgetful.

quelquefois/parfois/de temps en temps
Elle est distraite de temps en temps.

somewhere *adv*
somewhere
I left my umbrella somewhere.

quelque part
J'ai oublié mon parapluie quelque part.

soon *adv*
before long
We will be there soon.
See you soon!

bientôt/tout à l'heure
Nous serons bientôt arrivés.
A bientôt!/A tout à l'heure!

202

early   tôt
too soon   trop tôt
so soon   si tôt
sooner than we thought   plus tôt que nous n'avons pensé
sooner or later   tôt ou tard

as soon as   aussitôt que/dès que
We'll have dinner as soon as he arrives.   Nous dînerons aussitôt qu'il arrivera. [*Note: future tense*]

as soon as possible   le plus tôt possible/dès que possible

sorry   *adj*
(I'm) sorry! [*Excuse me*]   Oh, excusez-moi!/Pardon!
(I'm) sorry I'm late.   Je regrette d'être en retard.
    (Je suis) désolé(e) d'être en retard.
I'm sorry you aren't feeling well.   Je suis navré que vous ne vous sentiez pas bien. [*Note: subjunctive*]
I felt so sorry for him.   Il m'a fait beaucoup de peine.

sort   [*see* **kind**]

space
a space   un espace
Leave a space between the two chairs.   Laissez un espace entre les deux chaises.
outer space   l'espace/le cosmos
[*see also* **room**]

spare   *adj*
a spare tire   un pneu de rechange
in my spare time   à mes moments perdus

spare   *v*
to spare time, money
Can you spare a moment?   Tu as un moment?
I can't spare the time.   Je n'ai pas le temps.
Can you spare a dollar?   Tu peux me passer un dollar?

to do without
I can't spare the car today.

We can't spare him.

se passer de
Je ne peux pas me passer de la voiture
  aujourd'hui.
Nous ne pouvons pas nous passer de
  lui.

spell *v*/spelling *n*
a spelling mistake
he is good at spelling.
to spell (out)
How is that spelt?
How do you spell your name?
Can you spell it for me?

une faute d'orthographe
Il est bon en orthographe.
épeler
Comment (est-ce que) ça s'écrit?
Comment écrivez-vous votre nom?
Pouvez-vous me l'épeler?

spend *v*
money
I have spent all my money.

dépenser
J'ai dépensé tout mon argent.

time
to spend time doing sth
We spent half an hour exploring the
  beach.

passer
passer du temps à faire qqch
Nous avons passé une demi-heure à
  explorer la plage.

spoil [*see* **ruin**]

sports *n*
sports
to like sports
to play sports
to play a sport
winter sports

le sport [*Note: usually singular*]
aimer le sport/être sportif
faire du sport [*Note: not **jouer***]
pratiquer un sport [*Note: not **jouer***]
les sports d'hiver

stage *n*
[*in a theater*]
to be/to go on stage
at this stage
the first stage of the journey

la scène
être/entrer en scène
à ce stade
la première étape du voyage

Ø **stage** [*m*] means "an internship."

stair(s) *n*
[*a staircase*]
to go up/down the stairs
a moving stair

un escalier
monter/descendre l'escalier
un escalier roulant

stand v
to be standing
There is no more room; you will have
  to stand.

être/rester debout
Il n'y a plus de place; il faudra que
  vous restiez debout.

to stand up
Stand up when he enters.

se lever
Levez-vous quand il entrera.

indicating position
A man was standing by the window.

se tenir
Un homme se tenait près de la fenêtre.

to tolerate
I can't stand him.
I can't stand this any longer.

supporter/encadrer [fam]
Je ne peux pas l'encadrer.
Je ne peux plus supporter ça.

stay v
to remain
Stay there!
How many nights will you be staying?

rester
Reste là!
Combien de nuits voulez-vous rester?

to visit
I am going to stay at my friend's house
  for a week.
to stay overnight (with sb)

Je vais passer une semaine chez mon
  ami(e).
passer la nuit (chez qqn)

to live temporarily
Where are you staying?
I'm staying at my uncle's.

Où logez-vous à présent?
Je loge/Je suis chez mon oncle.

at a hotel
Where do you stay when you go to
  Paris?

descendre
Où descendez-vous quand vous allez à
  Paris?

other expressions
to stay up
I stayed up until 3 a.m.

ne pas se coucher/rester debout
Je ne me suis pas couché avant 3
  heures.

to stay out late
to stay in all day

rentrer tard
ne pas sortir de la journée

step n
to take a step (forward)
to hear footsteps
Mind the step!
You have to go up three steps.

faire un pas (en avant)
entendre un bruit de pas
Attention à la marche!
Il faut monter trois marches.

relatives
stepbrother/stepsister

demi-frère/demi-sœur

205

stepdaughter/stepson/stepmother stepfather	belle-fille/beau-fils/ belle-mère/ beau-père [Note: **beau-/belle-** also can mean "in-law."]

still *adj*

Keep still!	Reste tranquille!
Sit/stand still!	Tiens-toi tranquille!

still *adv*

[*up to the present moment*]	encore/toujours
He is still in Europe.	Il est encore en Europe.
I still don't understand.	Je ne comprends toujours pas.

Encore also means "again." **J'ai encore mal aux dents** could mean "I still have a toothache" or "I have a toothache again." **Toujours** also means "always." **Elle est toujours chez sa mère** could mean "She is still at her mother's" or "She is always at her mother's."

stomach *n*

the stomach	l'estomac(m)/le ventre
a stomach ulcer	un ulcère à l'estomac
I have a stomachache.	J'ai mal au ventre.
to lie on one's stomach	s'allonger sur le ventre

The French make a clear distinction between **l'estomac** (the digestive organ) and **le ventre** (the belly or tummy).

stop *v*

to stop	arrêter
Stop the car!	Arrêtez la voiture!
to stop (doing sth)	cesser de [+*infinitive*]
	s'arrêter de [+*infinitive*]
The lecturer has stopped talking.	Le conférencier a cessé de parler.
My watch has stopped.	Ma montre s'est arrêtée.
to prevent	empêcher
They stopped me from coming in.	On m'a empêché d'entrer.

store *n*

a (department) store	un (grand) magasin
[*large*] variety or food store	une grande surface
[*see also* **market**]	

stove *n*
[*a heater*] une chaudière/un poêle
[*for cooking*] une cuisinière
an electric/gas stove une cuisinière électrique/à gaz

straight *adj*
straight droit(e)/raide
a straight nose un nez droit
a straight line une ligne droite
a straight skirt une jupe droite
straight hair les cheveux raides

straight *adv*
Go straight on/ahead. Allez tout droit.
The church is straight ahead. L'église est droit devant vous.

strange *adj*/**stranger** *n*
strange bizarre/étrange
a stranger un inconnu (une inconnue)

Ø **étranger(ère)** means "foreign" or "a foreigner."

street *n*
the main street la rue principale/la grand'rue
the man in the street l'homme de la rue

stress *n & v*
the stress of city life le stress de la vie urbaine
to be stressed out être stressé
stressful stressant
to stress the importance of sth souligner l'importance de qqch
to stress a syllable accentuer une syllabe

student *n*
[*in elementary or high school*] un(e) élève
[*in higher education*] un(e) étudiant(e)

study *v*
He is studying math. Il fait des études de maths.
He is studying for an exam. Il prépare un examen.
I have to study hard this weekend. Je dois travailler dur ce weekend.
  Je dois bosser [*fam*] ce weekend.

subject *n*
topic

on the subject of...	au sujet de.../à propos de...
to change the subject	changer de sujet

in school

	la matière
English is my favorite subject.	L'anglais est la matière que je préfère.

subscription *n*

to take out a subscription (to a magazine)	s'abonner (à une revue)/prendre un abonnement

succeed *v*

to succeed in life/in business	réussir dans la vie/dans les affaires
Did you succeed in convincing them?	As-tu réussi à les convaincre?
to succeed to the throne	succéder à la couronne

successful *adj*

to be successful	réussir
He is very successful.	Il a bien réussi.
a successful business	une entreprise prospère

such *adj & adv*
followed by a noun

	tel (telle)/pareil (-eille)
such a noise	un tel bruit
such waves	de telles vagues/des vagues pareilles

followed by an adjective

	si/tellement
such a small amount	une si petite quantité
such interesting ideas	des idées tellement originales

suddenly *adv*

[*all of a sudden*]	soudain/tout d'un coup [*Note:* **soudainement** *is less used.*]
Suddenly the rain stopped.	La pluie s'est arrêtée tout d'un coup.

sue *v*

to sue sb	poursuivre qqn en justice

suit *n*

a man's suit	un complet/un costume
a woman's suit	un tailleur/un ensemble
a legal suit	un procès
to bring a suit against someone	intenter un procès contre qqn

suit v

to suit sb	convenir à/aller à qqn
Does that day suit you?	Est-ce que ce jour vous va?
That suits me very well.	Cela me convient parfaitement.
That color suits her.	Cette couleur lui va bien.

suitable adj

suitable	qui convient/approprié
suitable clothing	les vêtements appropriés
That time is the the most suitable for me.	C'est l'heure qui me convient le mieux.
This program is not suitable for children.	Ce n'est pas une émission pour les enfants.

supply v

to supply sth	fournir qqch
The clerk supplied me with the information.	L'employé m'a fourni le renseignement.

Ø **supplier** means "to beg."

support v
to hold up

The roof is supported by a beam.	Le toit est supporté par une poutre.

to provide for financially

He supports his mother.	Il subvient aux besoins de sa mère. Il fait vivre sa mère.
His parents support him in school.	Ce sont ses parents qui paient ses études.

to be in favor of

to support (a cause)	soutenir/être en faveur de/être pour
to support a candidate	soutenir/appuyer un(e) candidat(e)
to support a team [sports]	être supporter d'une équipe

Ø **supporter** also means "to put up with," "to tolerate."

suppose v

to be supposed to	être censé [+infinitive]
He was supposed to give a speech.	Il était censé faire un discours./Il devait faire un discours.

surgery [see *operation*]

suspect *v*
to suspect sb of a crime — soupçonner qqn d'un crime
to suspect sth — se douter de qqch
I suspected as much! — Je m'en doutais!

suspicious *adj*
causing suspicion — louche/suspect(e)
a suspicious individual — un individu louche

feeling suspicion — méfiant(e)/soupçonneux(-euse)
She's very suspicious. — Elle est très méfiante.
I am suspicious of his motives. — Je soupçonne ses mobiles.

swear *v*/**swearword** *n*
[*to take an oath*] — prêter serment/jurer
[*to curse*] — jurer/blasphémer
a swearword — un juron

sweater *n*
a sweater — un tricot/un lainage/un chandail

sweet *adj*
naturally sweet-tasting — doux (douce)
sweet wine — du vin doux

sweetened — sucré
sweet tea — du thé sucré
something sweet — une sucrerie

good-natured — gentil(-ille), doux (douce)
She is very sweet. — Elle est très gentille.

swim *v*
to swim — nager
I learned to swim when I was eight. — J'ai appris à nager à l'âge de huit ans.
to swim [*as a sport*] — faire de la natation
to swim across a lake — traverser un lac à la nage

sympathetic *adj*
sympathetic — compatissant(e)/compréhensif(-ive)
to be sympathetic to sb — être compatissant envers qqn
She has a very sympathetic husband. — Elle a un mari très compréhensif.

Ø **sympathique** (often shortened to **sympa**) means "nice" or "likeable."

sympathize *v*

I sympathize [*feel sorry for*] you.	Je vous plains.
I sympathize with you in your grief.	Je compatis à votre douleur.
I can sympathize with [*understand*] your point of view.	Je comprends votre point de vue.

Ø **sympathiser (avec qqn)** means "to get on well (with somebody)."

sympathy *n*

to express sympathy (for a bereavement)	présenter ses condoléances
a sympathy card	une carte de condoléances

Ø **sympathie** means "a liking" (for somebody).

≡ T ≡

take *v*
in general

Take your time.	prendre
	Prenez votre temps.
Do you want this? — Yes, I'll take it.	Vous voulez ceci? —Oui, je le prends.
[*in a store*]	
to take the bus/the train	prendre l'autobus/le train

to take things somewhere — porter/emporter

to take clothes to the cleaners	porter des vêtements chez le teinturier
Take your books (with you).	Emporte tes livres.

to take people somewhere — emmener

to take the children to the movies	emmener les enfants au cinéma
Shall we take your brother along?	On emmène ton frère?

to take sth from sb — prendre qqch **à** qqn

I took her coat.	Je lui ai pris son manteau.

time taken

How long will it take you to do that?	Combien de temps vous faudra- t-il pour faire cela?
It took her five hours to do it.	Il lui a fallu cinq heures pour le faire.
	Elle a mis cinq heures à le faire.

other

to take a trip/a walk	faire un voyage/une promenade
to take a class	suivre un cours
to take an exam	passer un examen

Emporter and **emmener** mean "to take to another place"; **apporter** and **amener** [*see* ***bring***] mean "to bring to the place where you are."

take in *v*
a thing

We have to take/bring in the chairs.	Il faut rentrer les chaises.
They took/brought the car into the garage.	Ils ont rentré la voiture dans le garage.
to take in a garment	rétrécir un vêtement

a person — faire entrer

Take/show her into my office.	Faites-la entrer dans mon bureau.

take off *v*

to take off (a garment) — retirer/enlever (un vêtement)
Take off your clothes. — Déshabillez-vous.
to take a day off — prendre un jour de congé
The airplane takes off at ten. — L'avion décolle à dix heures.
When do we take off? — A quelle heure partons-nous?

take out *v*

to take the dog out — sortir le chien
to take the children out — sortir les enfants
Take your hands out of your pockets. — Retire tes mains de tes poches.
hot food to take out — des plats chauds à emporter

take up/down *v*

to take the wine down to the cellar — descendre le vin dans la cave
to take the luggage down to the lobby — descendre les bagages dans le hall
Take your friends up to your room. — Fais monter tes amis dans ta chambre.

tall   [*see* **big**]

tape *n & v*

Scotch tape — le scotch/le ruban adhésif
tape measure — un centimètre
tape player/recorder — un magnétophone
cassette tape — une cassette
to tape record — enregistrer sur bande/sur magnétophone

taste *v*
of person tasting — goûter
Do you want to taste this? — Tu veux goûter?
I'll let you taste this cheese. — Je te ferai goûter ce fromage.
wine tasting — la dégustation des vins

of thing being tasted — avoir un goût
This tastes funny. — Ça a un drôle de goût.
This tastes good! — C'est bon! Ça a bon goût!

teach *v*
to teach sb sth — apprendre qqch à qqn
to teach the students the alphabet — apprendre l'alphabet aux élèves
to teach the dog to beg — apprendre au chien à faire le beau

to teach, as a profession — enseigner
He teaches Greek and Hebrew at the high school. — Il enseigne le grec et l'hébreu au lycée.

teacher

teacher *n*
[*in general*]   un enseignant/une enseignante
[*in high school or university*]   un professeur
[*in primary school*]   un instituteur/une institutrice/un
                                                    maître/une maîtresse

telephone   [*see phone*]

television *n*
to watch television   regarder la télévision
to see sth on television   voir qqch à la télévision
TV [*fam*]   la télé/le petit écran [*fam*]
TV set   un téléviseur/un poste (de télévision)
TV screen   l'écran [*m*]
TV program   une émission
TV program listings   le programme
TV channel   la chaîne
TV remote control   la télécommande/le zappeur [*fam*]
to turn on [*the TV*]   allumer/ouvrir
to turn off [*the TV*]   éteindre/fermer

tell *v*
Tell me what to do.   Dis-moi ce que je dois faire.
Don't tell her I'm here.   Ne lui dites pas que je suis là.
to tell the truth   dire la vérité
to tell someone a story   raconter une histoire à quelqu'un
I told them about my vacation.   Je leur ai parlé de mes vacances.
                                   Je leur ai raconté mes vacances.

tend *v*
to tend to   avoir tendance à
He tends to eat too much.   Il a tendance à trop manger.

test *n*
in school   une interrogation (écrite/orale)
a (written/oral) test/quiz   une épreuve/un contrôle

medical   une analyse
I had some blood tests done at the   Je me suis fait faire des analyses de
  clinic.   sang à la clinique.
[*see also exam*]

214

than *conj*
[*in comparisons*]
She runs faster than you.
Better late than never!

que
Elle court plus vite que toi.
Mieux vaut tard que jamais!

thank *v*
to thank sb for sth
She thanked me for coming.
Thank you.
Thank you very much.
Thanks to them, I was able to finish.
More coffee? — No thanks.

remercier qqn de/pour qqch
Elle m'a remercié d'être venu.
Merci./Je vous remercie.
Merci beaucoup./Merci bien.
Grâce à eux, j'ai pu terminer.
Un peu plus de café? — Merci. [*Note:*
merci *can mean "thanks" or "no
thanks," depending on the context or
tone of voice.*]

that *conj*
[*introducing a noun clause*]
We hope (that) you will stay.
She knows (that) they've already
   arrived.
I think you know her.

que
Nous espérons que vous resterez.
Elle sait qu'ils sont déjà arrivés.

Je crois que tu la connais.

In English the conjunction "that" is often omitted, but in French **que** may not be
omitted.

that [*dem pron & adj: see* **this**]

that *rel pron*

qui [subj]
que [obj]
dont [*Note: used if verb takes* **de**]

the pen that's in the drawer
the magazine (that) I was reading
the people (that) we know
the students that are taking the exam
   today
the notebooks (that) she needs

the person (that) I was talking about

le stylo qui est dans le tiroir
la revue que je lisais
les gens que nous connaissons
les étudiants qui passent l'examen
   aujourd'hui
les cahiers dont elle a besoin [*Note:
Verb takes* **de**.]
la personne dont je parlais [*Note: Verb
takes* **de**.]

In English the pronoun "that" is often omitted, but in French **qui, que,** and **dont**
may not be omitted.

the one/the ones/those *dem pron*

celui qui	ceux qui [*subj*]
celle qui	celles qui
celui que	ceux que [*obj*]
celle que	celles que

The one (that is) on the desk is mine.	Celui qui est sur le bureau est à moi.
Take the ones (that) you like best.	Prenez celles que vous aimez le mieux.
all those who are present	tous ceux qui sont présents

followed by "of"

	celui dont
the one of which I was speaking	celui dont je parlais
the ones (that) he's afraid of	ceux dont il a peur

with other prepositions

the one on which/with which/in which	celui sur lequel/avec lequel/ dans lequel
What chair? — The one you're sitting on.	Quelle chaise? — Celle sur laquelle tu es assis.

their *adj*

[*possessive*]

	leur/leurs
They've sold their house.	Ils ont vendu leur maison.
I know their parents.	Je connais leurs parents.

theirs *pron*

[*possessive*]

	le leur/la leur/les leurs
Theirs is bigger than mine.	La leur est plus grande que la mienne.

them *pron*

	les [*dir obj*]
	leur [*indir obj*]
	eux/elles [*disj*]
I didn't see them.	Je ne les ai pas vus.
He often phones them.	Il leur téléphone souvent.
We are leaving with them.	Nous partons avec eux/elles.

themselves [*see* **self**]

then *adv*

next

	puis/ensuite
I came home, then I cooked dinner.	Je suis rentré, puis j'ai préparé le dîner.

at that time

	à ce moment-là/à cette époque-là

At that time we were living in Spain.	A ce moment-là nous habitions en Espagne.

consequently
Do you know him? Then you can introduce us.

alors
Tu le connais? Alors tu peux nous présenter.

there *adv*

Have you ever been to France? — Yes, I've been there twice.
Put it over there.
Is your brother there? — No, he's not here.
there is/there are
There aren't any towels.
There's the Eiffel Tower!

Etes-vous déjà allé en France? — Oui, j'**y** suis allé deux fois.
Mets-le **là-bas**.
Est-ce que ton frère est **là**? — Non, il n'est pas **là**.
il y a
Il n'y a pas de serviettes.
Voilà la tour Eiffel!

these   [*see* **this** & **this one**]

they   *pron*

ils/elles [*subj*]
eux/elles [*emph*]
on [*impersonal*]

Your books? — They're on the shelf.
I don't know, but they know.
[*people, one*]
That's what they say.

Vos livres? — Ils sont sur le rayon.
Moi, je ne sais pas, mais eux le savent.
on
C'est ce qu'on dit.

thing   *n*
in general
something
There are things you don't know.

une chose
quelque chose
Il y a des choses que tu ne sais pas.

an object
She has some lovely things in her apartment.

un objet
Elle a de beaux objets dans son appartement.

belongings
Where did she put my things?

les affaires
Où a-t-elle mis mes affaires?

a thingamajig, whatsit
First you have to press the thingamajig.

un truc/un machin/un bidule
Il faut d'abord appuyer sur le truc.

other
I haven't a thing to wear.
That's not my thing.

Je n'ai rien à me mettre.
Ce n'est pas mon rayon.

think

think v
turn one's thoughts toward
What are you thinking of?
He never thinks of his friends; he only thinks of himself.

penser **à** qqn/qqch
A quoi penses-tu?
Il ne pense jamais **à** ses amis; il ne pense qu'**à** lui-même.

opinion
What do you think of that?

I thought that was stupid.
What did you think of the play?

Qu'est-ce que tu penses **de** cela?
Qu'**en** penses-tu?
J'ai trouvé ça stupide.
Comment avez-vous trouvé la pièce?

believe
I think he's right.

penser/croire
Je crois qu'il a raison.

third adj
the third house on the left
We ate a third of the pie.
a third party
the third world

la troisième maison à gauche
Nous avons mangé un tiers de la tarte.
un tiers
le tiers-monde

this/that pron

ceci [*c' before* **est**]
cela [*c' before* **est**]
ça [*fam*]

Drink this; don't drink that.
What's this/that?
This/that is the city hall.

Bois ceci; ne bois pas cela.
Qu'est-ce que c'est que ça?
C'est l'hôtel de ville.

this/that/these/those adj
this/that
these/those
I don't recommend this/that bakery.

They don't know these/those girls.
This hotel is less expensive than that one.

ce (cet)/cette
ces
Je ne recommande pas cette boulangerie.
Ils ne connaissent pas ces jeunes filles.
Cet hôtel-ci est moins cher que celui-là.

In French, a distinction is not normally made between "this" and "that," but **-ci** or **-là** may be added for emphasis or clarification.

this one/that one these/those pron
this one/these

celui-ci   ceux-ci
celle-ci   celles-ci

that one/those — celui-là ceux-là / celle-là celles-là

Which wine do you prefer? — This one is drier. — Quel vin préférez-vous? — Celui-ci est plus sec.

Our plums are riper than those. — Nos prunes sont plus mûres que celles-là.

those [see *the one*, *this* & *this one*]

thousand *n*
a thousand/one thousand — mille [*Note: no article*]
five thousand — cinq mille [*Note: no "s"*]

thousands *n*
thousands of people — des milliers de gens

through *prep*
to go through the park — traverser le parc
She got her job through her uncle. — Elle a eu son poste par l'intermédiaire de son oncle.

through the tenth of May — jusqu'au dix mai
all through the night — (pendant) toute la nuit
through a tunnel — sous un tunnel
through the window — par la fenêtre
through my own fault — par ma faute
Are you through? — Tu as fini?

throughout *prep*
place — partout dans
throughout the country — partout dans le pays

time — durant/pendant
throughout the evening — pendant toute la soirée
throughout his life — durant toute sa vie

ticket *n*
[*bus, Metro*] — un ticket
[*air, train, show, game*] — un billet
a one-way ticket — un (billet) aller
a round-trip ticket — un (billet) aller-retour

traffic violation — un P.-V. (procès-verbal)/une contravention

I got a (parking) ticket. — J'ai attrapé une contravention (pour stationnement interdit).

tidy

tidy *adj*
[*of a person's habits*]   ordonné(e)
[*of a person's appearance*]   soigné(e)
[*of a place, room, desk*]   bien rangé(e)/en ordre

tidy *v*
to tidy   mettre de l'ordre dans/ranger
Tidy your room.   Range ta chambre.
You should tidy your things.   Tu devrais mettre de l'ordre dans tes affaires.

till [*see* **until**]

time *n*
in general   le temps
How time flies!   Comme le temps passe vite!
Do you have time to go to the bank?   Avez-vous le temps de passer à la banque?
We don't have much time left.   Il ne nous reste pas beaucoup de temps.
part-time/full-time   à plein temps/à temps partiel
Can you finish in time?   Tu peux finir à temps?

clock time   l'heure [*f*]
What time is it?   Quelle heure est-il?
to be on time   être à l'heure
daylight saving time   l'heure d'été

occasion   la fois
I've been to that country three times.   Je suis allée trois fois dans ce pays.
How many times?   Combien de fois?
the first/last time   la première/dernière fois
several times   plusieurs fois
many times   souvent
sometimes   quelquefois/de temps en temps

historic period   l'époque [*f*]
at the time of Napoleon   au temps de/à l'époque de Napoléon
At that time there were no cars.   A cette époque-là il n'y avait pas de voitures.

point in time   le moment
at the present time   en ce moment
At that time there was no one on duty.   A ce moment-là il n'y avait personne de service.

simultaneously
She was laughing and crying at the same time.
They arrived at the same time as you.

en même temps/à la fois
Elle riait et pleurait à la fois.

Ils sont arrivés en même temps que toi.

to have a good time
We had a good time.
Have a good time!

s'amuser
Nous nous sommes bien amusés.
Amuse-toi bien!/Amusez-vous bien!

tip *n*
a gratuity
to give/leave a tip
Is the tip included?

un pourboire
donner/laisser un pourboire
Est-ce que le service est compris?

a recommendation, a lead
He gave me a few tips on boarding houses.

un tuyau
Il m'a donné quelques tuyaux sur les pensions.

tired *adj*
to be tired
to get tired
to be tired of [*fed up*]
I'm tired of hearing you say that.

être fatigué(e)
se fatiguer
en avoir assez/en avoir marre [*fam*]
J'en ai marre de t'entendre répéter ça.

to *prep*
to go to a place
to go to the market/the butcher's (shop)
to go to the opera the races

aller **au** marché/**à la** boucherie

aller **à** l'opéra/**aux** courses

to go to somebody's home or place of work
to the butcher's

aller **chez** qqn

chez le boucher [*Note the difference between* **chez** *and* **à**: **chez** *le boucher (a person) but* **à** *la boucherie (a place).*]

to the doctor's/to the dressmaker's
to my house/John's house/my cousins' place

chez le médecin/**chez** la couturière
chez moi/**chez** Jean/**chez** mes cousins

geographic
to Paris
to France
to Canada
to the United States

à Paris [*a city*]
en France [*a feminine country*]
au Canada [*a masculine country*]
aux Etats-Unis [*plural*]

221

together

to+infinitive
To leave is to die a little.	Partir, c'est mourir un peu.
There's nothing to eat.	Il n'y a rien **à** manger.
That's hard to understand.	C'est difficile **à** comprendre.
It's hard to understand her explanation.	Il est difficile **de** comprendre son explication.

in order to
	pour
I wrote them to express my disappointment.	Je leur ai écrit **pour** exprimer ma déception.

other
to be kind/nice to sb	être bon (bonne) **pour** qqn/gentil(-ille) **pour** qqn
to bet ten to one	parier dix **contre** un
the train to Dieppe	le train **de** Dieppe/à destination de Dieppe
Is this the road to Strasbourg?	C'est bien la route **de** Strasbourg?

together *adv*
They wrote it together.	Ils l'ont écrit ensemble.
Don't all answer together.	Ne répondez pas tous à la fois.
We should get together soon.	Il faut qu'on se revoie bientôt.
We get together on Mondays at the café.	Nous nous réunissons le lundi au café.
I'm planning a family get-together.	J'organise une réunion de famille.

toilet *n*
in a home
	les cabinets [*m pl*]/les waters [*m pl*]/le petit coin [*fam*]
Where is the bathroom/toilet?	Où sont les cabinets?

public
	les toilettes [*f pl*]/les W.C. [*Note: pronounced vé cé*]
women's/men's toilet	les toilettes de dames/de messieurs
Where is the toilet/bathroom/restroom?	Où sont les toilettes?

fixture
toilet bowl	la cuvette (de toilette)

"Toilet" is usually referred to in the plural in French. **Salle de bains** [*f*] is used only for a room with a bath. **Toilette** [*f*] is also used for dress, as in **vous avez une belle toilette**, or for washing, as in **elle fait sa toilette**.

too *adv*
too, too much
It's too expensive.
I ate too much.

trop
C'est trop cher.
J'ai trop mangé. [*Note: Do not add*
beaucoup.]

in addition, also
me too
She can sew and knit too.

aussi
moi aussi
Elle sait coudre et aussi tricoter.

top *n*
at the top of the page
from top to bottom
on top of the mountain

en haut de la page
de haut en bas
au sommet de la montagne

topic *n*/**topical** *adj*
a topic of conversation
an essay topic
a topical subject

un sujet de conversation
le sujet d'une dissertation
un sujet d'actualité

tour *n & v*
to take/make a tour
[*of a region, a country*]
[*of a building, city*]
to tour [*a place*]
I'll give you a tour of the campus.
a day tour
to tour the area
a (group) tour
a package/set price tour

faire un voyage
un voyage/un tour/un circuit
une visite
visiter
Je vous ferai visiter le campus.
une excursion
faire une excursion dans la région
un voyage organisé/accompagné
un forfait/un voyage à forfait

toward(s) *prep*
direction
towards the north/towards Calais

vers/en direction de
vers le nord/vers Calais

attitude
his feelings toward his father

envers/à l'égard de
ses sentiments envers son père

town *n*
They don't live in town; they live in the
country.
to be out of town
My home town is Marseilles.

to go downtown

Ils n'habitent pas en ville; ils habitent à
la campagne.
être en voyage/en déplacement
Je suis originaire de Marseille.
Je viens de Marseille.
aller en ville

traffic

downtown Chicago	le centre de Chicago
to downtown [*road sign*]	direction centre-ville

traffic *n*
rush hour traffic	la circulation des heures de pointe
The traffic is light/heavy.	Il y a peu/beaucoup de circulation.
traffic lights	les feux (de signalisation)

Ø **trafic** [*m*] usually refers to drug traffic.

train *v intrans*
to train (for)	s'entraîner (pour)
He's training for the race.	Il s'entraîne pour la course.

train *v trans*
to train a dog	dresser un chien
to train an athlete	entraîner un sportif
to train an employee	former un employé

Ø **traîner** means "to drag."

training *n*
[*sports*]	l'entraînement
[*background, education, experience*]	la formation

transcript *n*
a school transcript	un dossier scolaire/un relevé de notes

transfer *v*
university
to transfer to another university	aller dans une autre université

job
to be transferred to another office/ another town	être muté dans un autre bureau/une autre ville

transportation
to transfer [*plane, bus, train*]	changer d'avion/d'autobus/de train prendre une correspondance
Transfer to the Vincennes line.	Prenez la correspondance pour Vincennes.

translate *v*
to translate from English to French	traduire de l'anglais au français

Translate into French.

Traduisez en français.

transportation   *n*

[*in general*]
(public) transportation
means of transportation
Do you have transportation?

le transport
les transports (en commun)
les moyens de transport
Vous avez une voiture?
Comment faites-vous pour y aller?
On vous emmène en voiture?

Ø   **transportation** [*f*] is very little used.

trash   [*see **garbage***]

treat   *n & v*
I'll treat you to a drink.

It's my treat. [*I'm paying.*]
That will be a great treat for her.

Je t'offre un verre/un pot [*fam*].
Je te paie un verre.
C'est moi qui offre./Je t'invite.
Ça lui fera grand plaisir.

medical
to treat a patient
to be treated for

soigner un malade
se faire soigner pour

trip   *n*
to take a trip to London/Morocco/
   Europe
[*see also **tour***]

faire un voyage à Londres/au Maroc/en
   Europe

trouble   *n*
problem
to be in trouble
engine trouble
What's the trouble?
to have a lot of trouble with

un ennui/une difficulté
avoir des ennuis
des ennuis de moteur
Qu'est-ce qui ne va pas?
avoir de gros ennuis avec

effort
It's not worth the trouble.
to go to great trouble to do something

It's no trouble.

la peine/le mal
Ça ne vaut pas la peine.
se donner beaucoup de mal pour faire
   quelque chose
Ça ne me dérange pas.

tuition   *n*
tuition cost
Tuition is going up.

les frais de scolarité
Les frais de scolarité augmentent.

tuition fee
Have you paid your tuition?

les droits d'inscription
As-tu payé tes droits d'inscription?

turn *n*
a turn (in the road)
to make a left turn
to do someone a good turn
It's your turn (to play).
Whose turn is it?

un tournant
tourner à gauche
rendre service à quelqu'un
C'est à toi (de jouer).
A qui le tour?/C'est à qui?

turn on/off *v*
[*a light, stove, TV, etc.*]
to turn on
to turn off

allumer/ouvrir
éteindre/fermer

twice *adv*
I take aspirin twice a day.

Je prends des cachets d'aspirine deux
  fois par jour.

type *n*
in printing
printed in small/large type

les caractères [*m pl*]
imprimé en petits/gros caractères

the sort, kind
that type of person

le genre/l'espèce [*f*]
ce genre de personne/une personne de
  ce genre

Ø **un type** in colloquial French means "a guy."

type *v*
to type (on a typewriter)
to learn typing
a typist

taper (à la machine)
apprendre la dactylo
un(e) dactylo

typo *n*
[*typing error*]
[*printing error*]
[*spelling mistake*]

une faute de frappe/une coquille
une faute d'impression
une faute d'orthographe

U

u-turn *n*

to make a U-turn | faire demi-tour

un-

[*negative prefix*] | [*French has many different equivalents for this prefix.*]

unable | **in**capable
undressed | **dés**habillé(e)
uneatable | **im**mangeable
unessential | **non** essentiel(-elle)
unfriendly | **peu** aimable
unhappy | **mal**heureux(-euse)
unimportant | **sans** importance
unrecognized | **mé**connu(e)
uneducated | ignorant
unhurt | sain et sauf (saine et sauve)
unemployed | chômeur
unusual | insolite/exceptionnel(-elle)

uncomfortable *adj*
things
This chair is uncomfortable. | inconfortable/peu confortable
an uncomfortable situation | Cette chaise n'est pas confortable.
 | une situation pénible

people

 | [*Note:* **inconfortable** *is not used of people*]
to be uncomfortable [*position*] | être mal
I'm uncomfortable in this narrow bed. | Je suis mal dans ce lit étroit.
You look uncomfortable. | Vous n'avez pas l'air bien.
[*state of mind*] | être mal à l'aise/être gêné(e)
I am uncomfortable when he's around. | Je me sens mal à l'aise quand il est là.
[*see also* **comfortable**]

under *prep*
under | sous/au-dessous de
to go under a bridge | passer sous un pont
The key is under the doormat. | La clé est sous le paillasson.
to wear a T-shirt under a sweater | porter un T-shirt sous un pull
underwear | les sous-vêtements/les dessous

227

underneath

less than	moins de
to be under 21	avoir moins de 21 ans/être mineur(e)
children under 6	les enfants au-dessous de 6 ans
	les enfants de moins de 6 ans
to do sth in under twenty minutes	faire qqch en moins de vingt minutes
other expressions	
to work under sb	travailler sous les ordres/sous la direction de qqn
to be under the impression that	avoir l'impression que
under the circumstances	dans ces circonstances
under the law	selon la loi
under the terms of the contract	selon les termes du contrat
Everything is under control.	Tout est en ordre.

underneath *adv*

underneath — en dessous
Put this underneath. — Mets ça en dessous.

unfortunate *adj*
to be regretted

regrettable/fâcheux
an unfortunate occurrence — un incident regrettable

unlucky

malheureux
an unfortunate man — un individu malheureux
You have been most unfortunate. — Tu n'as vraiment pas eu de chance.

unfortunately *adv*

Unfortunately, we are unable to attend the reception. — Malheureusement, nous ne pourrons pas assister à la réception.

unit *n*

a unit of academic credit — une unité de valeur

university *n*

the university — l'université/la faculté/la fac [*fam*]
to study at a university — faire des études universitaires
a university town — une ville universitaire
a university professor — un professeur d'université

unless *conj*

unless — à moins que [+*subjunctive*]
— à moins de [+*infinitive*]

228

[*Note: The infinitive form is preferred when the subject of both verbs is the same.*]

I'll come by at 6 unless my bus is late.	Je passerai à 6 heures, à moins que mon bus ait du retard.
I'll come by tonight unless I am tired.	Je passerai ce soir, à moins d'être fatigué.

unlike *prep*

Unlike his father, he is lazy.	A la différence de son père, il est paresseux.
It's unlike him to be late.	Ça ne lui ressemble pas d'être en retard.

until *conj*

until	jusqu'à ce que [*+subjunctive*]
Let's stay here until the rain stops.	Restons ici jusqu'à ce que la pluie s'arrête.
I'll be here until I finish.	Je resterai jusqu'à ce que je termine.

after a verb in the negative

avant que [*+subjunctive*]
avant de [*+infinitive*]
[*Note: The infinitive form is preferred when the subject of both verbs is the same.*]

I won't know anything until I get his letter.	Je ne saurai rien avant de recevoir sa lettre.
We won't begin until you get here.	Nous ne commencerons pas avant que tu (n') arrives.

until *prep*

until	jusqu'à
Our guests stayed until Saturday.	Nos invités sont restés jusqu'à samedi.

after a negative

avant

We are not leaving until 3 o'clock.	Nous ne partirons pas avant 3 heures.

up *adv*

to go/come up	monter [*conjugated with* **être** *if there is no object; with* **avoir** *if there is an object*]
I went up.	Je suis monté.
I went up the steps.	J'ai monté les marches.
to take/bring sth up	monter qqch [*Note: conjugated with* **avoir**]

upset

I took my suitcase up to my room.	J'ai monté ma valise dans ma chambre.
to get up	se lever
It's up to you (to decide).	C'est à toi de décider.

upset *adj*
[*offended*]	vexé(e)/contrarié(e)
[*sad*]	triste/attristé(e)
She is upset about her son's divorce.	Le divorce de son fils lui fait de la peine.
	Elle est triste à cause du divorce de son fils.
She is very upset.	Elle est bouleversée.
to have an upset stomach	avoir mal à l'estomac

upstairs *adv*
upstairs	en haut
He works upstairs.	Il travaille en haut.

us *pron*
us	nous
She never speaks to us.	Elle ne nous parle pas.
Come with us.	Viens avec nous.
Call us tomorrow.	Appelez-nous demain.
Let's [*let us*] go/try/see.	Allons/essayons/voyons.

U.S. [United States] *n*
the U.S.	les E.-U. (Etats-Unis)

use *n*
to make use of sth	faire usage de qqch
What's the use?	A quoi ça sert?/A quoi bon?/Ça ne sert à rien.
It's no use crying.	Ça ne sert à rien de pleurer.
Can I be of any use?	Est-ce que je peux être utile?

use *v*
to use	utiliser/se servir de
He's learning to use these tools.	Il apprend à utiliser ces outils.
I used the computer to write my article.	Je me suis servi de l'ordinateur pour rédiger mon article.
What is this used for?	A quoi sert ceci?/A quoi est-ce que ça sert?
It's used for digging.	Ça sert à creuser.
I could use some coffee!	Je prendrais bien du café!

230

Ø **user** means "to wear out."

used *v*
[*to express a habit in the past*]

[*verb is in imperfect; adverb **autrefois** may be added.*]

When I was small I used to spend my vacation at my grandparents' house.

Quand j'étais petit je passais mes vacances chez mes grandparents.

The villagers used to speak in dialect.

Autrefois les habitants du village parlaient en dialecte.

used *adj*
accustomed

to get used to sth — s'habituer à qqch
I can't get used to it. — Je ne peux pas m'y habituer.
to be used to doing sth — être habitué(e) à faire qqch/avoir l'habitude de faire qqch

I'm not used to it. — Je n'y suis pas habitué./Je n'en ai pas l'habitude.

second-hand — d'occasion
a used car — une voiture d'occasion

Ø **usé(e)** means "worn" or "worn out."

usual *adj*
usual — habituel(-elle)
at the usual time — à l'heure habituelle
as usual — comme d'habitude

usually *adv*
usually — d'habitude/normalement/généralement
I am usually at home on Mondays. — Je suis normalement chez moi le lundi.

utility *n*
public utilities — les services publics
to pay the utilities — payer les charges

≡ V ≡

vacancy *n*
[*a job opening*]
[*in a hotel*]
We have no vacancies.
"No vacancies."

un poste vacant
une chambre libre
L'hôtel est complet./C'est complet.
"Complet."

vacation *n*
vacation
to take a vacation
to go on vacation
to spend the vacation in Europe
vacation plans
paid vacation
The French have five weeks of paid
  vacation.

les vacances [*Note: always plural*]
prendre des vacances
partir en vacances
passer les vacances en Europe
des projets de vacances
des congés payés
Les Français ont cinq semaines de
  congés payés.

valuable *adj*
a valuable object

un objet de valeur

Ø **valable** means "valid" or "worthwhile."

various *adj*
different
There are various ways to tackle the
  problem.

différent(e)s
Il y a différentes façons d'aborder le
  problème.

several
Various friends of mine have said the
  same thing.

plusieurs
Plusieurs de mes amis ont dit la même
  chose.

verse *n*
a verse (of a poem)
to write in verse

une strophe (d'un poème)
écrire en vers

Ø **vers** [*m*] also means "a single line of poetry."

very *adv*
very

très

232

very interesting	très intéressant(e)
very much/very many	beaucoup/énormément
I like it very much.	Je l'aime beaucoup. [*Note: Do not use* **très** *with* **beaucoup.**]
They have very many friends.	Ils ont énormément d'amis.

vest *n*
[*sleeveless jacket*]   un gilet

Ø **veste** [*f*] means "a jacket."

video *n & v*
a videotape	une bande vidéo
a videocassette	une cassette vidéo
a videorecorder (VCR)	un magnétoscope
to make a video recording	enregistrer sur bande vidéo/sur magnétoscope
a video camera	un camescope

visit *v*
to visit [*a place*]	visiter
You must visit the Louvre.	Il faut visiter le Louvre.
to visit [*a person*]	rendre visite à qqn/aller voir qqn
We visited her yesterday.	Nous sommes allés la voir hier.
I am going to visit my aunt for a few days.	Je vais passer quelques jours chez ma tante.

visitor [*see* **guest**]

vivid *adj*
a vivid blue	un bleu vif/éclatant
a vivid color	une couleur vive/éclatante
a vivid description	une description vivante
a vivid imagination	une imagination vive

volunteer *adj & v*
[*an unpaid worker*]	un(e) bénévole
to do volunteer work	faire du travail bénévole/travailler bénévolement
a volunteer army	une armée de volontaires
to volunteer to do sth	se proposer pour faire qqch
She volunteered to do the dishes.	Elle s'est proposée pour faire la vaisselle.

≡ W ≡

wait *v*

to wait for sb/sth

Wait for me!

We have been waiting for the bus for twenty minutes.

to wait tables [*in a restaurant*]

I can't wait [*I am unable to*]

I can't wait. [*I'm longing to*]

I can't wait to tell him about it.

I can't wait for vacation!

attendre qqn/qqch [*Note: no preposition*]

Attends-moi!

Nous attendons l'autobus depuis vingt minutes.

servir à table/faire le service

Je ne peux pas attendre plus longtemps.
Il m'est impossible d'attendre.

Je meurs d'envie/d'impatience.

Je meurs d'envie de lui en parler.

Vivement les vacances!

waiter/waitress *n*

a waiter

a waitress

un garçon/un serveur

une serveuse [*Note: not **servante***]

walk *n & v*

the action of walking

The baby has begun to walk.

It feels good to walk.

marcher

Le bébé a commencé à marcher.

Ça fait du bien de marcher.

to go for a walk

to go for a short walk/a long walk

to walk the dog

se promener/faire une promenade

faire un tour/une randonnée

promener le chien

as opposed to driving

He walks to his office.

Shall we walk or take the car?

aller à pied

Il va au bureau à pied.

On y va à pied ou en voiture?

simple change of location

He walked over to the door.

Il est allé à la porte.

warm *adj*

weather, temperature

It's warm today.

It's nice and warm in here.

Il **fait** chaud aujourd'hui.

Il **fait** bon ici.

a thing

The coffee is not warm enough.

Le café n'**est** pas assez chaud.

Le café **est** tiède.

a person
I'm too warm.   J'**ai** trop chaud.
My coat keeps me warm.   Mon manteau me tient chaud.
warm-hearted   chaleureux(-euse)
a warm welcome   un accueil chaleureux

warmly   *adv*
to dress warmly   s'habiller chaudement
to greet sb warmly   acceuillir qqn chaleureusement

wash   *v*
to wash [*oneself*]   se laver
Wash your hands!   Lave-toi les mains!
to wash dishes   faire la vaisselle
to wash clothes   faire la lessive/laver le linge
to bring in/fold the wash   rentrer/plier le linge
a washing machine   une machine à laver
a dishwasher   un lave-vaisselle

waste   *n & v*
to waste money/food/energy   gaspiller de l'argent/de la nourriture/de l'énergie
to waste one's time   perdre son temps
She wasted three hours typing that.   Elle a perdu trois heures à taper cela.
It's a waste of time.   C'est une perte de temps.

watch   *v*
to watch television/a sporting event/a show   regarder la télévision/une épreuve sportive/un spectacle
[*to look after*]   surveiller/garder
Can you watch the children for a while?   Peux-tu garder les enfants pendant un moment?
Watch out!   (Faites) attention!
Watch your step.   Attention à la marche.

way   *n*
manner
the way to do sth   la façon/la manière de faire qqch
to do sth the right/wrong way   bien faire/mal faire qqch
That's not the way to do it!   Ce n'est pas comme ça qu'il faut faire!
the American way of life   le mode de vie des Américains

route, path, road
to ask/show the way to...   demander/indiquer le chemin de...

Could you tell me the way to the Arc de Triomphe?	Pour aller à l'Arc de Triomphe, s'il vous plaît?
Is this the way to the station?	C'est bien le chemin de la gare?
to go the wrong way	se tromper de chemin/de route
I saw it on my way here.	Je l'ai vu en venant ici.
Which way did you come?	Par où êtes-vous passé?
This way, ladies and gentlemen.	Par ici, messieurs-dames.
a one-way street	une rue à sens unique

distance

It's a long way (from here).	C'est loin (d'ici.)
It's way over there.	C'est très loin là-bas.

other expressions

By the way...	A propos...
There's no way to get in.	Il n'y a pas moyen d'entrer.
You are in my way.	Vous m' empêchez de passer./Vous me gênez.
The work is under way.	Le travail est en cours.
No way!	Pas question!

we *pron*

we	nous
we Americans	nous autres Américains

wealthy *adj*

His family is very wealthy.	Sa famille est très riche./Sa famille a de la fortune.

weather *n*

What's the weather like?	Quel temps fait-il?
The weather is hot/cold.	Il fait chaud/froid.
We've had good weather.	Il a fait beau.
the weather report [*on TV, radio*]	la météo/le bulletin météorologique

wedding *n*

the wedding	le mariage/les noces [*f pl*]
to go to a wedding	assister à un mariage
to be in a wedding [*as bridesmaid or best man*]	être demoiselle d'honneur/garçon d'honneur
to have a church/civil wedding	se marier à l'église/à la mairie avoir un mariage religieux/civil
on their wedding day	le jour de leur mariage
a wedding dress	une robe de mariée
a wedding ring	une alliance
silver/golden wedding (anniversary)	les noces d'argent/d'or

week   *n*

a week	une semaine/huit jours
Come back in a week.	Revenez dans huit jours.
two weeks	quinze jours/deux semaines
three weeks	trois semaines

weigh   *v*/weight   *n*

to weigh	peser
How much do you weigh?	Combien pèses-tu?
I weigh 140 lbs.	Je pèse/Je fais 64 kilos.
to lose weight	perdre du poids/maigrir
to gain weight	gagner du poids/grossir
He has lost/gained a lot of weight.	Il a beaucoup maigri/grossi.

welcome   *adj*
in response to "thank you"

You're welcome.

Je vous en prie./Il n'y a pas de quoi./ De rien. [*Note: Europeans do not feel the need for an automatic response to "thank you."*]

to make sb welcome

You are welcome here.	Vous êtes le/la bienvenu(e)/les bienvenu(e)s.
Welcome to our home.	Soyez le bienvenu chez nous.

giving permission

You are welcome to stay as long as you want to.	Vous pouvez rester aussi longtemps que vous voudrez.
You are welcome to use my room.	Ma chambre est à votre disposition.

welcome   *n & v*

to welcome sb	accueillir qqn/souhaiter la bienvenue à qqn/faire bon accueil à qqn
They gave us a warm welcome.	Ils nous ont accueillis chaleureusement.
Welcome to our town. [*official sign*]	Bienvenue à notre ville.

well   *adv*
successfully, satisfactorily

You dance well.	bien Tu danses bien.
He did well on his exam.	Il a bien réussi à son examen.
Well done!	Bravo!

of health

to feel well

se sentir bien

what

Are you well?	Ça va?/Vous allez bien?
I'm very well, thank you.	(Je vais) très bien, merci.
	Ça va bien, merci.
	Je suis en (pleine) forme.
to get well	se remettre
Get well soon!	Remets-toi vite!
to look well	avoir bonne mine

what *inter adj*

	quel quels
	quelle quelles
What time is it?	Quelle heure est-il?
What news?	Quelles nouvelles?
What size are you?	Quelle taille faites-vous?
[*see also* **which**]	

what *exclam*

What a...!	Quel/Quelle...!
What a good idea!	Quelle bonne idée!
What a fool!	Quel idiot!
What a nuisance!	Quelle plaie! [*fam*]
What!	Quoi!/Comment!
What! Six o'clock already!	Comment! Déjà six heures!

what *inter pron*
in a direct question

	Qu'est-ce qui...? [*subj*]
	Qu'est-ce que/Que...? [*obj*]
	quoi [*after a preposition*]
What happened?	Qu'est-ce qui s'est passé?
What are you doing?	Qu'est-ce que vous faites?
	Que faites-vous? [*literary style*]
What did he say?	Qu'est-ce qu'il a dit?
What are you writing with?	Avec quoi écris-tu?
What are you thinking about?	A quoi penses-tu?
What is he afraid of?	De quoi a-t-il peur?

What is/are...?

	Quel/quelle est...?
	Quels/quelles sont...?
What is your phone number?	Quel est votre numéro de téléphone?
What is your favorite tune?	Quel est ton air préféré?
What are your initials?	Quelles sont vos initiales?

when asking for a definition

	Qu'est-ce que c'est que...?
What is a Jerusalem artichoke?	Qu'est-ce que c'est qu'un topinambour?

other common questions

What? [*please repeat*]	Comment?
What is your name?	Comment vous appelez-vous?
So what?	Et après?
What's the use?	A quoi bon?
What if it rains?	Et s'il pleut?
What about going to a movie?	Si on allait au cinéma?
What else?	Quoi encore?/Quoi d'autre?

in indirect questions

ce qui [*subj*]
ce que [*obj*]
quoi [*obj of preposition*]

Do you know what's happening?	Savez-vous ce qui se passe?
Can you tell me what they decided?	Pouvez-vous me dire ce qu'ils ont décidé?
Do you know what it's made of?	Sais-tu en quoi c'est fait?

what *rel pron*

ce qui [*subj*]
ce que [*obj*]
ce dont [*used if verb takes **de***]

Small children don't know what is dangerous.	Les petits ne savent pas ce qui est dangereux.
What you wrote is illegible.	Ce que vous avez écrit est illisible.
What I need is a little peace.	Ce dont j'ai besoin, c'est d'un peu de calme.

whatever *adj*

quel/quelle que soit
quels/quelles que soient

He'll do it, whatever the risks (may be).	Il le fera, quels que soient les risques.

whatever *pron*
no matter what

quoi que [+*subjunctive*]

Whatever I say, you contradict.	Quoi que je dise, tu dis le contraire.

all that . . .

(tout) ce qui [*subj*]
(tout) ce que/ce dont [*obj*]

Take whatever you want.	Prends (tout) ce que tu veux.
He gives her whatever she asks for.	Il lui donne tout ce qu'elle demande.
We'll buy whatever we need.	Nous achèterons ce dont nous aurons besoin.

when *conj*
when

quand

239

It was spring when we got married.

When shall we go to the zoo? — When it stops raining.

Phone me when you get there.

lorsque [*literary style*]
C'était le printemps quand nous nous sommes mariés.
Quand allons-nous au zoo? — Quand il s'arrêtera de pleuvoir. [*Note:* **quand** *takes future tense when meaning is future.*]
Téléphone-moi aussitôt que tu arriveras. [*Note: future tense*]

whenever *conj*
no matter when
I can leave whenever you want me to.

quand
Je peux partir quand tu voudras.

every time that . . .
Whenever I try to phone, the line's busy.

chaque fois que/toutes les fois que . . .
Chaque fois que j'essaie de téléphoner, la ligne est occupée.

whether *conj*
whether

si [*Note:* **si** *meaning "whether," unlike* **si** *meaning "if," may be followed by a verb in the future or the conditional.*]

I don't know whether I'm free.
Do you know whether she would accept?
I wonder whether the mailman has come.

Je ne sais pas si je serai libre.
Savez-vous si elle accepterait?

Je me demande si le facteur est passé.

which *inter adj*

quel   quels
quelle   quelles

Which color do you like best?
[*see also* **what**]

Quelle couleur préfères-tu?

which (one) *inter pron*

lequel   lesquels
laquelle   lesquelles

Which (one) do you want?
Which ones do you want?
Which one are you thinking of?
Which ones do you need?
Which of you haven't paid?

Lequel/laquelle veux-tu?
Lesquels/lesquelles veux-tu?
Auquel/à laquelle penses-tu?
Desquels/desquelles as-tu besoin?
Lesquels d'entre vous n'ont pas payé?

The forms of **lequel** contract with the prepositions **à** and **de**, giving the following
forms: **auquel, auxquels, auxquelles, duquel, desquels, desquelles.**

which   *rel pron*

qui [*subj*]
que [*obj*]
lequel [*obj of preposition*]

a dog which bites — un chien qui mord
the letter (which) we received — la lettre que nous avons reçue [*Note: que may not be omitted*]

the knife with which I cut the bread — le couteau avec lequel je coupe le pain
the hotels to which I wrote — les hôtels auxquels j'ai écrit

of which — dont
the theory I'm talking about — la théorie dont je parle
the problem I'm afraid of — le problème dont j'ai peur
the works he is most proud of — les oeuvres dont il est le plus fier

In contemporary English, "which" is often replaced by "that"; see **that** [*rel pron*].

whichever   *adj & pron*
You can serve whichever wines you have. — Vous pouvez servir les vins que vous avez.
Buy whichever one you want. — Achète celui que tu veux.

while   *conj*
time — pendant que
en [+*present participle*]

Stay here while I get the car. — Reste ici pendant que je vais chercher la voiture.

We watched the sunset while we had dinner. — Nous avons regardé le coucher du soleil en dînant.

whereas — tandis que
My brother likes jazz, while I prefer classical music. — Mon frère aime le jazz, tandis que moi, je préfère la musique classique.

who/whom   *inter pron*

Qui/Qui est-ce **qui**...? [*subj*]
Qui/Qui est-ce **que**...? [*obj*]
qui [*obj of preposition*]

Who lives here? — Qui habite ici?
Qui est-ce qui habite ici?

Who(m) did you see last night? — Qui as-tu vu hier soir?

who/whom

To whom did you give the package?/ Who did you give the package to?	Qui est-ce que tu as vu hier soir? A qui as-tu donné le paquet?

who/whom   *rel pron*

	qui [*subj*]
	que [*obj*]
	qui [*obj of prep*]
people who read	les gens qui lisent
the actors (whom) I admire	les acteurs que j'admire [*Note:* **que** *may not be omitted*]
the woman with whom they work	la femme avec qui ils travaillent

of whom

	dont
the friends of whom she spoke	les amis dont elle parlait
the man of whom the children are afraid	le monsieur dont les enfants ont peur

In English, the relative pronouns "who" and "whom" are often replaced by "that." See **that** [*rel pron*].

whoever/whomever   *pron*
anyone who

Whoever comes will find the house empty.	Quiconque viendra trouvera la maison vide.
Whoever wants to can come.	Tous ceux qui veulent venir le peuvent.

no matter who

Whoever you are, you may not come in.	Qui que vous soyez, vous n'avez pas le droit d'entrer.
You can invite who(m)ever you please.	Tu peux inviter qui tu veux.

in a question

Whoever did that?	Qui a pu faire ça?

whole   *adj & pron*

in the whole world	dans le monde entier
the whole apple	la pomme entière/toute la pomme
the whole of Paris	tout Paris
We saw the whole thing.	Nous avons tout vu.

whose   *inter adj & pron*

Whose...?	A qui...?

242

Whose backpack is that?/Whose is that backpack?	A qui est ce sac à dos?
Whose shoes are these?	A qui sont ces chaussures?

whose   *rel pron*
[*of whom*]

dont

an actor whose name I forget

un acteur dont j'ai oublié le nom [*Note: word order*]

a writer whose ideas are controversial

un écrivain dont les idées sont contestées

why   *adv & conj*

Why didn't you tell me?	Pourquoi est-ce que tu ne m'as rien dit?
I don't know why I'm so tired.	Je ne sais pas pourquoi je suis si fatigué.
That's why she refused.	Voilà pourquoi elle a refusé.
That's the reason (why) we can't stay.	C'est la raison **pour laquelle** nous ne pouvons pas rester. [*Note: not* ***pourquoi***]

willing   *adj*

to be willing	bien vouloir
They are willing to lend us the money.	Ils veulent bien nous prêter l'argent.

wish   *n & v*

to make a wish	faire un souhait
to wish sb a happy birthday	souhaiter bon anniversaire à qqn

to want

désirer/vouloir

I don't wish to see her.

Je ne veux pas la voir.

contrary to reality

I wish I were there now!	Je voudrais être là maintenant!
I wish he he were here!	Je voudrais qu'il soit là!
I wish I had known!	Si (seulement) j'avais su!

with   *prep*

a man with a beard	un homme **à** barbe
the girl with (the) long hair	la fille **aux** cheveux longs
a hat with a wide brim	un chapeau **à** large bord
tea with milk/with lemon	du thé **au** lait/**au** citron
red with shame/white with fear	rouge **de** honte/blanc **de** peur
covered with snow	couvert **de** neige
filled with water	rempli **d'**eau
to be angry with sb	être fâché(e) **contre** qqn

243

within

to be pleased/satisfied with	être content(e)/satisfaite) **de**
I saw it with my own eyes.	Je l'ai vu **de** mes propres yeux.
He walked in with his hands in his pockets.	Il est entré les mains dans les poches. [*Note: no preposition*]
to be "with it"	être dans le vent/être branché(e)/être câblé(e) [*slang*]

within *prep*

within the walls	à l'intérieur des murs
within 20 km of Bordeaux	à moins de 20 km de Bordeaux
within 24 hours	dans les 24 heures

without *prep*

without	sans
without a coat	sans manteau [*Note: no article*]
without a (single) word	sans une parole [*Note: article used for emphasis*]
He left without saying goodbye.	Il est parti sans dire au revoir. [*Note: infinitive after **sans**]

word *n*
in general

the words in the dictionary	les mots du dictionnaire
the right word	le mot juste
What is the word for...?	Quel est le mot pour...?
What's the word for...in French?	Comment dit-on...en français?
in other words	autrement dit

spoken or sung

Those are his very words.	Ce sont ses propres paroles.
I don't know the words to this song.	Je ne sais pas les paroles de cette chanson.

work *n*

She likes her work.	Elle aime son travail.
to go to work	aller travailler
to look for work	chercher du travail/un emploi
to be out of work [*unemployed*]	être au chômage
My carpenter does good work.	Mon menuisier travaille bien.
an art work/a literary work	une œuvre d'art/de littérature
the complete works of Molière	les œuvres complètes de Molière
[*see also **job**]	

work *v*
people   travailler
I work nights.   Je travaille la nuit.
to work full-time/part-time   travailler à plein temps/à temps partiel

things   marcher/fonctionner
My watch doesn't work.   Ma montre ne marche pas.

worker *n*
[*in general*]   le travailleur/la travailleuse
She is a fast worker.   Elle travaille vite.
manual, blue-collar worker   l'ouvrier [*m*]/l'ouvrière [*f*]
white-collar, clerical worker   l'employé(e)

worn out *adj*
worn-out shoes   des chaussures usées
I am worn out!   Je suis à bout de forces!
                                                  Je n'en peux plus!
                                                  Je suis crevé(e)! [*fam*]

worry *v*
to worry/be worried   s'inquiéter/être inquiet(-ète)/ s'en faire
She is worried about her husband.   Elle s'inquiète pour son mari.
Don't worry (about me).   Ne t'en fais pas (pour moi).
She's a worrywart.   C'est une éternelle inquiète.

worse/worst *adj*
worse   plus mauvais(e)
                                                  pire [*with abstract nouns*]
the worst   le plus mauvais/la plus mauvaise
                                                  le pire/la pire/les pires
a worse grade   une plus mauvaise note
the worst grade in the class   la plus mauvaise note **de** la classe
the worst thing that could happen   la pire chose qui puisse arriver

worse/worst *adv*
worse   plus mal
the worst   le plus mal [*invar*]
I feel worse today.   Je me sens plus mal aujourd'hui.
They all play badly, but you play the   Ils jouent tous mal, mais c'est toi qui
  worst.   joues le plus mal.

worth *adj*
to be worth (a sum of money)   valoir (une somme d'argent)

245

would

How much is this vase worth?	Combien vaut ce vase?
It's not worth it./It's not worth the trouble.	Ça ne vaut pas la peine.
This book is worth reading.	Ce livre vaut la peine d'être lu.

would *v*
polite request

I would like to see the manager please.	Je voudrais voir le gérant, s'il vous plait.
Would you please make room for me?	Pourriez-vous me faire un peu de place?

conditional

You would recognize her if you saw her.	Tu la reconnaîtrais si tu la voyais.
You would have recognized her if you had seen her.	Tu l'aurais reconnue si tu l'avais vue.

habitual action in the past

When we were young we would dance all night.	Quand nous étions jeunes nous dansions toute la nuit. [*Note: imperfect tense*]

wrong *adj & adv*
mistaken or incorrect

to be wrong	avoir tort
You think he is dishonest, but you are wrong.	Tu crois qu'il est malhonnête, mais tu as tort.
to get sth wrong	se tromper de qqch
I went to the wrong address.	Je me suis trompé d'adresse.
You took the wrong bag.	Vous vous êtes trompé de sac.
I did this all wrong.	J'ai fait ça de travers.

morally wrong

It's wrong to steal.	C'est mal de voler.
What's wrong with that?	Quel mal y a-t-il à cela?

trouble

What's wrong (with you)?	Qu'est-ce que tu as?
Is anything wrong?	Il y a quelque chose qui ne va pas?
No, nothing's wrong.	Non, tout va bien.
	Non, ça va.

X

x-ray *n*
an X-ray
to have an X-ray

I had an X-ray taken.

une radiographie/une radio
se faire radiographier/se faire faire une radio

Je me suis fait faire une radio.

Y

year *n*
a year

un an/une année [*Note: For difference in usage, see* **day.**]

with a date, a number
the year 2000
ten years from now
The baby will soon be a year old.

l'an
l'an 2000
dans dix ans/d'ici dix ans
Le bébé aura bientôt un an.

at regular intervals
every five years
once a year

l'an
tous les cinq ans
une fois par an

when modified
Happy New Year!
the school year
a sabbatical year
during/in the course of the year
in his/her tenth year
several years
for many years
a few years

l'année
Bonne année!
l'année scolaire
une année sabbatique
pendant/au cours de l'année
dans sa dixième année
plusieurs années
pendant bien des années
quelques années

yet *adv & conj*
however
He's very rich, yet he's not happy.

pourtant/cependant
Il est très riche; pourtant, il n'est pas heureux.

you

not yet	pas encore
They're not home yet.	Ils ne sont pas encore rentrés.

you *pron*
[familiar]

tu *[subj]*
te *[obj]*
toi *[disj]*
vous

[formal or plural]	vous
It's up to you to decide.	C'est à vous de décider.
I'll go and enquire; you stay here.	Je vais me renseigner; toi, reste là.
I'll write to you.	Je vous écrirai.

your *adj*
[familiar]
[formal or plural]
your notebook
your homework
your address

ton/ta/tes
votre/vos
ton cahier/votre cahier
tes devoirs/vos devoirs
ton adresse/votre adresse [*Note:* **ton** *is used before a feminine noun beginning with a vowel.*]

yours *pron*
[familiar]

[formal or plural]

le tien   les tiens
la tienne   les tiennes
le vôtre   les vôtres
les vôtres   les vôtres
[*Note: circumflex accent*]

My car is older than yours.

Ma voiture est plus vieille que la tienne/la vôtre.

yours sincerely
in a business letter
[from merchant to client, employee to boss, etc.]

Je vous prie de croire, Monsieur/ Madame, à l'expression de mes sentiments dévoués.

[from client to merchant, boss to employee, etc.]

Je vous prie d'agréer, Monsieur/ Madame, l'expression de mes sentiments distingués.

in a personal letter

(Bien) cordialement à vous/En toute amitié/Bien amicalement

These are a few examples of the phrases used in correspondence. There are many variations.

yourself [*see* **self**]

Z

zero *n*

zero

below/above zero

Zero degrees Centigrade=32 degrees
  Fahrenheit.

Our team was leading five to zero.

zéro

au-dessous de/au dessus de zéro

Zéro degré centigrade égale 32 degrés
  Fahrenheit.

Notre équipe menait de cinq à zéro.

zip *n*

zip code

le code postal

zipper *n*

a zipper

une fermeture éclair

NTC'S LANGUAGE DICTIONARIES

The Best, By Definition

Spanish/English
Vox New College (Thumb-index & Plain-edge)
Vox Modern
Vox Compact
Vox Everyday
Vox Traveler's
Vox Super-Mini
Cervantes-Walls

Spanish/Spanish
Diccionario Básico Norteamericano
Vox Diccionario Escolar de la lengua española
El Diccionario del español chicano

French/English
NTC's New College French and English
NTC's Dictionary of *Faux Amis*
NTC's Dictionary of Canadian French

German/English
Schöffler-Weis
Klett's Modern (New Edition)
Klett's Super-Mini
NTC's Dictionary of German False Cognates

Italian/English
Zanichelli New College Italian and English
Zanichelli Super-Mini

Greek/English
NTC's New College Greek and English

Chinese/English
Easy Chinese Phrasebook and Dictionary

For Juveniles
Let's Learn English Picture Dictionary
Let's Learn French Picture Dictionary
Let's Learn German Picture Dictionary
Let's Learn Italian Picture Dictionary
Let's Learn Spanish Picture Dictionary
English Picture Dictionary
French Picture Dictionary
German Picture Dictionary
Spanish Picture Dictionary

English for Nonnative Speakers
Everyday American English Dictionary
Beginner's Dictionary of American English Usage

Electronic Dictionaries
Languages of the World on CD-ROM
NTC's Dictionary of American Idioms, Slang, and
  Colloquial Expressions (Electronic Book)

Other Reference Books
Robin Hyman's Dictionary of Quotations
British/American Language Dictionary
NTC's American Idioms Dictionary
NTC's Dictionary of American Slang and
  Colloquial Expressions
Forbidden American English
Essential American Idioms
Contemporary American Slang
NTC's Dictionary of Grammar Terminology
Complete Multilingual Dictionary of Computer
  Terminology
Complete Multilingual Dictionary of Aviation &
  Aeronautical Terminology
Complete Multilingual Dictionary of Advertising,
  Marketing & Communications
NTC's Dictionary of American Spelling
NTC's Classical Dictionary
NTC's Dictionary of Debate
NTC's Mass Media Dictionary
NTC's Dictionary of Word Origins
NTC's Dictionary of Literary Terms
Dictionary of Trade Name Origins
Dictionary of Advertising
Dictionary of Broadcast Communications
Dictionary of Changes in Meaning
Dictionary of Confusing Words and Meanings
NTC's Dictionary of English Idioms
NTC's Dictionary of Proverbs and Clichés
Dictionary of Acronyms and Abbreviations
NTC's Dictionary of American English
  Pronunciation
NTC's Dictionary of Phrasal Verbs and Other
  Idiomatic Verbal Phrases
Common American Phrases

Polish/English
The Wiedza Powszechna Compact Polish and
  English Dictionary

For further information or a current catalog, write:
National Textbook Company
a division of *NTC Publishing Group*
4255 West Touhy Avenue
Lincolnwood, Illinois 60646-1975 U.S.A.